A Bit of a Stretch

'Honest and authentic. Atkins perfectly captures the madness, hope and despair of prison. Please read this.'

Professor David Wilson – founding Director of the Centre for Applied Criminology at Birmingham City University and former prison governor

'An important, urgent and entertaining memoir. It made me laugh, cry my eyes out and think hard, not only about forgiveness, but about love and life in general. An essential read.'

Sathnam Sanghera – author of *The Boy with the Topknot*

About the Author

Chris Atkins is a BAFTA-nominated filmmaker. His documentaries *Taking Liberties* and *Starsuckers* were critically acclaimed and made front-page news. He has also worked extensively with *Dispatches* for Channel 4 and BBC *Panorama*. Following his release from prison, he is now back in North London, filming documentaries and writing.

A Bit of a Stretch

The Diaries
of a Prisoner

Chris Atkins

Atlantic Books
London

Published in hardback and trade paperback in Great Britain in 2020 by
Atlantic Books, an imprint of Atlantic Books Ltd.

10 9 8 7 6 5 4 3 2 1

A CIP catalogue record for this book is available from the British Library.

Hardback ISBN: 978 1 83895 015 6
Trade paperback ISBN: 978 1 83895 103 0
E-book ISBN: 978 1 83895 016 3

Printed in Great Britain

Atlantic Books
An imprint of Atlantic Books Ltd
Ormond House
26–27 Boswell Street
London
WC1N 3JZ

www.atlantic-books.co.uk

To Nazia, the best friend anyone could ever have.

And for Kit, obviously.

Contents

Preface

It's about 10 p.m. I'm locked in my cell, H2-09, with my padmate, Gary, a likeable young Scouser who's nearing the end of his sentence for smuggling cannabis. We're watching a film set in an American prison. Not for the first time, I reflect on how popular culture gives an oddly false impression of life inside. The on-screen criminals are ripped, tanned and seemingly possess all their faculties. It's a far cry from the emaciated, spice-addicted souls who surround me in Wandsworth, many of whom are mentally ill.

There's a jangling of keys outside, and our cell door is unlocked. Standing in the doorway is Mr Hussain, a young screw I get on reasonably well with.

'Evening, Chris,' he calls to me. 'I've just dropped Rob off next door. He's having a right mental.'

'It's not my shift.'

The officer shrugs. 'None of the other Listeners will talk to him.'

My curiosity is piqued. 'Give me a minute.'

I put on some flip-flops and head out the door. I currently live at the more salubrious end of H Wing, which is an enormous Victorian prison block. The ground floor is dark and deserted, except for a couple of rats sniffing around the bins. We walk down the landing and Hussain opens the door to the Listener Suite. This name is quite misleading, as it's basically two derelict cells knocked together. The windows are broken and the temperature is barely above freezing. It's harshly lit by a couple of strip lights and it stinks of cigarette smoke. There's no furniture except for three plastic chairs and a revolting toilet in the corner. It resembles a 1970s police interview room and is hardly an ideal space for giving emotional support to vulnerable inmates. Nonetheless, this is where I do most of my work as a Listener. I have recently been trained by the Samaritans to help prisoners who are suicidal, self-harming or just losing their minds. I've now been Listening for several months, and witness more suffering in a single day than I would have previously seen in a whole year.

Sitting waiting for me is Rob, a rather large prisoner in his late twenties.

'I'll leave you to it,' says Officer Hussain as he locks us in.

Rob is sweating profusely, and glares at me through enormous bloodshot eyes. He's wearing his prison clothes inside out, with crazy gibberish scrawled all over the fabric, and he is obviously having some form of psychotic episode. Over the last couple of months, I've become quite accustomed to meeting people suffering severe mental illness in prison. Most of the time they are far more likely to be the victim of violence from other inmates rather than the perpetrator. That said, Rob looks seriously scary. I cautiously sit down on the seat furthest away from him. 'Hi, I'm Chris. How are you feeling this evening?'

'What the FUCK are you asking me that for?' he hisses. It's around this point that I regret coming in here alone. Listeners are technically supposed to work in pairs at night, just in case we get stuck with a dangerous inmate. But over Christmas, our numbers have plummeted, while call-outs have soared, so the rules have fallen by the wayside.

'Right, sorry, stupid question, sorry.' I notice that Rob has half a comb sticking out of his hair, and I'm unsure if this is a fashion statement or a potential weapon.

'What do you know about quantum mechanics?' he demands.

'Quite a bit as it happens,' I say. 'I actually studied physics at Oxford, and that was the only part I found interesting.'

We spend the next 10 minutes discussing wave–particle duality.

'I'm seriously impressed with your knowledge,' I say warmly, congratulating myself on building up such a strong rapport.

He nods and leans in conspiratorially. Assuming that he's finally going to open up about his inner turmoil, I lean in too. Instead, he grins like the Grim Reaper and says, 'Sing me a song or I'll slit your throat.'

Introduction

My spell behind bars coincided with the worst prison crisis in history. In 2016, there was a 27% increase in prisoner assaults nationally, with assaults on staff up by 38%. The number of self-inflicted deaths had more than doubled since 2013, with 113 prisoners taking their own lives.[1] The president of the Prison Governors Association said that conditions were 'the worst we have ever seen'.[2]

I spent nine months in Wandsworth before being shipped out to an open prison, which was like the Ritz in comparison. This book charts my unlikely and often surreal experiences through those crazy months, and tries to explain why our jails are in such dire straits. Prisons are frequently in the news, and the crisis is usually blamed on drugs and plummeting officer numbers. These are definitely real issues, but for me, the main problem, which hardly gets any airtime, is that prisons are extraordinarily badly run. If Wandsworth was a hospital, patients would be discharged with far more diseases than when they arrived. If it was a school, pupils would graduate knowing less than when they enrolled. The management was so grossly inept that if they were running any other part of the public sector, they'd be immediately sacked. But prisons exist in a vacuum, where the authorities can tightly restrict all outgoing information and cover up their own incompetence. Free from public scrutiny, Wandsworth and other prisons are able to continue failing on an epic scale.

I was perhaps unique in Wandsworth, as I'd spent years making documentaries. I knew that the biggest barrier to capturing a decent story is access. It's often very difficult getting into interesting places, as the gatekeepers don't want anyone seeing what's going on. Even when access is granted, film-makers are often put under such tight restrictions that we only film what they want us to see. But in Wandsworth, I was just another prisoner. I had no press pass, minders or aggressive PRs telling me not to ask interesting questions. This unfettered access gave me a front-row seat for the extraordinary chaos that unfolded in Wandsworth every day. I kept detailed notes of everything I witnessed, which formed the basis of this book. I hope my unvarnished account will provide a strong argument for urgent prison reform.

I have to admit that before my incarceration, prison reform wasn't something I spent much time thinking about. Why on earth should law-abiding citizens concern themselves with what happens to a bunch of criminals? Well, having spent a considerable amount of time in the system, I can now think of two key reasons. Firstly, most reasonable people would agree that everyone should be treated with minimum standards of decency and care, even if they've done something wrong. Whatever your baseline for humane treatment, I can guarantee British prisons are falling way below it. A recent HM Inspectorate of Prisons report details 'some of the most disturbing prison conditions we have ever seen – conditions which have no place in an advanced nation in the 21st century'.[3] Far from being the 'holiday camps' described by numerous tabloids,[4] I saw how British prisons are brutalising teenagers to a lethal degree.

Osvaldas Pagirys was just 18 when he was arrested for stealing sweets. He was held in Wandsworth during my time there, and was found with a noose around his neck on five separate occasions. The authorities treated his mental illness as bad behaviour, and he was sent to the punishment block. One evening he pressed the emergency button, but officers took 37 minutes to arrive. The teenager was found hanging and unconscious, and died shortly afterwards. At the inquest, the jury found that this delay, along with general poor treatment, had contributed to his death.[5]

I didn't meet Osvaldas, but while working as a Listener, I sat with lots of similarly disturbed teenagers. Anywhere else they'd be treated as human beings who needed urgent medical help. But because they were in prison, often on pathetically trivial offences, they were shouted at like animals and locked up permanently in a concrete box. The spiralling suicide rate means that many of them will not survive.

If this doesn't swing it, then you might want to think about the cost. Prisons are supposed to rehabilitate inmates so they don't inflict further harm on society. On that basis, your hard-earned taxes are being flushed down the drain, as Britain has the worst reoffending rate in Europe, with 48% of ex-prisoners being reconvicted within one year of release.[6] The cost of reoffending alone is estimated at £15 billion,[7] more than three times the entire prison budget. This means that your house may well have been burgled by someone who has already served several jail sentences. If British prisons functioned effectively, you'd still have your laptop and silverware.

However, this book definitely isn't an earnest lecture on criminology and penal policy. Wandsworth was a cesspit of misery and despair, but I also found it darkly entertaining. Most prisoners were locked up for 23 hours a day, which meant they would do anything to get out of their cells. Several Muslims joined Alcoholics Anonymous, despite being strictly teetotal, just to attend the weekly meetings. Other prisoners claimed to be simultaneously Catholic, Jewish and Buddhist, simply to get unlocked for the various religious services. We had a new mindfulness programme called 'Tunnelling', which proved remarkably popular until it became clear that it involved teaching prisoners how to control their breathing rather than dig tunnels. Laughing at this ridiculousness was often the only way to get through.

When I first arrived, I was trapped in a cell all day, and was thus completely oblivious to how the jail was (not) functioning. As time went on, I became increasingly trusted, and gained access to hitherto restricted parts of the building. This enabled me to stick my nose into steadily darker corners of the Wandsworth machine, and witness increasingly disturbing events. I became a Listener after four months, and dealt with dozens of highly disturbed and vulnerable inmates.

My prison journey often felt like a deranged computer game. I'd fight my way through a level, dodging baddies and collecting tokens, before finally being confronted with a terrifying obstacle. Somehow I would manage to beat the challenge – be it getting more visits with my son, or escaping a psychopathic cellmate – only to discover a whole new level with even darker trials. Each level presented ever more shocking revelations about how the system was falling apart, as well as teaching me vital prison survival skills. I've structured the book around these ascending levels of madness, which illuminate progressively shocking aspects of British jails.

I'd never set foot inside a prison before, and had led a very different life to most of my neighbours. In many ways this makes my conviction more damning, as I'd squandered the life chances that had been denied to my fellow prisoners. So before I jump into the deep end, I should give some brief context, and explain how a lefty middle-class film-maker found himself banged up in one of the most notorious jails in the country.

I want to be clear that I did definitely do something wrong, and the events that led me to prison were largely my own fault. I first began producing films in the late 1990s, when the Blair government introduced tax breaks for the British film industry. Some enterprising accountants created investment schemes to enable bankers and footballers to avoid paying tax. These investors would notionally back a film, and a small amount of the cash would trickle down to the producers to spend on the production. Tax financing was subsequently used to make hundreds of British films, some of which we all know and love.

In the early 2000s, I was making pretty low-budget fiction feature films, all of which were part financed with these tax schemes. I then moved into documentaries, and directed a Michael Moore-style film attacking Tony Blair for undermining human rights during the War on Terror. *Taking Liberties* was released in cinemas in 2007, garnering excellent reviews and a BAFTA nomination. I then decided to tackle the media business, but no one was willing to pay for a movie that intended to burn our own industry. I pitched the film everywhere, and all I heard was a resounding no. The only person who said yes was an accountant called Terry Potter, who ran one of the funds that put tax money into movies.

By this stage, HMRC were closing the tax breaks. But Potter flew me out to France and told me that he'd developed a new film-funding scheme. He admitted that he'd made 'a few modifications' to circumvent HMRC's latest restrictions. It was clearly moving towards the darker end of the grey area, but to me, the scheme didn't sound that different from what was happening more broadly in the film industry at the time.

Bottom line, I should have been more concerned with checking out Potter's scheme, but I was desperate to get the film made. I can honestly say that while arrogance, hubris and a big ego definitely played their part in making me accept his offer, financial greed most definitely did not. I shook Potter's hand and agreed we should get on with it.

Over the next two years, we did as Potter instructed: setting up limited companies, raising inflated invoices on demand, and passing money between accounts. Only a small amount was retained by the production company, which was all spent on making the film. In retrospect, I realised it was wrong – possibly criminal – and I should have known better. However, Potter assured me it would not get us into trouble. I heard what I wanted to hear and quickly forgot about the funding, becoming consumed by what was an extremely ambitious production.

Notwithstanding the fact that I went to prison for the film, *Starsuckers* definitely includes some of my finest work. I secretly filmed Max Clifford boasting about how he protected his clients, specifically Mohamed Al-Fayed and Dustin Hoffman. We sold fake celebrity gossip stories to the tabloids to prove they didn't check facts. The *Sun*, the *Mirror* and the *Daily Star* all printed our nonsense about female pop stars being secretly obsessed with quantum physics. I also did a reverse undercover sting on several Sunday tabloid journalists who were trying to buy celebrity medical records. This exposed a widespread culture of unlawful behaviour in tabloid newspapers, including the *News of the World*.

Starsuckers finally premiered at the 2009 London Film Festival, and was released in selected cinemas. The *Guardian* splashed our exploits on the front page for two days running, prompting the *News of the World* to threaten to sue us for breaching *their* privacy. Max Clifford also threatened to take out an injunction against the film, and we had to beep Fayed and Hoffman's names out of the final edit. We got great reviews, and the film was broadcast on Channel 4 several times and released on DVD. Despite making a vast amount of noise, however, it didn't make a bean.

In 2011, the phone-hacking scandal shut down the *News of the World*. Lord Justice Leveson was tasked to investigate the press, and *Starsuckers* was screened to the inquiry, where I also gave detailed evidence. The judge's final report agreed with much of what was said in the film. Max Clifford was arrested for sex crimes in 2012;

I was subsequently interviewed by officers from Operation Yewtree and handed over all the tapes of my undercover filming. Clifford was convicted and sentenced to eight years, and in 2017 Fayed[8] and Hoffman[9] were accused of sexual misconduct in the wake of the Harvey Weinstein scandal (neither has been charged or convicted and both deny the accusations). By every measure, *Starsuckers* had vastly exceeded my expectations.

Once the production was over, I said goodbye to Potter and started making documentaries directly for TV. In 2012, I fronted a *Dispatches* for Channel 4, investigating corrupt private detectives who were running a black market in personal information. I then made another *Dispatches* about *Coronation Street* stars secretly promoting products on social media. It made the front pages of the *Sun* and the *Mirror*, and led to ITV threatening to sue Channel 4. Next I produced a BBC *Panorama* about bad practice in big charities, revealing that Comic Relief was secretly investing donations in arms companies, tobacco firms and alcoholic drinks manufacturers. I wrote and directed a fiction film for Channel 4 about a future in which UKIP actually won the general election. It became one of the most complained-about films of all time, triggering over 6,000 Ofcom complaints. I was pretty much at the top of my game.

But all this time HMRC had been digging into old film-funding schemes. Prolonged austerity had hardened public attitudes to tax dodging, and HMRC had long been vexed by the behaviour of the British film business. In 2014, 14 of us were charged with tax fraud, including Potter and several of his wealthy investors. It was two and a half years before I got to court, and during that time I stepped back from making controversial films. Not working 70-hour weeks actually enabled me to be a far better dad to my infant son Kit. I'd separated from his mother, Lottie, but we remained on very good terms, and Kit spent half the week with each of us.

Potter was convicted in September 2015, along with three City bankers, and my court date was set for May 2016. The evidence against me seemed mostly circumstantial, and the prosecution didn't deny that I hadn't been personally paid out of the scheme. However, I was party to some fairly damning emails, including one where I suggested that we delete the entire conversation. I'd made films accusing others of wrongdoing, and I had to be judged by the same standard.

The trial was a horrendous ordeal, and it felt as if I was being slowly squeezed by an enormous vice. It didn't help that I became addicted to sleeping pills, and was knocking back a bottle of wine and a pack of fags every night. I was convicted on 24 June 2016, hours after the EU referendum result had been announced. If I'd been on the jury, I'd probably have come to the same decision.

I was told to return to court a week later for sentencing. My barrister told me to expect at least six years. This terrifying figure was a consequence of me being convicted of conspiring to help Potter and the bankers attempting to defraud about £1,000,000. Only £85,000 had actually trickled down to the production company, which had all been spent on making the film, but on a conspiracy case everyone is responsible for the whole lot. Potter's scheme needed films to evade the tax, and my documentary was a crucial cog in the machine.

During that week, I was overwhelmed by a lot of love. Friends, family and former colleagues rushed forward with support and commiserations, and there was a feeling of 'there but for the grace of God' from several quarters. I went onto autopilot to deal with the admin of closing off my life, and cleared out my north London house. I had been warned that HMRC would potentially come after my assets, so it might well need to be sold. It was only when I had to sort out Kit's things that I completely cracked. Packing away children's toys has such horrible connotations that I kept having to tell myself that Kit was alive and well and playing in a nearby park. I was about to store the child seat for my bike, before realising that he would be miles too big for it by the time I got out.

My best mate Tom had a bit too much fun researching what I was allowed to take into prison, scouring numerous blogs about what to expect in jail. He ran round Camden sourcing the contents of a 'bang-up bag', principally tracksuits from Sports Direct, which seemed to be the lag's brand of choice. The blogs all advised that newbies take in a cheap watch, flip-flops, spare underwear and stamps. I also packed all the books that I'd been meaning to read for the past five years and had never got round to starting.

As my final hours of freedom ticked away, several people recommended that I write down everything I experienced in prison. In what follows, I've changed all the names unless I'm referencing public figures, quoting news reports, or writing about people who've given express permission to be identified. I've taken particular care with anything I heard while working as a Listener, and have altered some personal details to make identification impossible. Some of the dates have also been changed.

1

Trauma and Toothpaste

In which I check into E Wing – aka Beirut – and am surrounded by mentally ill drug addicts, but luck out with my first cellmate.

Things I learn:

1) How long I'll have to spend in Wandsworth

2) The grim realities of prison cuisine

3) A curious new version of apple bobbing

Things get so bad that I consider faking Christianity, and I eventually depart to the uplands of A Wing.

1 July 2016

I wake up at 7 a.m., and lie in bed hoping that this last week is only the remnants of a terrifying nightmare. Radio 4 is commemorating the Battle of the Somme, which began exactly a hundred years ago. If those young men could run at machine guns, then I can probably handle a stretch in prison. I walk over to Lottie's flat to have breakfast with Kit. He knows that something is up as soon as he sees I'm in my court clothes. I bought a new suit from M&S specifically for the trial, which Kit hated me wearing from day one.

As we play with his little cash register, he keeps saying, 'Hello, customer, what do you want to buy today?' When it's time to go, he gives me a hug goodbye. I don't want to leave. I'm really, really scared. He decides that I need another hug, and leans over and holds me extra tight. This releases a huge surge of confidence and energy that I've never felt before or since. I feel as if I'm cloaked in an impenetrable force field.

'I can do this,' I whisper to myself, and stride out the door.

I'm accompanied to the sentencing by Lottie's brother and her mum, Debby. She's been a tower of strength, and we had nightly debriefs in her garden throughout the trial. When we get out at London Bridge, the sun is streaming down, and we head round the corner to Southwark Crown Court. Three photographers are waiting for me and jostle to get my picture. One of them shouts, 'Good luck, mate!' and I walk up the steps for the last time.

In Court 5, my friends and family are packing out the public gallery. After a couple of minutes, Judge Beddoe whisks in. My barrister pleads for leniency, but when the judge starts speaking, he doesn't sound in a very forgiving mood. He accepts that I didn't know precisely what Potter was up to, but is going to punish me for facilitating the scheme. He says that I should get six years for the main count, and two years for a side count, which ought to run consecutively.

My internal ticker tape is now up to eight years. Prisoners usually serve half their overall sentence, so I'm constantly halving the figures to work out how long I'll be inside. I start zoning out as everything gets quieter and further away. Kit's hug is still protecting me. The judge then looks at me and says that my sentence is five years, and I'll serve two and a half inside. I suddenly snap back into the room as if I've been given defibrillation. 'Only five?!' I shout in my head. 'Get out of here before he changes his mind!' I stand up and give a moronic wave to the judge. The journalists in the press gallery look as if I've gone completely batshit as I bowl out the side door, where

I'm cuffed up to a custody officer who is a dead ringer for Eric Idle from *Monty Python*.

'Are you sure he said five?' I gibber.

'That's what you've got,' he replies, and presses a button to call the lift.

Not surprisingly, backstage is a lot shabbier than the customer-facing parts of the courthouse. It's like accidentally taking the service elevator in a hotel. The doors open into the basement, and I'm led to a small desk, where an officer takes some basic personal details. I'm then cuffed up to the young guard who sat in the dock with me during the trial. We got on quite well and I'd sometimes chip in on his Sudoku puzzle when we hit peak boredom.

'What happened?' he asks.

'Guilty on the lot. Got five years.'

He smiles sympathetically. 'From Judge Beddoe, that's not too bad. Cells are through here.'

On the wall is a large whiteboard listing the names of my fellow prisoners. Next to Cell 5 is scrawled *CLIFFORD*.

'Is that *Max* Clifford?' I ask the guard.

He nods proudly. Clifford is still serving his original prison sentence, but has now been hauled back to court to stand trial for more historic sexual assaults.

'I sort of know him,' I whisper.

The lad checks that no one else is around. 'Do you want to have a word?'

'Fuck yeah.'

There's a little round porthole on the cell door, and I peer inside. Clifford sits hunched at the back of a tiny windowless kennel. He looks nothing like the cocky king of PR I filmed eight years ago; rather he resembles a geriatric Osama bin Laden.

'Hi, Max!'

He edges up to the door, smiling carefully. 'Who is it?'

'It's me. Chris Atkins. I turned you over in my film *Starsuckers*.'

He looks extremely rattled, probably assuming that I've come to torment him further. 'What are you doing here?' he demands.

'I just got five years for fraud.' I hold up my cuffed hand to illustrate the point. 'For funding *Starsuckers*, funnily enough.'

His mood brightens. 'Right, OK then. How are things otherwise?'

'Yeah, not bad. Couldn't believe the Brexit result.'

'Incredible, wasn't it?'

'Madness. Good luck in your new case.'

'Cheers. Mind how you go.'

The guard leads me a few doors down. 'You're wasting away,' he says. 'You should have some lunch.' He's not wrong; I barely ate during the trial, and my weight has plummeted. Now that I know my fate, my appetite is flooding back. He offers a microwaved chicken curry, and I order two.

I'm locked in a dingy box, about three feet by five. It's the first time I've ever been detained against my will, but I feel oddly elated. The judge indicated that I might get eight years, so receiving only five seems like a lucky escape. After 20 minutes, the food arrives, but there's nothing to eat off. I balance the microwave container on my lap and bolt everything down like a starving dog, dropping much of it on my M&S trousers.

An hour later, I'm led through a holding bay and into a big white Serco van. I squeeze into a tiny box in the back. It makes flying Ryanair seem luxurious – there's no seat belt and the legroom is non-existent. The van drives out from under the courthouse and starts to crawl across south London. Through the darkened window I can see people with that Friday-afternoon spring in their step. I try and fail to come to terms with the fact that I won't be joining them for some considerable time.

The van finally pulls to a halt. I squint up at the sinister Gothic architecture looming above us. It looks like Castle Grayskull from the He Man cartoons. A gate opens, admitting us into a massive courtyard, and we reverse towards a vast Victorian prison wing. There are some Portakabins tacked onto the side, and a big sign says *HMP WANDSWORTH: RECEPTION*.

I'm let out of the van, and join six other prisoners inside one of the Portakabins. The room is pretty bashed up; in the corner is a loo cubicle with no door. The other inmates are all black, and much younger than me. One lad is shaking and twitching, I'm guessing through drug withdrawal. Everyone else is wearing tracksuits, while I stand awkwardly in my curried court clothes. One by one our names are called, and the others start heading round the corner to be processed. I'm the last to be summoned, and I walk hesitantly through. Standing behind a desk is an officer who presumably got the job based on his highly intimidating appearance. He's bald and bearded, with various sinister tattoos, and reminds me of the cave troll that skewers Frodo in *The Lord of the Rings*.

'Right, Atkins. You've just got five years, do you understand that?'

'Yes,' I reply as confidently as I can manage.

The troll looks me up and down. 'You're remarkably calm for someone who's received a long prison sentence. Are you a calm kind of person?'

I shrug. 'It's probably just the shock. I expect I'll completely lose my shit in a few days.'

He shrugs back. 'This is your first time inside, so let me warn you – this place is *full* of slime. Total vermin. Isn't that right, Dave?' The equally huge screw to his left grunts in agreement. 'Of the sixteen hundred prisoners in this joint,' the cave troll continues, 'there are about fifty I could have a reasonable conversation with. The rest are pond life.' At the time, this seems like an unfair slight on the population of Wandsworth.

'Do you smoke?' he asks.

'I just quit,' I reply, and mean it.

He fills in some forms. 'You stick out like a sore thumb, so the vultures will soon come knocking. Say no to *everything* and you'll be fine.' My photo is taken, I'm given a prison number – A8892DT – and then I'm locked in a holding cell on my own. The other arrivals were existing Wandsworth residents, so I'm the only newly sentenced prisoner being processed.

My system is flooded with adrenaline. I'm sharply focused on everything that's happening around me, only nothing is. It reminds me of when I did undercover filming, minus the constant reassuring knowledge that I could walk away at any moment. There's a poster on the wall: *Welcome to Wandsworth.* The photos show a spotlessly clean cell, a privacy curtain shielding the toilet area, and a small desk. Two jolly officers are smiling and waving at the camera. That doesn't look too bad, I think to myself.

I'm called out of the room and told to follow a winding grey path that feeds through reception. It's like a dystopian Yellow Brick Road, with flatulent prison officers instead of Munchkins.

First stop: clothing. I'm led into a little booth, and instructed to undress. I've been mentally preparing myself for the naked squat over a mirror, but the officer just gives me a cursory look. I've brought in the recommended cheap tracksuits, but apparently I won't be able to wear my own clothes until I've been inside a few months without causing trouble. In the meantime, I'll have to make do with prison-issue kit. I'm handed an overstretched pair of grey tracksuit bottoms that feel like they're held together by itching powder, and an enormous thick blue T-shirt that resembles the smocks worn by medieval peasants. The officer assures me that these garments have been thoroughly cleaned, but they nonetheless smell like someone's died in them. My court clothes are stuffed into my 'prop box', a flimsy black plastic crate that will store items I'm not allowed on the wings.

Next stop: property. A barrel-shaped screw produces my bang-up bag and empties my possessions onto a conveyor belt. Another officer starts removing prohibited items, which he then shoves into my prop box. I watch with eager anticipation to see what makes it through. It's like an austere version of *The Generation Game*. I lose the radio, quite a few toiletries and a hardback notebook. The officer inspects my brand-new Argos watch, and tosses that in the box too.

'Er, what's wrong with that?' I timidly ask.

'It's got a stopwatch,' he replies. To this day I have no idea why this causes a security problem in a prison.

Thankfully there is no restriction on my books, which all get thrown into a clear plastic bin liner with my other permitted items. The prison blogs advised bringing in some cash, and I have £100 in an envelope. This is taken by an officer, who assures me that it'll be added to my account.

Then it's medical. A nurse asks if I have any health problems, and I tell her that I'm physically fine. She says that I'll get a more thorough 'second-day screening' over the weekend.

All that remains is a series of interviews with various officers.

'Have you got anything sharp in your pockets?'

'Do you have any mental illnesses?'

'Have you got anything sharp in your pockets?'

'Do you have any mental illnesses?'

I'm asked the same questions over and over again; it reminds me of doing a press junket for a film: 'How did you come up with the idea for the movie? Has working on the film changed you at all? Have you got any drugs on you?' As in press junkets, a lot of the officers' questioning turns towards drugs. I can truthfully say that I'm completely clean.

'Are you a racist?'

'Are you a homophobe?'

'When did you last commit arson?'

I wonder who would actually answer these questions in the affirmative. Apparently this grilling is to ensure that it's safe for me to share a cell.

I'm given a 'non-smoker's pack', a small plastic bag containing tea, coffee, biscuits and chocolate. I ask about visits, and am told that I can have as many as I want in the first week. Another officer hands me a slip of paper with an eight-digit pin number on. 'This is your two-pound emergency phone credit. It'll let you call anyone in the next twenty-four hours. You might want to use it now, as you'll probably be banged up all weekend.'

I scurry to a battered blue prison phone on the wall and call Lottie. She answers, and the available credit starts plummeting downwards.

'I got five years!' I gasp.

'Are you OK?'

'I'm at Wandsworth now; it's not too bad so far. I can have as many visits as I want this week.'

'Everyone wants to come and see you. I'll sort out a rota.'

'How's Kit?'

'Fine, he's eating his tea and watching *Sarah and Duck*.'

'Tell him I love him.'

The credit is almost out, so I say goodbye. An officer ushers me into another holding room.

'Just hang here until someone can take you up to the wing.'

It feels like the calm before the storm. I fish out *The Constant Gardener*, and try and read the first page, but not a single sentence goes in. The door opens and my name is called, slightly pointlessly since I'm the only person in here. I pick up my bin liner of belongings and shuffle out.

A female officer leads me into a corridor that connects the reception Portakabins to the prison wing. 'The induction wing is a bit crazy at the moment,' she warns. The corridor can't be more than 20 feet long, but it takes forever to get to the end. She opens the final door, wishes me luck, and I step through the wormhole.

The first thing that hits me is the noise: yelling, banging, screaming, grunting, begging, barking, threatening, ranting, laughing, trading,

22

scoring, whining, arguing, fighting, howling, crying. It's as if someone has downloaded every single prison sound effect from the internet and is blaring them all out, dialled up to 11.

I'm standing on the ground floor of an enormous Victorian jail block, and it's about as prisony an environment as you could possibly imagine. The landing stretches out a hundred yards left and right, with cell doors running down each wall. Looming above are two more levels, with thin spurs along both sides. It looks like it last had a makeover when Oscar Wilde stayed here in 1895. It's basically *Porridge* infrastructure meets *One Flew Over the Cuckoo's Nest* personnel, and is awash with the most terrifying individuals I've ever seen. They mostly appear to be either severely mentally ill, off their heads on drugs, or both. If I was directing this scene in a film, I would complain that the set had been prisoned up far too much and dial down the existential wailing. Nothing in my life has prepared me for this moment. I have overdosed on blue pills, we've smashed through the looking glass and are now light years away from Kansas.

'Are you Atkins?'

I turn round to see a comparatively normal-looking man in a tracksuit. He's about 50, wearing thick plastic glasses and holding a clipboard.

'Yes,' I squeak.

'Didn't you just get sentenced by Judge Beddoe?'

'Er, yeah, got five years.'

He looks surprised. 'How did you manage that? The cunt gave me fourteen.'

I'm not sure what to say. I go for 'Sorry,' which doesn't really cut it.

He calls to another prisoner. 'STEVE! Steve!' An officious-looking bald man potters up.

'This is Atkins,' says the bespectacled prisoner. 'He just came in from Beddoe, only got a five.'

'Fucking what? That's just a parking ticket!' Steve storms off.

The bespectacled prisoner introduces himself. 'I'm Hitchins, the induction orderly.'

'Have you been here long?' I ask.

'Two years, living the dream. Let me find you a cell where you won't be sharing with a psychopath. Not as easy as it sounds.' He vanishes into the throng, while I stay where I am, refusing to believe that any of this is really happening. That officer was right – I do stick out like a sore thumb.

A drooling lad with a bilious skin rash drags a trolley past and hands me a soggy baguette.

'Is this lunch?' I ask.

'Dinner,' he giggles back.

Hitchins soon reappears. 'I've found you a good guy to move in with. Follow me.'

I grab my sack of possessions and totter off after him. He strides down the landing, completely impervious to the screeching prisoners milling around us.

'This is the truffle shuffle,' he explains. 'Junkies coming out for their methadone hits.' At the end of the landing are some iron stairs, and I follow Hitchins to the very top level. The whole wing stretches out in front of us. There is a hundred-foot drop down to the bottom level, and heavy netting is stretched across the huge gap, designed to break the fall of prisoners hurling themselves into the abyss. Right now, I know how they feel.

We head down the right-hand spur, past a series of blue cell doors. Hitchins is still firing information at me. 'Don't expect to get out much; then again, who'd want to be out with this lot? Over the weekend, there'll be constant bang-up.' I work out that this is prison jargon for being locked up for a long period of time.

He seems a useful person to have around. 'Do you live on this wing?' I ask.

'Fuck no. This is the worst wing in the prison; we call it Beirut. Right, this is you.'

We stop outside a cell marked *E4-36*. An officer appears jangling his keys and opens it up. I slip inside and the door clangs shut behind me. It's the heaviest noise I've heard in my whole life.

The cell is about six feet by twelve. My first instinct is to complain to the Advertising Standards Authority about the *Welcome to Wandsworth* poster in reception. It promised a spotlessly clean cell, but these walls are covered in demonic graffiti, and half the paint is peeling off. The bunk beds look like they'd collapse from sleeping on the bottom, let alone venturing onto the top. The mattresses are made from heavy-duty blue plastic, like those used in hospices, designed for the easy cleaning of bodily fluids. There's a wooden desk along the wall that's about a foot deep, with a couple of battered shelving units at each end. The chairs are white lumps of plastic, and at the back is a hideous toilet that doesn't have a seat. There's no privacy curtain, though someone has improvised with a prison-issue green sheet; its opacity is actually enhanced by the large brown stains. The floor is cold concrete, and it all smells pretty bad.

Sitting on the bottom bunk is a tanned bald man in his sixties. He has a thin face with wire-framed glasses, and is eating his dinner off a chair while watching TV.

'You look completely fucked, mate,' he says kindly. 'Do you want a cup of tea?'

I readily agree. He introduces himself as Ted, and explains that he's just been re-arrested in Spain, having previously absconded from a long sentence for drug smuggling.

I crawl onto the top bunk. I'm now thankful that I lost so much weight during the trial, as anyone over 10 stone would flatten the whole structure. My appetite has returned at the very moment I'm stuck in a place notorious for terrible food. I wolf down the manky baguette in seconds. I'm still starving, so I eat the entire pack of biscuits from my non-smoker's pack. We watch the evening news – the government is in meltdown following the EU referendum. My life and the country have seemingly pulled a handbrake turn at exactly the same moment. I can't help feeling that my incarceration and Brexit are somehow mystically interlinked. Ted's political views become apparent as he shouts, 'Go on, Nige!' every time Nigel Farage appears on screen.

Ted turns off the telly, and I lie in the sweltering dark. So this is what real trauma feels like. My left leg is twitching involuntarily, like a smashed cymbal that's still reverberating. I can taste the shock in my mouth. One minute I'm crushed by the realisation that I can't look after Kit for the foreseeable future. The next I'm fretting about cancelling my direct debits. Forget feeling the full legal force of the British government; I'm now fearful that I'll leave prison to the mother of all Netflix bills.

The noise from the wing is intense. Someone is repeatedly kicking their door, someone else is screaming at him to shut up, someone else is crying out for an officer, someone else wants to score drugs, someone else wants to borrow tobacco, someone else is going to cripple their neighbour for non-payment of an earlier tobacco debt, someone else has somehow got hold of a thumpingly loud stereo and is playing drill rap at such a volume that the walls throb. I'm a bit irked by this, remembering how my little analogue radio was confiscated in reception. The protective bubble from Kit's hug is fading, and dots start jumping in front of my eyes. I drift off and dream about the trial.

2 July

I wake from the best night's sleep I've had for weeks. It takes me a while to work out that I'm in prison and it's a Saturday. Ted is already up.

'When do we get unlocked?' I ask.

He laughs. 'We'll be lucky if we get out at all.'

Inmates keep coming up to our door and demanding tobacco.

'Skinny burn, please, I beg you!'

'Fam, you give me burn, I pay you back canteen.'

I start to stammer an apology, but Ted simply barks, 'Fuck off!'

I'm finding it nearly impossible to absorb my new surroundings. Instead I try to contemplate the bigger picture, and start to digest the fact that I'll be in prison for the next couple of years. This makes me feel even worse, so I go back to looking around the room. The graffiti is mainly incomprehensible, but near my bed someone has scrawled, *They can lock the locks, but they can't stop the clocks*. It's the first sensible thing I've heard since I arrived.

I slowly unpack my things, and pull out some photos of Kit.

'Toothpaste,' says Ted. I rummage in my bag and hand him a tube of Colgate. 'No, you idiot, use toothpaste to stick your photos to the wall.' I do as instructed, and it holds surprisingly well. Ted winks and points to his head. 'Up here for thinking, down here for dancing,' and motions to his feet.

The door unexpectedly opens, and an officer shouts, 'S and Ds!' This is 'Social and Domestics', a brief window to get out of the cell to do whatever needs doing. Ted takes charge of the schedule. 'I need a crap; why don't you go and see what the showers are like.'

I nervously head out onto the landing, where the other residents are also spilling out, and am directed to the shower room, which is on the opposite spur. I walk into a wall of steam, and I'm overwhelmed by the stench of marijuana mixed with human waste. I now realise why the prison blogs strongly recommended flip-flops, as the floor is ankle deep in plastic bags, razors, floss and shampoo bottles. There are only six shower heads, and the place is heaving with bodies. I quickly undress and dive in. It takes me a moment to clock that everyone else is showering in their pants. Being the only naked person in the room isn't exactly helping my efforts to remain inconspicuous.

We're unable to lock the cell door, so Ted and I take turns to keep watch. He borrows my flip-flops and goes for a shower, and I'm soon visited by our next-door neighbour. He has a couple of gruesome facial scars and several missing teeth.

'I see you've got a TV,' he drawls in a thick Birmingham accent. I really wish Ted was here. 'I haven't got a TV,' he continues.

'Sorry about that,' I stammer. I have no idea how to end this conversation.

'The screws wouldn't gimme one. They said I should borrow yours.' I steadfastly refuse to take the hint. He peers into our cell, his beady eyes alighting on a copy of the *Sun* on Ted's bed. 'You've got a newspaper as well!' he says accusingly.

I feel cornered, fearful that I'll get shanked over a tabloid newspaper that I hate. Mercifully Ted soon reappears, his antennae twitching at the potential home invasion. The Brummie scuttles away.

'What did that inbred want?' Ted demands. I'm flushed with pride as I recount how I held back the marauding hordes.

After that, we're locked up for the rest of the day. I always thought that inmates were coy about discussing their crimes, but Ted is more than happy to talk about his colourful career. He was initially arrested in 2004 for importing rather a lot of cocaine. 'A lot' turns out to be 115 kilos. The police raided his house, and found 2,000 Ecstasy tablets, a dozen fake passports, £500,000 in cash, a pepper spray and 12 grams of cannabis. He is still smarting over the last item. 'That hash was just for personal use – I never sell anything less than a bleeding kilo.'

He was charged with multiple drugs conspiracies. The evidence against him was overwhelming, so he pleaded guilty and got a 17-year sentence. That meant eight and a half years in prison. He started out at Woodhill, the notorious Category B jail frequented by murderers and terrorists, and ended up at an open prison that allowed offenders out to work in the local community.

'I landed a great number working as a lifeguard at the local swimming pool,' he says. 'Perfect place to pick up single mums – talk about mouth to mouth.'

A few months before the end of his sentence, he did a runner and went 'on his toes' to Spain.

'Why did you abscond so close to the finish line?' I ask.

"Cos of my POCA,' he grunts.

The Proceeds of Crime Act (POCA) enables the government to confiscate criminals' assets. Offenders are ordered to pay back the fruits of their crimes, and can receive more jail time if they don't cough up.[1] Ted was clearly very good at his job, and had built up a large collection of houses and cars, and the CPS tried to get the lot. He was hit with a £2 million bill, and told that if he didn't pay, he'd get additional years on his sentence.

In Spain, he lay low and enjoyed the sun for four years. A few days before I was sentenced, he was rudely arrested at Malaga airport under a European Arrest Warrant. He was wearing little more than a shirt and shorts.

'I'll have to serve out the rest of the original sentence, plus the additional time for the outstanding POCA. Probably a couple of years.' He says this with mild irritation, as though he's been stuffed with a larger than expected hotel bill.

I tell him how I came to be in prison, and it feels really good to admit everything to someone in similar straits. Ted is thankfully approving of my crime, as it involved misappropriating money from the British government.

'How did they nail you in the end?' he asks.

'Basically because of a single email. I suggested deleting the whole email chain, and then forgot to do it.'

'You stupid fucking bastard!' He is quite annoyed at me for being such a terrible criminal.

3 July

I keep failing to get my head round my situation. It's like trying to look at a whole mountain while hanging off the side of it. A five-year sentence means I'll serve two and a half years, which is 30 months. Even saying that figure out loud makes me weak at the knees. Ted knows the system backwards, and maps out how my prison journey will progress from here. As a white-collar criminal on my first offence, I'll definitely qualify for Cat D status, which is the gateway to open prison. Unfortunately, I can only get made Cat D once I have less than 24 months to serve. This means I'll have to spend at least six months in Wandsworth.

Two pieces of pink A4 paper are randomly shoved under the door.

'These are the canteen sheets,' advises Ted.

The canteen is basically the prison shop. We can order toiletries and groceries, which get delivered a week later. My £100 hasn't yet been credited to my account, so I only have 50p to spend. Ted is sitting on the giddy sum of £1, and deduces that we've both been put on the unemployed rate of 50p per day. It's darkly ironic that I've been convicted of conspiracy to rob a million quid and Ted has been jailed for importing £10 million of cocaine, but we haven't got enough between us to buy a pack of Hobnobs. The coffee in my non-smoker's pack is dwindling fast, so I order three sachets of Nescafé.

The evening wears on, and the wing chorus cranks up. Many of our neighbours are keeping themselves fit by pulverising their cell doors.

'Where do they get the energy?' I wonder aloud.

'These lowlifes are all riddled with drugs,' replies Ted.

This seems a pretty ironic criticism, given his line of work. 'How do you know they aren't on drugs that you've supplied?'

'None of these scumbags could afford my drugs,' he scoffs. 'They're all fucked on spice.'

The spice is right

Spice is a synthetic version of cannabis. It used to be a 'legal high' but was criminalised in 2016,[2] which did nothing to dent its popularity. This drug is the reason why 50% of prisoners look like extras on a zombie film, with saucer white eyes, flaky skin and a twitchy step. It's by far the most popular choice inside, and people who'd normally take other drugs switch to spice while in jail. It doesn't show up on standard drugs tests,[3] it's mostly undetectable by sniffer dogs and can even be soaked in paper and posted in.[4] Spice attacks are commonplace; prisoners will suddenly hit the deck without any warning. It's even a hazard for those who don't intend to take drugs. An old man nearly died after smoking a cigarette he'd rolled out of dog ends that happened to contain more than tobacco. The lethal potency is actually part of the marketing; one particularly virulent strain of spice is known as 'Man Down'.[5] A report found that one in five addicts actually picked up their habit while serving their sentence,[6] one of many examples of how prison increases crime. I never touched any drugs during my sentence; I can't imagine anything worse than coming down in a rancid prison cell.

We remain locked in the cell for the rest of the day, and sit on our beds watching TV. The shock of imprisonment has made me extremely weak, so it's just as well I have to loaf about, as I'm not much good for anything else.

4 July

I wake up slowly.

'How did you sleep?' asks Ted

'I keep dreaming about the trial.'

He gives me a stern look. 'You need to cut that out. That's all in your past and you have to focus on your future.' I agree with his wise words. 'You need to start dreaming about prison life. Like how you're going to get bummed in the shower.' He laughs like a drain and I can just about crack a smile.

The toilet is so revolting that I haven't had a crap for three days. I feel like I'm at the battered end of a music festival. There's no seat, and the stains are so bad that I feel unsafe just hovering above it. The sink doesn't have a plughole or taps – the water is button-activated and frequently runs dry. I'll cover myself in soap, but then nothing emerges to rinse it off. My frustration at the appalling conditions suddenly makes me feel guilty. Halfway through complaining, I'll hear Judge Beddoe's voice in my head, accusing me of blowing the money earmarked for prison toilets on the *Starsuckers* animation sequences.

A screw unlocks our door and shouts, 'Induction!' We're led round the other side of the landing to a classroom. There are two rows of computers, and we watch a PowerPoint presentation on how the prison supposedly works. All inmates have to do a job or an education course, which will mean much more time out of the cell. There's also information on visits, phone calls and post. I'm trying to take it all in when our Brummie neighbour sidles up next to me.

'My mate's on telly tonight,' he hisses. I look round for Ted, but he's already buggered off. 'I'll just borrow your TV to watch him. I'll bring it straight back.' It gives some indication of my mental state that I don't immediately discount this request. In my defence, I've worked in the media for years and my friends often appear on TV, so it does seem vaguely plausible.

I foolishly give an inch. 'I'll have to ask my cellmate, it's his TV.' The Brummie looks like the telly is as good as his.

An orderly gives me an induction booklet, which is a wedge of photocopied A4 pages, and I'm sent to a classroom on the landing below.

'You need to do your English and maths tests,' another orderly instructs. I take the assessments a tad more seriously than the other inductees – two young lads are rolling joints, while an eastern European guy mutters darkly to himself. The orderly quickly marks my paper. 'Forty-four out of forty-five. Well done.'

I can't let this slide. 'What did I get wrong?'

He rolls his eyes. 'It doesn't matter. You got level two; it's the highest there is.'

'What education courses can I sign up to?'

'None. All the main prison wings have just been shut down for the summer. Lack of staff.'

I'm confused. 'So what do we do?'

He yawns. 'Stay banged up in your cell. Gonna be like this till August.'

I'm staggered that hundreds of men are simply locked in cells all day. No wonder most of them are going round the twist.

I return to our cell, where the Brummie is lurking with intent outside. I say to Ted, 'So, er, the guy next door wants to borrow the TV.' Ted looks like I've just proposed to him, but I stumble on. 'Um, a mate of his is on a show tonight. He just needs to borrow it for an hour.' It's only once the words are out of my mouth that I realise how ridiculous this sounds.

'He hasn't got a bleeding mate on TV, you sap!' Ted barks incredulously. 'And if he has, it's on fucking *Crimewatch*.' I curse myself for being so naïve.

In the afternoon, we are opened up for exercise. We all troop down the stairs and head out through a side door into the blazing sun. The yard is massive, about 70 metres in diameter. On one side is the towering Victorian prison wing. It's caked in gunge, as if a shit bomb has been detonated on the set of a Tim Burton movie. The other sides are enclosed by a high metal fence with razor wire along the top. After languishing in a tiny box, I find the expanse of space quite a shock.

There are about 80 other prisoners in the yard, and they immediately start coalescing around ethnic lines. The atmosphere is thick with aggression as everyone eyes each other up. I keep playing the opening bars of *West Side Story* in my head. A single screw stands by the door back onto the wing, looking like he'd happily leg it at the first sign of trouble. Ted and I walk round the perimeter; I have to stop myself physically clinging to his arm. He's one of the oldest people here, but he still carries an air of incendiary menace. After a few circuits he suddenly approaches a bunch of muscular lads doing press-ups. They chat briefly, and then Ted walks back to me. 'I just told them I was doing a seventeen stretch for a hundred and fifteen Ks of Charlie,' he whispers. 'We're not going to get any hassle.'

The sunshine and fresh air does me a lot of good. After an hour, the screw calls time, and we're herded straight back to our cells.

My daily routine quickly centres around the only two opportunities to get out of the cell. On a good day we get S&Ds in the morning and exercise in the afternoon. On a bad day, one or both are cancelled. The bad days outnumber the good.

6 July

I am desperate to call home. There are blue prisoner phones at the end of each landing, but we need a pin number to make calls. My initial emergency credit has long gone, and I've submitted the necessary forms to get a permanent pin. I then hear that there's a four-week backlog. I know I have a big support network outside, but as all communication is severed, I start to feel isolated and abandoned. When I first arrived, I was told that I could have unlimited visits in the first week. During S&Ds, an officer informs me that this is only for remand prisoners – inmates who have been charged but not convicted. Sentenced cons like me can only have one induction visit, and thereafter only two visits a month, each just an hour long.

I cannot believe that this will be the only contact I'll get with my son. Until my imprisonment, Kit lived with me for half the week, and the prospect of near total separation is devastating. I tell an officer that I was given a bum steer on the visits, and she lets me use the office phone. Thankfully Lottie answers, and we agree that she should visit on her own first, and judge if it's appropriate for Kit to come later.

'Are you OK?' she asks.

'I'm completely fine,' I lie. I can see the officer is running out of patience. 'What's all the gossip on the outside about?'

Lottie takes a deep breath. 'You.'

I return to the cell and discover a pile of correspondence on my bed. It's a combination of old-fashioned letters and printed emails. These are from the emailaprisoner.com service, which pretty much does what it says on the tin. It's fantastic to finally hear from friends and family. Everyone has been googling Wandsworth and apparently my new home has a terrifying reputation. I reply to every missive, but it's been a while since I've written with a pen, and my joined-up handwriting is unintelligible. I end up writing in shouty block capitals, which will do nothing to alleviate any concerns that I've lost my marbles.

I'd always assumed that though prison cuisine would taste bad, there'd at least be enough of it. However, both the quantity and quality are straight out of a Victorian workhouse, except that we don't even get to do any work. The 'breakfast pack' consists of a toddler's serving of cereal, two jam sachets (with nothing to spread it on), sugar, tea bags, coffee whitener (but no actual coffee) and a fun-size carton of milk. I consume all this by 8 a.m. and am starving again by 9.

Lunch is the only purportedly hot meal of the day, and is served around 11 a.m. We're unlocked and head to a small servery on the landing below. A derisory portion of something barely edible is slapped onto a plastic plate. Occasionally there are a couple of slices of bread. We then totter back up to the cell, and by the time we tuck in, the food is anywhere between lukewarm and stone cold. Around 4 p.m., our door is opened and a cackling prisoner dumps two mushy baguettes on the side. If we're lucky, there's an item of stale fruit and a Penguin bar.

The induction booklet insists that this is all the nutrition a grown man needs, but if I fed it to Kit I'd be prosecuted for parental neglect. Ted says the only way to survive is to buy additional food from the canteen. I can't wait until Friday for my first delivery.

7 July

I become consumed with anxiety about when Lottie is coming to visit. Ted maintains a level head in the face of all frustrations. 'The beginning is always the worst. Once you've got through the first week, it gets slowly better.' He's spent years in prison, and teaches me some of his extensive jail skills. He fashions a bin out of a cardboard box and lines it with newspaper.

'Don't chuck in any leftover food,' he warns. 'It'll rot in this heat, and stink the place out. Always bung food waste down the toilet.' He demonstrates by flushing some bread and orange peel. I give it a go, and panic when an apple core doesn't go down. I keep flushing but it refuses to disappear, like a nauseating game of apple bobbing.

'Just be patient,' advises Ted. '*Everything* sinks once it's absorbed enough water,' he adds ominously, giving me the willies.

An officer suddenly opens the door. 'ATKINS! VISIT!' I leap off the bed, which nearly causes it to collapse, and quickly try to make myself presentable. This is a tall order, as I haven't shaved in a week or showered for three days. I follow the officer down to the gates at the end of the landing that connect the wing to the 'centre'. This is a massive domed hexagon at the heart of the prison structure, with six colossal wings feeding off it.

The perfect prison

The main part of Wandsworth follows the classic Victorian 'spider' design, where six wings radiate out from a central point. This structure was pioneered by the nineteenth-century philosopher Jeremy Bentham, who tried to create the perfect prison, believing that inmates would behave if they thought they were always being watched.[7] However, given the utter carnage that was usually unfolding at Wandsworth, Bentham's theory seemed somewhat flawed. Nobody ever gave a stuff about being watched, and prisoners seemed happy to run around dealing drugs, getting in fights and wrestling with officers.

I'm led into a revolting holding room, full of smoking inmates. We're all issued with purple bibs, presumably to identify us as prisoners, though looking round this group, I doubt anyone would be confused about who we were.

The visits hall is enormous, and Lottie is waving at me from a nearby table. We hug and sit; neither of us can keep a straight face about how utterly weird this is. She's been allowed to bring in £5 to spend, which I beg her to convert into coffee and food. She queues up at the café hatch, and I survey the hall. There are about 40 tables in six rows. Each table has three seats on one side for visitors, with one seat on the other side for the prisoner. In the far corner, there is a children's section, with toys, books and a small soft play area, giving me some hope that Kit can visit soon.

Lottie returns laden with sustenance, which I immediately start wolfing down. She looks at me as if I've just returned from a tour of Vietnam. She says that Kit is fine, but that he's realised something is up. Before I was sentenced, I told him that I'd done something wrong and would have to go on quite a long time-out. He seemed to accept the principle, but obviously not the duration of the time I'd be away. Lottie agrees that he should come and visit as soon as possible. I'm massively grateful for her strength and support, and not for the first time I tell myself that I had a child with the right woman.

The visit puts a spring in my step, and reminds me that I haven't been completely forgotten. During the next S&Ds, I ask an officer if my son has been cleared to visit. The screw looks me up on NOMIS, the prisoner database, and sees that Kit still isn't approved.

'We have to do criminal background checks. It can take a few weeks.'

'He's three,' I reply. The officer shrugs, as if this detail is completely immaterial.

8 July

The good news is that I haven't had a cigarette for a week. I really only smoked while drinking, so an absence of alcohol has made quitting fags a lot easier. Other prisoners occasionally offer me 'two's up', which is basically taking sloppy seconds on their roll-up, but I've managed to resist the temptation. The bad news is that my sense of smell is returning in the last place you'd want to redevelop your nasal abilities. The wing stinks of decaying sweat and weapons-grade disinfectant.

Friday is canteen delivery day. In the afternoon, our door is unlocked and I skip to the landing below like a child on Christmas morning. They hand over my bag, and my heart sinks. It's a large clear plastic sack, and my coffee sachets only take up 1% of its capacity, horribly accentuating the pathetic size of the order. I look enviously at other prisoners lugging bags full of chocolate, cereal and tinned curry. Back in the cell, I realise that I've accidentally been given an extra coffee sachet, and I'm suddenly ecstatic again.

Ted has invested his £1 in gravy granules. 'There isn't a meal in prison that can't be improved with a dollop of gravy. That includes most of the desserts.'

9 July

We don't get out at all over the weekend. The temperature goes through the roof and the sun shines mercilessly into the cell, turning it into a sauna. The windows were clearly designed with security as a greater priority than ventilation, and don't open at all. The door has a thin vertical glass observation panel, and there's a metal flap on the outside that isn't quite closed. I can peek out onto the landing like a demented curtain twitcher, seething about the prisoners larking around outside.

'How come they're out of their cells?' I demand.

'Some will have got out for the Sunday service,' Ted replies. 'Others are junkies who're unlocked for their meds. A lot of these fuckers tick both boxes, so they can pick up their methadone and then sell it in church.' I seriously consider faking a heroin problem and/or Christianity just to stretch my legs.

In the afternoon, we prepare for a stroll in the yard, but a screw shouts out that exercise is cancelled as it's raining. This is contradicted by the cloudless blue sky, which is clearly visible from our window.

Ted deals with the vicious bang-up by taking extended siestas. I tell him he's spent too long in Spain. 'Not long enough,' he growls back.

11 July

I read the prison induction booklet cover to cover. A great deal of it is utterly at odds with everything I've experienced so far. We can supposedly visit the library once a week, but none of the officers know about this and one screw questions whether there even is a library in the prison. There's allegedly a weekly kit change, where we can exchange prison clothes, sheets and towels. I've been wearing the same rags for a fortnight and I'm desperate to get clean clobber. When I ask an officer about the kit change, he just laughs and walks away. There is a whole section on 'purposeful activity'; an officer confirms that practically all such activity has been cancelled due to staff shortages. The only place where prisoners can do jobs and educational courses is Trinity, which is a separate unit for sentenced prisoners. This sounds like the place to be, and I beg to be moved there.

'Got to wait until you're categorised,' replies the officer. All prisoners are given a security categorisation between A (murderers and terrorists) and D (low-risk criminals, who end up in open prison).[8] I should be made Cat C for the first six months, so I can at least get to Trinity.

'How long until that happens?' I ask.

'Could be weeks. There's a massive backlog.'

He suggests moving to one of the other main wings in the meantime. 'Anywhere is better than here. A Wing isn't so bad – there aren't as many crackpots.'

Ted is wary of moving. We get on pretty well, and we've avoided any serious problems on E Wing. Shifting location might split us up. I'm terrified of sharing a flight of stairs with most of the people I've met inside, let alone bunking up with them.

14 July

S&Ds are cancelled, and then exercise is called off as well. Ted cracks and agrees to move, but insists that we stick together. 'It's not where you go, it's who you're with.' I tell the officer that we want to move to another wing, and he offers us a double cell on A Wing. We snap it up, and quickly throw all our stuff into bin liners. We're escorted into the centre and through a double gate.

A Wing has much the same structure as E Wing, but there's markedly less screaming and door-kicking. We are led to a cell on the 'Twos'.

Cell A2-10 is the same size as our former pad, but is in much better condition. The walls are mainly graffiti-free, the bunk beds are structurally sound, and the window actually lets in air.

'There's no fucking kettle,' observes Ted.

The screw doesn't give a toss. 'There's a long waiting list for replacements,' he tells us, and leaves without even indicating if we'll be added to the bottom of it. This is disastrous news. I've been drinking tea constantly since I've been inside. I also ordered some noodles from the canteen, which I've been looking forward to all week. My despair is heightened by the realisation that this is going to be the norm from now on.

For the first few days in prison I was in reasonably good spirits, buoyed by the body's natural reaction to trauma, in much the same way that people often laugh and joke following a fatal prognosis. But the comforting glow of adrenaline has now worn off, and my prospects look extremely bleak. I am going to be banged up for at least 22 hours a day until I'm categorised, which could take weeks. I can't phone home, and Kit still isn't approved as a visitor, so I have no idea when I'll see him again.

And I can't even make a cup of tea.

2

Lockdowns and Love Actually

In which I progress through three different prison wings, with the bang-up getting steadily worse. The authorities continue to block my son from visiting, and the separation becomes unbearable.

Things I learn:

1) The futility of submitting application forms

2) How to phone home

3) The delicate notion of shittiquette

I get trapped in a temple of porn with a deranged Romanian, but fortuitously jump the property ladder into Little Hampstead.

15 July

At noon we are opened up for lunch. In the queue, I check out my new neighbours, who are mostly twice my size. Many seem to be from eastern Europe. The food is a bit better, and the servery workers are reasonably jolly. One of them recognises Ted.

'Ted! What's going on!?'

'Fuck me, it's, er, Mike?' Ted ventures.

'Yeah, mate, we were in Springhill.' Mike is about 18 stone and has an impressive beard.

Ted is in his element. 'Of course! That must have been six years back. How you doing?'

Mike smiles coyly. 'Back in on an eighteen stretch. What about you?'

'Went on me toes to dodge the confiscation. Just got busted in Spain.'

'Nightmare. You got everything you need?'

'Just moved in, but there's no cunting kettle.'

'Let me see what I can do.'

I totter round the end of the hotplate, struggling to carry all the various items. Suddenly I feel a hand on my arm. My blood runs cold; I assume that I'm getting jumped. I turn to see Mike surreptitiously wedging a small kettle under my arm. He gives me a wink, and I mouth, 'Thank you.'

Back in the cell, I make a cup of tea, and bounce off the walls with happiness. This emotional yo-yoing continues for some time. A small setback will send me off a cliff, and a nugget of good fortune feels like I've won the lottery.

16 July

The authorities are still probing Kit's criminal history, so I have my next visit with just Lottie again. It's brilliant to see her, but we are running on completely different clocks. I have to speed up massively to keep up with her, and I'm completely exhausted by the end.

As our visitors leave the hall, I chat to a gregarious Australian called Scott. He lives on Trinity, the separate Cat C unit, and is effusive about the better conditions.

'It is *so* much better than the main wings. We usually get gym at seven thirty, then do education and jobs most of the day. We're out practically all the time.' This sounds like paradise compared to my current regime.

Later on, I ask an officer if I can move to Trinity, and he looks me up on NOMIS, the creaking prisoner database. 'Sorry, mate, you're still uncategorised. You can't move to Trinity until you're a Cat C.'

17 July

It's Kit's birthday and I hit an all-time low. I still haven't received a phone pin, so I'm unable to call out. Brandishing a photo of Kit, I find the only female officer on duty.

'Sorry to disturb you, miss.' Female screws are all called 'miss', like we're at school. 'It's my son's fourth birthday and I still can't call home.'

She lets me use her office phone, and I get a couple of minutes with Kit while he blows out the candles. The officer is furious that I'm still without phone access. 'Wandsworth is the shittest prison I've ever worked in. There are never any fucking staff and the governors are all cunts.' She tells me to fill out another phone pin application, and promises to take it to the relevant office.

I get another huge bundle of letters and printed emails. I'd arranged to take Kit on holiday to France with my friends from university, and they've obviously had to go without us. People are Facebooking photos of me playing with everyone's kids on previous trips. It feels as close as you can get to being dead without actually dying. I've always wanted to know what it would be like to attend my own funeral, and I guess this is the next best thing.

18 July

Theresa May has been anointed as prime minister, and she unveils her first cabinet. Liz Truss is promoted to Justice Secretary, taking ultimate responsibility for the nation's prisons.[1] This surprises everyone, not least Liz Truss herself, who walks into Downing Street looking as if she knows as much about prisons as I did when I entered Wandsworth.

Truss announces that she will continue the reform programme that was the brainchild of her predecessor, Michael Gove. 'I am under no illusions about the scale of the challenge we face ... I am clear that the vital work of prison reform will continue at pace.'[2]

Reformed characters

I arrived in Wandsworth just as it became the very first 'reform prison', spearheading a radical new policy designed to tackle the escalating prison crisis. Suicides, assaults, self-harm and reoffending were at record levels, and the reform programme was intended to solve all these problems. It gave unprecedented powers to Wandsworth's new executive governor, Ian Bickers, allowing him control over the £35m budget, and autonomy over how the prison was run. Bickers was quoted as saying that Wandsworth was not fit for purpose, and pledged to transform the jail in 18 months.[3] SPOILER ALERT! Things didn't exactly go to plan ...

Watching the TV brings out Ted's ugly side, and he keeps unleashing intolerant tirades at the news. I reluctantly have to reappraise his political stance from 'ardent Brexiteer' to 'borderline racist'. The news shows a boat overloaded with refugees, and Ted shouts, 'Let the fucking cockroaches drown!' My middle-class liberal sensibilities go into a tailspin. I instinctively want to challenge these outbursts, but Ted has been my prison mentor and protector, and I don't want to poison the atmosphere. I'm also terrified that his xenophobic rants will be overheard. White Brits are definitely an ethnic minority in Wandsworth, and there are a lot of black and Muslim guys on this wing.

One afternoon the BBC reports a surge in knife crime, and Ted carps that 'It's just a bunch of black bastards stabbing each other.'

There is a sudden vocal explosion outside our locked door.

'WHAT YOU SAYING ABOUT MY PEOPLE?! I'M GONNA CUT YOU UP!'

Through our observation panel I can see the bulging red eyes of a seething prisoner staring in. He looks like he's been infected by the Rage Virus in *28 Days Later*, and my heart stops. Even Ted goes white. We then hear a huge laugh.

'TED! I is only messing with you, innit. It's Reggie! Remember me?!'

Ted looks as though he's just been given the all-clear from a cancer scare. 'Yeah, Reggie! How's it going?'

Reggie too knows Ted from a previous prison, and I meet him in the exercise yard later on. He's about six foot six, and appears to have fallen into a cauldron of steroids as a baby. He tells us about a recent run-in with a Tornado squad, the double-hard officers who are sent in to quell riots. While the screws got tooled up outside Reggie's cell, he covered himself in baby oil, a technique pioneered by veteran prison lunatic Charles Bronson that prevents anyone getting a grip on you. He also squirted oil all over the floor. He acts out the scene where three Tornado officers stormed his cell and went arse over tit. This scrap got him carted off to the block (aka the segregation unit, where troublesome inmates are kept in total isolation). He is in stitches while he tells us his story. I'm laughing out of nervous fear.

We return to the cell and find a large sack of bananas on the floor.

'That'll be from Mike,' says Ted. 'I did a few favours for him back in Springhill.' I really don't want to know what they were.

19 July

I finally get issued with my phone pin. When we're opened for S&Ds, I run to the phone at the end of the landing and call Lottie and Kit. The wing is extremely noisy and I can't make out a lot of what Kit is saying, but it's an intense relief to finally hear his little voice. Before

I came inside, we'd usually use FaceTime, and he doesn't understand why he can't see me on the phone. I'm limited to five minutes per call, and the charges are stuck in the 1990s. I've put £4 on my phone credit, but this gets burned up calling Lottie's mobile. I resolve to hear Kit's voice every day, but this is no easy task. There's always a hefty queue for the phones, and scary prisoners frequently push in. If my call goes to voicemail then I'm blocked from calling again for 10 minutes, so I can easily blow most of my S&Ds trying to get through.

20 July

The incessant lockdown gets most awkward when we need to take a crap. Basic human decency dictates that this activity is best undertaken alone, but nature eventually prevails over dignity. Sometimes we just have to get on with it, and I'm introduced to the art of 'shittiquette' – how to lay a turd while being considerate towards your cellmate.

This afternoon Ted randomly turns up the TV volume and then discreetly disappears behind the curtain. I don't realise what he's up to, and I get increasingly angry at the Victoria Derbyshire show, which is discussing a Twitter spat between Kanye West and Taylor Swift.

'Why do we have to watch this crap?' I demand.

'So you don't have to listen to mine,' replies Ted. 'I'm chopping one off. I only put it on so you don't hear my noises.'

'I'd rather listen to you having a shit, to be perfectly honest.'

The A Wing shower room is marginally less revolting than the one on E Wing, though the floors are still awash with detritus. It's a major faff dealing with my glasses, which I precariously balance on a nearby pipe. I always scrub myself raw, as I have no idea when I'll be able to shower again. Today my frenetic washing knocks my glasses into the razors and dental floss, and one of the lenses pops out. This is a disaster, as it's my only pair and I'm practically blind without them. I instinctively bend over to rescue them, realising too late that this is the last thing one should do in a prison shower.

I hunt through the trash with my arse in the air, really wishing I'd worn some pants into the shower. I eventually find the lens, but need something to screw the frame back together again. There are some maintenance staff up on the top landing, and I tap one of them on the shoulder.

'Hi, guys, sorry to bother you. Any chance I could borrow a small screwdriver?' They shake their heads and walk away quickly.

I recount this to Ted, who laughs himself silly. 'They thought you wanted it to stab someone, you dipshit.' Instead I cannibalise a biro top, and manage to twist in the tiny screw. It's unlikely to stay in for long, and I fill in the first of many healthcare applications asking to see an optician.

At or around this time I start showering in my pants.

21 July

I ask an officer to look at my NOMIS file, which reveals that Kit still hasn't been authorised to visit. Peering at the screen, I notice a big 'C' next to my name.

'Does that mean I've been made a Cat C?'

'Yup.'

'Can I move to Trinity?' I ask breathlessly.

'Sure, I'll put you on the list. You'll go this afternoon.'

I break the news to Ted, who is furious that I'm abandoning him for pastures new. He's still uncategorised, so won't be able to come with me. My impending departure leads to an uncomfortable atmosphere in the cell, like the last days of a relationship, and I pack my things in silence.

As the afternoon turns to evening, it becomes obvious that I'm not going anywhere today. I wretchedly unpack again, while Ted grins to himself. This uncertainty continues for the next two days, and I turn into a febrile wreck. Every time a screw approaches, I assume I'm about to move, and jump off the bed ready to go. When the officer walks past without stopping, I'm completely crushed.

Ted is unsympathetic. 'It won't be any better over there, you know.' I realise this is just jealousy – Trinity is obviously vastly superior – and I bite my tongue.

22 July

A female officer suddenly unlocks the door. 'Atkins? Why aren't you ready?' I hurl my stuff into bags, and Ted helps me pack. Suddenly we're friends again. I thank him for his kindness, and for making the start of my prison journey just about bearable. We even stretch to a hug.

I go down to the far end of the wing with five other prisoners. I'm giddy with excitement, and can't wait to start my new life on Trinity. We're led out of a back door into blazing sunlight, and I lug my bags towards a smaller building nearby. The officer leads us up some steps, and we go in through a big rusty metal door. Inside is a slightly smaller version of where I've just left. The cell doors are the same, the banging is the same; I even recognise one of the more colourful characters from E Wing.

Trinity is essentially a mini version of the main prison: a smaller domed centre with three wings protruding from it. An officer resembling the Milky Bar Kid leads me to the top of K Wing and opens up K4-09. Sitting inside is a man in his forties, with jet-black skin and a deeply irritated expression. I offer him my hand, but he completely ignores it and in broken English pleads with the officer not to move me into his cell. The Milky Bar screw tells him to lump it, and I drag my stuff over the threshold.

My reluctant new cellmate is from Sri Lanka, and I work out that his name is Yogi. At least the cell is a pleasing improvement. It has a kettle and a TV, and the bunks are built into the wall. The window actually opens to let a nice breeze in. Now that I'm on the top floor, I can just about see London's skyline by standing on the loo.

It's Friday, and I can't wait for my canteen delivery. On my last order I was allowed to spend a whopping £10. Half went towards phone credit, and the rest I splurged on coffee, tomato ketchup and tinned mackerel. Later on, an officer opens the door, accompanied by a couple of prisoners handing out the canteen bags. Yogi is given his groceries, but there is nothing for me.

'Any idea what's happened to my canteen?' I ask.

'You've just moved here from A Wing,' replies the officer. 'Your order was probably delivered there, so it should come across here on Saturday.'

It never arrives.

Can't complain

I submitted several 'Comp 1' complaint forms asking for a refund for my missing groceries. After taking longer than some murder investigations, the complaints department finally responded in December. They concluded that my canteen was received by someone, but they could not identify who it was. They offered me a full refund, with just one small caveat: I had to provide written confirmation from an officer that I didn't receive my order. This is known as 'proving a negative'. It's a philosophical hot potato that is sometimes used to undermine atheism, as it's impossible to prove the non-existence of God. There were 500 residents on Trinity, and over 8,000 canteen bags would have been delivered in the intervening months. Asking an officer to testify that I didn't receive some groceries in July would have got me laughed off the wing. The authorities were clearly asking for unobtainable proof to avoid coughing up.

23 July

It's Saturday, and we're opened up at 8.30 for S&Ds. This turns out to be only 45 minutes long, and includes our exercise time as well. Yogi and I agree to take turns watching the cell, and he goes off for a shower while I take the first shift. When he fails to return on time, I get increasingly agitated. He eventually saunters back after half an hour and finds my anger highly amusing. I run off and try to shower and phone home in just 10 minutes. The shower room is the worst yet: a total swamp. There's a small exercise yard adjacent to K Wing, and I dart out into the sun. I don't even make a single lap before the officer calls time, and we're then locked up for the rest of the day.

24 July

During S&Ds, I bump into Scott, the chatty Australian whose tales of Trinity lured me over here. He's wearing his own clothes and clutching a clipboard.

'How're you doing, Tiger?' he asks with a massive cheesy grin.

'I have to say, this place is not living up to your glowing description.'

'Jeez, sorry about that.' Scott starts rattling off details about my new home, and it becomes clear that he's lived here for some considerable time. 'There are three wings on Trinity,' he continues. 'Your problem is that you're on K Wing, which is where they keep all the nutjobs. Do *not* move to G Wing, whatever you do. All the normal people are on H Wing; we get loads more time out of our cells.'

'How do I get to H Wing?' I plead.

'You need to catch one of the officers in a good mood. I'd strongly advise signing up to a course, then you'll get unlocked for freeflow on weekdays. That's when inmates who have jobs and education can leave the wing.'

Later, I queue up to see an officer.

'Guv, I really think I belong on H Wing.'

'It's Enhanced prisoners only on H Wing.' He looks me up on NOMIS. 'You've only just arrived, so you're currently on Standard.' He's referring to my IEP level, which dictates what privileges I can access. 'After three months you can apply to be Enhanced, and then you can move to H Wing.' This means that I'll be stuck on K Wing for at least another nine weeks.

Disincentivised and underprivileged

The IEP (Incentives and Earned Privileges) scheme was heavily tightened up by former Justice Secretary Chris Grayling. He declared that 'It is not right that some prisoners appear to be spending hours languishing in their cells and watching daytime television.'[4] Four years later, the majority of Wandsworth's residents were stuck in their cells watching TV for 23 hours a day, so Grayling's reforms were hardly a screaming success. The IEP system is essentially the merit/demerit scheme I had at prep school, now being applied to crack addicts. Every prisoner has an IEP level:[5]

- Entry (newbies): covers the first two weeks; heavily restricted privileges
- Standard (plebs): two visits a month; have to wear prison clothes and can only spend £15 on the canteen
- Enhanced (swots): four visits a month; can wear own clothes and spend £37 on the canteen
- Basic (naughty corner): punishment regime; TVs are confiscated and inmates are locked in their cells all day

'Positive IEPs' are awarded for good behaviour, and 'negative IEPs' for bad. It wouldn't have been out of place for them to start issuing stickers.

This is a really simplistic summary; the IEP rules are in fact absurdly complicated. Hockey shirts and quilted coats are also banned and prisoners are limited to three pairs of pyjamas, ten pairs of socks and two shower caps.[6]

I'm dying to get stuck into my stack of books, but it's impossible to read as Yogi watches TV constantly and has assumed control over the remote. This afternoon we sit through *Love Actually*, which is comfortably my most hated film of all time. I've often joked that my idea of hell is being trapped in a room and forced to watch Richard Curtis films, and now it has come to pass. Yogi is chortling away, so I explain that the movie is a misogynistic fantasy. 'The female characters only exist to be courted by men, and it's furthering a deeply unequal neo-capitalist society.' This does not convince him to change the channel.

Yogi is also a ridiculously loud snorer, and I instinctively want to lean over and give him a mild kick. On reflection, I realise that the snoring has its advantages, enabling me to have a cheeky wank while I know he's definitely asleep.

25 July

On weekdays our door is opened at 8 a.m. for freeflow. Yogi heads out for his IT course, and I beg him to sign me up to the same class. He just gives me a pained smile and slinks away.

Hours later, an officer walks past, and I call through the locked door. 'Guv, GUV! Is there any way I can get on a course, any course? I'm going crazy in here.'

'Fill out a general app.'

Papers, please

The lifeblood of Wandsworth's ancient bureaucracy was the general application form, aka the general app, which still used the old carbon-copy system. These administrative relics were the stock answer to all my problems:

My canteen never arrived – fill in a general app.

My son is still not approved to visit – fill in another general app.

My glasses are broken and need fixing – talk to the general app.

At first I went a bit general-app crazy and started to flood the system. Later on, I chatted to a couple of friendly kids who were finding prison a barrel of laughs, possibly due to the joint they were openly passing between them. They both claimed to be cleaners, but didn't take their duties particularly seriously.

'It's all about getting out, bruv, you get me? Man gotta beat the bang-up. You need a cause to stay out the cells, you know what I'm sayin'?'

'Well I should be getting on an IT course soon,' I said confidently. 'I've filled out a bunch of general apps.'

They exploded in hysterics, and pointed to a nearby bin liner full of shredded paper. 'Those are your fucking apps, rude boy!'

27 July

Even the smallest level of human contact is a blessing. Whenever anyone comes to the cell door, I leap up to greet them as though I've been stranded on a desert island. This afternoon an elderly staff member peers in through the observation panel. He looks like a retired maths teacher, his glasses hanging round his neck on a cord.

'I don't suppose you'd be interested in a workshop on dry lining?' he asks.

'YES!' I reply, a bit too forcefully.

'Do you know what dry lining is?'

I yelp, 'Yes!' again, fearing that ignorance will bar me from the course.

'Excellent, I won't have to waste time explaining it. I'll put you on the list.' He shuffles away, and I instinctively reach to my pocket for my iPhone to google 'dry lining'. This is a habit I really need to get out of. I don't even have any pockets.

29 July

I'm queuing outside the wing office when an incandescent prisoner marches to the front.

'Marbles has shat in the showers *again!*' he yells.

I've thankfully already had a shower today, so I find this hilarious, but nobody else sees the funny side. Marbles is a tall Bangladeshi prisoner who is wandering around with his trousers halfway down to his ankles.

I eventually speak to an officer, who reveals that Kit is finally allowed to enter Wandsworth. I race to a phone and call Lottie, and she applies to visit immediately.

31 July

A slip appears under my door: *Activity allocated – dry lining. Starting 2 August.* I'm over the moon, although none the wiser about what dry lining actually is.

I return from S&Ds to find Yogi hurriedly packing his stuff. He cagily admits that he's moving to H Wing, which is infuriating, as he isn't Enhanced either. I interrogate him about how he's escaped K Wing, and he reveals that room moves are organised in an office on the Twos landing.

I sprint downstairs and burst through the door as politely as I can. One of the more affable screws is peering up at a huge wooden board on the wall that is straight out of a 1950s hotel. There are hundreds of little slots representing all the cells on Trinity, and index cards showing where each prisoner lives.

'Afternoon, guv. My cellmate's moving to H Wing, are there any more spaces?'

The screw looks at me quizzically, with one eyebrow raised. 'Are you on full-time work?'

I brandish my slip. 'I'm about to start dry lining.'

'What's dry lining?'

I'm not ready for this curveball. 'Well, it's, er, quite commonplace these days ... More and more prisons are starting to develop, er ... It's good for long-term ...'

I peter out, while the officer peruses the board.

'You won't be able to share with your cellmate; he's moving in with someone else.'

I try to say 'Bummer' without sounding sarcastic.

'There's one space free with a Romanian fella.'

'I'll take it.'

'We never have any problems with Romanians, always as good as gold. Get your stuff downstairs pronto.' He doesn't ask if I'm Enhanced.

I run back to the cell. Yogi's already departed, and has snaffled the kettle, the remote control and all my clear plastic bin bags. I don't really care, I'm ecstatic to be joining the hallowed ranks of H Wing. I chuck everything into a sheet, tie it up and head downstairs.

'You're in H3-19,' says the officer. 'You can make your own way there.'

H Wing has an identical structure to K Wing, but the atmosphere is distinctly calmer. I go up to the Threes – the second landing up – and find my cell. The door is locked, and the occupant is peering out through the observation panel. He has cropped blonde hair and a hard face, and eyes me suspiciously.

'You come here?' He speaks with a thick eastern European accent.

'Yes.'

'Do you smoke?'

'No,' I reply, and smile.

'You sure you don't smoke?' he asks a little louder.

'I definitely don't smoke.'

He nods and disappears back into the cell. A few minutes later, he returns to the door with a dark expression.

'Do you smoke?' he demands again. This throws me a bit, as I thought we'd resolved the issue.

'No, I still don't smoke.' I want to somehow prove that I haven't had a fag for a month. Hopefully his insistence is due to his strong aversion to smoking, rather than a serious mental illness.

An officer soon opens the door, and I enter my new home. I'm immediately overwhelmed by a deluge of pornography. I'd assumed that the internet had decimated the demand for porn mags, but this cell has clearly kept the market going. Every last bit of wall, and indeed the ceiling, is coated in tits and vaginas. There is smut on the inside of the cupboard doors, the underside of the bunk bed and even on the window frames. Standing in the middle of it is a stocky, square-jawed man in his forties, who introduces himself as Dan. I feel we're going to have a better relationship than I had with Yogi.

'Why you here?' he grunts.

I try to explain my fairly convoluted crime, but he quickly gets bored. I ask him what he did prior to being in prison.

'I worked the London Underground.'

'That's fascinating,' I say brightly. 'Were you a train driver?'

His eyes narrow. 'I was pickpocket.'

Notwithstanding the saturation porn, the cell is pretty clean. Dan gives me a bizarre guided tour, showing me the various scouring pads he uses for cleaning the dishes and the sink. The door opens for afternoon S&Ds, and he hands me a key to the cell. This is beyond thrilling, as there's now no need to stand guard. I head down to the ground-floor landing. Scott is marching around patting people on the back.

'Welcome to the Ritz!' he calls to me. 'Come and meet the rest of the White Collar Club.'

I follow him into his cell, which turns out to be enormous. It's basically two normal cells knocked together, and resembles a small studio flat. There's a separate sleeping section, and a big seating area with a large table. A group of guys are playing board games, and Scott introduces me to his cellmate, Lance. He's around 30, and overly proportioned, both in height and girth, resembling an adult Billy Bunter fallen on hard times.

'Ah, *you're* Atkins. Film chap. Where did you go to school?' He has a loud public-schoolboy manner that is utterly out of place.

Scott and Lance have got this large cell as a perk of being Listeners – prisoners trained by the Samaritans to comfort other inmates who are suicidal or self-harming. Their room also serves as a common room for the white-collar fraternity, and they insist that I'm welcome at any time.

1 August

Dan and I eat lunch side by side at the tiny desk in our cell. He makes a barbed comment about my elbow straying onto his side of the table. I jovially point out that we have less than two feet of desk space each, so we shouldn't stress the odd roving elbow, but he throws an aggressive sulk. I remove a couple of pairs of tits from the wall by my bed so that I can put up photos of Kit. Dan gets quite cross, but he grudgingly allows me to stick limited pictures on top of the porn. This significantly diminishes the emotional impact of seeing my only son, as Kit is now engulfed in images of degraded women. Dan then ticks me off for using the wrong scouring pad to clean the sink. I usually give as good as I get in a row – I even (maybe misguidedly) yelled at the prosecutor to 'grow up' during my cross-examination in court. But Dan looks like he's been in a few prison scraps, so I just cravenly apologise. At least I can look forward to tomorrow, which is the start of my dry-lining experience.

2 August

At 8 a.m., our door is unlocked for freeflow. The landing is seething with dozens of inmates stomping around, while screws shout at everyone to hurry up. I still have no idea what dry lining is, or where it's situated. Thankfully, one of the White Collar Club, Nigel, is on the same course, so I tag along with him.

We go out the back door into the open air. The main prison wings loom in front of us, and round to our left is a line of decrepit corrugated-iron buildings. One of the workshops has a new sign outside: *Bounceback – Dry Lining*. I'm reminded that *Bouncing Back* was the title of Alan Partridge's autobiography, in which he had a nervous breakdown and drove to Dundee in his bare feet. We go into the workshop, and I'm quite thrown by its huge size. A month trapped in a prison cell has made me really agoraphobic. There are a dozen other prisoners in the class, which is run by a strapping Russian builder called Uri.

It transpires that dry lining involves putting up internal walls and ceilings. The first few days are to be spent studying health and safety, and I diligently start filling in my folder. One of the other students, Dylan, talks throughout the lesson. He has a shaved head and angry ears, and is the last person you'd want to meet in a dark alley. That said, you'd easily hear him rabbiting away from the other end of the alley, allowing you to leg it before you crossed his path. I find it difficult to concentrate on the Working at Height Regulations (2005) while he noisily recounts how he outran three cops across a Hammersmith rooftop.

At 11 a.m., someone shouts 'Freeflow!' and we all head back to the wing, where we're banged up over lunch. We are then unlocked for afternoon freeflow at 2.30, and I have another dry-lining session until 4.15. H Wing then has S&Ds until 6 p.m., so I'm now getting about six hours out of the cell instead of one.

When I return home, Dan starts shouting at me for leaving the lights on. His anger is baffling. I can't fathom why a Romanian pickpocket is so concerned about HMP Wandsworth's electricity bill. I point out that the problem is easily remedied by switching the light off, but this falls on deaf ears.

A big bundle of letters and emails has been dumped on my bed. The mailroom is evidently as inefficient as the rest of the prison, as some of this correspondence is three weeks old. As I carefully open each one, savouring their contents, I suddenly realise that Dan is standing next to me, seething because he hasn't got any mail. His girlfriend has promised to write to him, and he's convinced that her letter's got mixed up in my pile. I sift through the embarrassingly large stack of post, but it's all addressed to me. Dan seems quite upset, so I crack a light-hearted joke.

'Don't worry dude, I'll write to you instead!'

I immediately realise that this was a hideous mistake. Dan's mood goes so black that I think the lights have actually dimmed, and I feel dozens of topless models eyeballing me reproachfully. I climb onto the top bunk and try to open the rest of my mail in silence. After a few minutes, Dan starts rummaging around in one of his boxes. I peer down to see him painstakingly measuring our desk with a ruler. He then draws a line halfway across it with a pencil, as if he's marking the UN's border between North and South Korea. He twists a screw into the desk at the midpoint before flouncing the two feet back to his bed.

I wait for a bit, then gingerly climb down to the desk. It's bloody uncomfortable having a sharp screw right by my elbow, but I try to ignore it and start penning a letter to my brother. The minutes tick by and I don't hear anything from my cellmate, so I grab a quick glance behind me. While Dan is certainly tucked up with his eyes closed, he is definitely not asleep. From the activity under his sheet, it's obvious that he's wanking furiously, about three feet away from where I'm sitting. Now admittedly I did craftily knock one out on K Wing, but I had the decency to wait until Yogi was snoring. Dan has no such inhibitions, and I suspect that he's trying to freak me out, which he fully succeeds in doing. I grab my letter and scramble back up to my bunk.

3 August

Dan starts to engage in bodily functions as loudly and frequently as possible. I'm woken up by the sound of him having a crap, during which he hacks up phlegm for 10 seconds and then gobs it into the sink. He belches so loudly that it echoes round the cell, followed by a couple of explosive farts. At lunchtime, he waits until I'm eating before urinating without pulling the curtain. Anywhere else, this display of human sound would be a source of amusement, even possibly an entry on *Romania's Got Talent*, but in this confined space it's highly destabilising. His next tactic is to refuse to say a single word to me. I'll ask if he wants the radio or the TV on, and he'll just completely blank me. Then while I'm watching something he'll aggressively grab the remote and change the channel.

Being locked up with Dan makes me feel physically threatened for the very first time. I start to unravel, flinching every time my back is turned, and I can barely sleep. At every stage of my Wandsworth journey I've convinced myself that the next step will solve all my problems, whereupon now I've walked into a whole new world of pain.

4 August

I crawl into the dry-lining workshop totally wrung out. Nigel soon notices that something is up, and I tell him about my nightmare cellmate. After class, I tiptoe back to the cell, bolt down my lunch and sit on the bed feeling sorry for myself.

Suddenly Nigel appears outside our locked door and grins through the observation panel. 'Martyn's cellmate has just gone to open prison. Do you want to move in with him?' Martyn is another white-collar guy, whose cell is directly opposite Lance and Scott.

'Fuck yeah!' I cry out. My whole body lifts up as if I'm being pulled by an invisible string. I'm suddenly not scared of Dan any more; this lifeline has robbed him of his power. I have to stop myself humming the Hallelujah Chorus while I pack my things. When I pull Kit's photos off the wall, I accidentally tear Dan's precious porn mags. He winces at this destruction and silently sticks his tits back on the wall, and I actually feel a bit sorry for him.

Martyn is in his forties, with ginger hair and a cheery twinkle in his eye. He hands me a key and exclaims, 'Welcome to H2-13!' as though I've come to stay the weekend in his garden cottage. The cell is spotless, full of ingenious cardboard shelving and hooks made out of matchsticks. The lighting is far softer than previous cells, with several pages from the *Sunday Times* magazine stuck over the strip light in the ceiling.

Martyn explains that this is *the* prime location on H Wing. 'We're often one of the first cells to be unlocked, which means we can get to the showers first.' The rest of the White Collar Club all live down this end of the landing; basically it's the prison equivalent of Hampstead. Shamefully, I have somehow tumbled into the most prestigious part of the prison, and I lie on the bed buzzing with my good fortune.

3

Showers and Slips

In which my son is finally allowed to visit. I despair at only seeing him twice a month, and try to increase contact by becoming the screws' bitch.

Things I learn:

1) The dangers of Islamic extremism

2) The secret identity of the Trinity governor

3) Never steal a towel from a naked wet Scotsman

I collect enough brownie points to get more visits, but am beaten by the evil boss. Victory is finally snatched thanks to a pack of Haribo.

5 August

It doesn't take me long to settle in to my new cell. Martyn has an infectiously cheerful manner, and my mood takes a dramatic swing upwards. He used to be the managing director of Deutsche Bank, but was recently convicted of insider trading and got four and a half years.[1] He's only been in Wandsworth seven weeks longer than me, but acts as though he's been inside for ages. He deals with incarceration by keeping as busy as possible, and works as both the education orderly and the chaplaincy orderly.

'Why don't you come to chapel on Sunday?' he asks.

'I'm a screaming atheist, so it would be grossly hypocritical.'

'You'll get the whole morning out of the cell.'

'I'm in.'

Martyn puts my name on the Protestant service list. Sunday morning we assemble in a little chapel room tacked onto K Wing. The congregation is made up of the White Collar Club, various committed Christians, and Marbles, who famously defecated in the K Wing showers. He lurches around in varying states of inebriation and undress, clutching a milk carton. Steve, the chaplain, does a fairly decent sermon and we have a jolly sing-song.

We do indeed get the rest of the morning out on the wing. I write to Ted telling him to get his arse over here.

6 August

Kit is finally coming to visit. I have no idea what impact the last five weeks will have had on him. For the previous three years he'd been living with me half the week, and would usually insist on sleeping in my bed. Since coming inside, I've had nightmares about him not recognising me, or refusing to talk.

I walk into the visits hall looking like an anorexic Robinson Crusoe in a purple bib. Kit sprints up and hugs me tight. 'Daddy! Read me a story!'

He's been obsessed with books since he was a baby, and he sits on my lap while I read him several Mr Men books. He's just had his fourth birthday, and he tells me all about his new toys. We don't talk about why Daddy is living in this strange building. He's clocked that I'm not at home any more, but he's unlikely to understand the reason for my incarceration. I can barely get my head round it myself.

I neck a lot of coffee and wolf down a pie, while Kit drinks Ribena and mainlines chocolate. Despite the bizarre surroundings, it is extremely uplifting to sit with my family for just a little while.

It's like I've been watching an incomprehensible film in Russian and someone has briefly turned on the subtitles. When the hour is up, we have a group hug, and they disappear out of the room. I assumed that the visit would boost my spirits, but it suddenly hits me that I'm only allowed two visits a month. I won't see Kit again for another fortnight.

I stagger back to Trinity feeling as if my foundations have just been detonated. A sign proclaims that *Maintaining family ties is vital for prisoners' rehabilitation.* This was recently echoed by Liz Truss, who said that 'a prisoner's family is the most effective resettlement agency'.[2] Given the derisory visits allowance, these statements just twist the knife even further.

I tell Martyn how terrible I feel about being separated from my son. He empathises, as he has two young kids of his own. 'It'll get a lot better once your IEP level goes up to Enhanced. Then you'll get a visit every week.'

The rules state that I have to wait three months to become Enhanced. I tell Martyn that I don't really care about wearing my own clothes, but I can't bear to wait that long to see Kit every week.

He laughs dismissively. 'Fuck waiting three months. The IEP system is so complicated that hardly anyone understands it. I got made Enhanced after just five weeks.' He suggests I do a bit of serious boot-licking to get some positive IEPs on my file, and then pitch myself to a senior officer.

I resolve to disappear up as many screws' arses as possible.

7 August

My brown-nosing crusade coincides with the regime getting squeezed on all sides. Morning freeflow is pushed back to 8.30, afternoon freeflow doesn't start until 3, and the end of S&Ds creeps earlier to 5.30. This results in 90 minutes' less time out of the cell. Both freeflow and S&Ds start being randomly cancelled without notice, just as another heatwave kicks in. Like so many other problems in Wandsworth, the diminishing regime is a direct consequence of officer numbers being hacked to the bone.

Grayling's folly

Between 2010 and 2015, the number of prison officers was cut by a third, to 23,746. This was despite the number of prisoners remaining stable at around 85,000.[3] Chris Grayling drove through the cuts, and introduced a voluntary exit scheme for the most experienced officers, who promptly left in droves. An elderly officer once told me that in the previous three months, he'd said goodbye to colleagues with a combined total of 700 years' service. Astonishingly, some of these old-timers were then rehired on short-term contracts at vast public expense, just to plug the gaps.[4] Grayling appears a lot in this volume, which is ironic as he once attempted to ban prisoners from receiving books.[5] This spiteful measure was overturned following a furious reaction from the literary community.[6] He then took his unique leadership skills to the Department of Transport.[7] Anyone who is reading this on a delayed train will at least be comforted to know that Grayling has previous when it comes to destroying public institutions.

The increasingly tighter schedule means that I'm unable to speak to Kit every day. He's often with his childminder until 5.30, by which time our S&Ds are over. When I do get through, Lottie puts me on speakerphone to facilitate the conversation. This worked well previously, but it's a nightmare when I'm calling during S&Ds. There are no booths – the phones are just tacked to the wall – and there are always noisy games of table tennis, snooker and table football going on. The din is so loud that it's often impossible to hear what Kit's saying. Today I can just make out that he's planning a tea party this afternoon.

'Daddy, can you come to my party?'

I go back to the cell and cry my eyes out.

9 August

I spend more time hanging out in Scott and Lance's palatial pad. Scott does about six different jobs, and is constantly in demand from officers and prisoners alike. He flies around clutching a clipboard that contains almost mystical power to get doors unlocked. Lance, the outsized public schoolboy, also has several jobs, but never seems to do any of them. He mostly loafs about his cell, eating constantly and holding court. Today he recounts how he was given three and a half years over an unpaid bar tab at the Savoy. I'm shocked at the severity of the sentence, though I soon discover that he pretended to be Elon Musk and lived in a hotel suite for weeks. He was remanded in Wandsworth, and had to wait six months to get to court. Just before the sentencing, he gave all his possessions away on the wing, assuming that whatever sentence he received would be covered by the time already served.

The hearing did not go well. 'The judge turned fucking puce,' he says cheerfully. 'He didn't even mention me by name, just screamed, "Three and a half years! Now clear the dock!"' Lance crawled back to Wandsworth still with more than a year to serve and desperately tried to reclaim his telly so he could see himself on *Newsnight*.

Lance doesn't take prison remotely seriously. He loves schoolboy pranks, and will frequently barge into our cell and pretend to have a crap in our toilet. One time he convinces an officer to hand me a fake application form stating that my transfer to HMP Hull has been approved. I soon retaliate and submit a property application in his name requesting a small rock hammer and a poster of Rita Heyworth.

11 August

Lance sticks his grinning head round our door. 'There are a couple of jobs going handing out visit notification slips. They offered it to me but I simply cannot be fucked.'

This presents a fantastic opportunity to worm my way into the screws' good books. Martyn and I snap the jobs up. We're given two clear plastic A4 pockets full of paper slips informing prisoners of impending visits. The IT revolution has clearly passed Wandsworth by, as the slips have all been written out by hand.

'I'll do H Wing,' suggests Martyn. 'You can do G.' He hands me a spare clipboard, which feels like a torch being passed between Olympians.

To say that the power goes to my head is an understatement. Flushed with bureaucratic authority, I march to the end of H Wing, where a gaggle of prisoners are trying to argue their way through the locked gate. I wave my clipboard at the officer. 'Got to deliver these slips to G Wing!' I call officiously. The screw allows me to pass, and I have to restrain myself from clicking my heels.

Passing through the big black gates of G Wing, I feel like I'm entering Mordor. The air is thick with satanic screaming and the sound of doors being kicked. I beetle round the landings handing out the slips. Several are missing, so I have to verbally notify some of the prisoners about their visits. After I've knocked on a few doors, I soon realise why Martyn gave me G Wing. One guy demands to know who's visiting him, and when I say I don't know, he goes ballistic. Another lad has an unexpected legal visit, which sends him into gibbering despair. I later learn that this usually means the police are coming to serve new charges. Many inmates just lie on their beds in a vegetative state and don't even acknowledge my existence. Quite a few demand that I bring them burn or drugs from nearby cells. When I decline, they scream abuse.

I find the experience mildly traumatising, and scurry back to the sanctuary of H Wing. Everyone else is now locked away, apart from Martyn, who's drinking tea in Lance and Scott's cell. They find my G Wing baptism of fire hilarious. After a while, a screw comes to lock us up. Our new jobs have given us an additional 45 minutes out of the cell, and Martyn breaks out some Jaffa cakes to celebrate.

12 August

Delivering the visit slips on G Wing continues to be pretty nerve-racking. I'm walking along the Fours when an officer calls me from the landing below.

'Hey, do us a favour and give a message to the guy in 4-20.'

I leap at the excuse to curry favour with officialdom. 'Course, guv! Whatever you need!'

'Just tell him he can't have his meds today, ta.'

I beetle down to 4-20 and tap on the locked door. 'Afternoon. I just wanted to let you know that you can't have any medication today.' The prisoner attacks the door with such ferocity that he smashes the observation panel. I jump out of the way to avoid the broken glass. The screw walks away chuckling, and I limp off twitching in fear, resolving to quit delivering these bloody slips.

Scott is at the end of the landing. 'You're not going to fall for that old chestnut again, are you?' He picks up a phone receiver and starts to dial.

I had no idea we could call from different wings. 'Do these phones work?'

'Of course,' says Scott. 'I never call from H Wing during S and Ds; it's full of screaming cunts. I always phone from G Wing when it's locked down. It's quiet, and there are no queues.'

Apart from a couple of spice dealers nipping between doorways, G Wing is pretty much deserted. I call Lottie and have the best conversation with Kit since I've been in prison. As I leave the wing, I spot the screw who stitched me up, and ask if I can have a positive

IEP for my trouble. He agrees to write a nice note on my file, and I actually skip back to the cell.

I start calling home from G Wing while I'm delivering slips, and add more family and friends to my phone pin. I tape their numbers to the inside of my clipboard, so I can craftily snatch a call when the opportunity arises.

13 August

I return to the cell to see Martyn decked out in a pristine Sports Direct tracksuit. Becoming Enhanced has eventually gained him access to his prop box, and he's cast aside his prison clothing. We are now visibly poles apart, and I feel like Baldrick lurking behind Blackadder. Martyn now has an incredible £37 to spend on his canteen sheet, and generously orders extra goodies to share out. He also buys a duvet, and unpacks it as if he's unlocking a brand-new Porsche. I'm still stuck with a horrible itchy orange prison blanket, and I experience a torrent of middle-class envy that only heightens my desperation to become Enhanced.

Martyn and I have become increasingly competitive. A few doors down from us is a mini gym. It's essentially two cells knocked together, and contains some creaking fitness machines. Access to the exercise yard is pretty haphazard, so I endeavour to get into the gym every day to do some running. Martyn starts logging our times for 5K, and produces a spreadsheet listing our achievements. I keep pushing myself faster and faster, just to beat his personal bests.

14 August

I'm already sick of the H Wing shower room, which is down on the Ones – the basement level. There's hardly any ventilation, steam fills the air and condensation drips from the ceiling, which is just above my head. The changing area is an inch deep in water, and it's always rammed with bodies. A hundred and eighty prisoners have to share six shower heads, in two opposing rows. Today I'm showering directly opposite a disabled Scottish guy. He's very stocky and has an ironclad jaw, and he tries to wash while clutching a pipe. I hop out and pull my tracksuit bottoms on over my dripping-wet pants.

As I start to leave, I hear an angry Hibernian roar. 'YOU STOLE MY FOOKIN' TOWEL!' The naked crippled Scotsman is in hot pursuit with a raised fist.

'No I didn't!' I stammer, and back into the darkened corridor. He follows me out, and a couple of young prisoners start shrieking with laughter. I protest again, but realise in horror that I already have my towel round my neck – the one I'm holding must be his. I'm appalled at my error; robbing the disabled is like stealing from a church. I try to apologise, but the hyena-like cackles from our audience make communication impossible. The Scotsman snatches his towel back and barges back into the shower room, grunting like Rab C. Nesbitt.

I return to the cell and hurriedly change my pants, which is highly appropriate given what's just transpired. I slowly calm down, and devise a plan to remedy the situation. Martyn has a stash of spare towels, and he said I could help myself. I take one and head back to the shower room, where the Scotsman is getting dressed awkwardly. I offer him a fresh towel as a peace offering. Assuming that I've come to taunt him further, he leaps up, fists primed. The spectators can't believe that our show has a second act, and they howl with laughter as I run away again. I lock myself in the cell, realising that I've just made things 10 times worse.

Martyn returns, and I confess to accidentally robbing an angry naked Scotsman. Martyn pisses himself. 'Angus does have some temper issues, but he's a softie really.' He disappears, and returns moments later with Angus, who is no longer waving his fists around. I grovel an abject apology. Angus is fairly sheepish about his overreaction, and I insist on giving him the other towel.

15 August

Dry lining moves on to practical work. We're issued with overalls, boots and gloves, and I'm ecstatic to get two blue Bounceback T-shirts. Nigel and I start erecting plasterboard walls, which is extremely therapeutic. I try to blend in with the other dry-liners, but my excessive education sometimes makes me painfully conspicuous.

Uri, the Russian instructor, explains to the group how to work out the area of a circle. 'The area is equal to the radius squared, multiplied by pi, which is 3.14.'

My father spent a lot of money on my education, and I don't want it to go to waste. 'Er, actually, pi is an irrational transcendental number, which has numerous means of calculation, but 3.14 isn't one of them.'

Dylan, the wild-eyed lad with crazy ears, starts giving me funny looks. I retreat to the back of the workshop and discover a store of bin liners, scouring pads and detergent. These are impossible to source on the wing. I discreetly stuff a load of cleaning contraband down my absurdly oversized prison trousers and smuggle it back to the cell.

16 August

The regime continues to be scaled back. Martyn and I become consumed with getting unlocked to fulfil our basic human needs:

1) Grabbing five minutes alone to have a crap
2) Phoning our kids
3) Taking a shower

The shower room is always rammed during S&Ds, and sometimes the screws call time before I've got to the front of the queue. We are constantly trying to slip into the shower room at other times to have a proper scrub in peace. Today there is an official notice outlawing showers outside S&Ds; negative IEPs will be issued for showering at any other time. I'm astonished that a British public institution is actually punishing adults for cleaning their bodies. Even the

Victorians realised that personal hygiene was crucial to prevent disease.

This becomes known as the War on Washing. One day Martyn and I make it in outside S&Ds and both enjoy a good long soak. A huge officer suddenly appears; he's about six foot three and has tattoos on his knuckles. I manage to hide, but Martyn is right in the line of fire – covered in soap, wearing his huge prison-issue boxer shorts, with his hand up his arse.

'What the hell are you doing in here?!' the screw yells.

'I'm having a wash,' Martyn replies, trying to suppress a giggle.

'You've got thirty seconds to get out, or you'll get a nicking!' This is how some officers refer to a negative IEP, trying to make the demerit sound more sinister.

The War on Washing causes much aggravation across the prison. The chaplaincy organises an Eid feast, but the Muslims on K Wing aren't allowed a shower beforehand. One lad begs an officer to let him out, insisting that it's disrespectful to attend Eid without washing.

'Just use the sink in your cell,' barks the officer.

Half an hour later the wing starts flooding, and the screws discover water flowing out from under the Muslim prisoner's door. They open it up to see the lad lying injured on the floor, and water gushing from the wall where the sink has come off. The idiot took the instruction to use the sink too literally, and tried to have a shower by standing up in his basin, which promptly collapsed under his weight.

18 August

I now do the visit slips just before the end of S&Ds, to maximise my time out of the cell. The gate out of H Wing usually attracts a dozen or so prisoners trying to escape the impending bang-up, some obviously hustling tobacco and drugs. Flashing my slips to the officer always gets me allowed through, but this soon provokes jealousy from the surrounding inmates.

Today a young black lad sidles up to me as I'm waiting by the gate. 'Hey, give me some of them slips.'

I don't want to make enemies, but I daren't lose this passport to my evening calls home.

'Sorry, mate, they gave them to me to hand out.'

He hisses 'Guvboy' at me threateningly.

Days later I'm handing out the slips on G Wing, and the same guy is hopping between doorways. He clocks me and marches up. 'Hey! Let me have them slips. Prison rules, you get me. Always share the slips.'

'Those aren't the rules I've been told,' I mutter, and step round him. The lad is pretty stocky and could easily flatten me, so I peg it up the stairs while he shouts 'Guvboy!' after me again.

I discuss this later with Martyn. He's been targeted by the same character, who we christen Guvboy. It seems there is lurking resentment towards the White Collar Club from various quarters, who are understandably miffed that we have monopolised all the best jobs.

Let the white one in

In a strange mirror of wider society, the more educated and affluent prisoners quietly carved out the best jobs and places to live. This was actively enabled by the prison being so understaffed, as the officers relied on inmates to keep the place running. The authorities believed that ex bankers and accountants were unlikely to abuse these roles by dealing drugs, so white-collar inmates were instinctively favoured for trusted jobs. The flip side was that the rest of the prison's population – which had a disproportionately high proportion of young black men[8] – had less time out of their cells. I often felt guilty about being sucked into this bubble of white privilege; it was yet another example of how the most vulnerable people on the outside often got the worst deal behind bars too.

19 August

There's never freeflow on Friday afternoons. The entire prison is shut down while a group of trusted prisoners hand out the canteen. Just before lunch, Martyn bounces into the cell with exciting news.

'Two of the canteen delivery guys have just been caught with phones and put on Basic. I've pulled some strings, and we're going to fill their shoes.'

I can hardly believe our luck. I've begun to dread the horrible bang-up on Fridays, and delivering canteen will undoubtedly push me further up the greasy pole.

After lunch, we head out to the exercise yard, where there's a large pile of black packing boxes. We drag two stacks through to G Wing, and start lugging the boxes up the stairs. Inside are dozens of clear plastic sacks containing all the prisoners' canteen orders. We carry the bags down the landings and dump them outside the relevant cells. This allows us to have a good nose at what everyone else has ordered.

'Oh look, 4-15 has got some of those lavender joss sticks.'

Meanwhile, the doors are being kicked senseless by inmates who've been locked up for days.

Bang bang bang. 'I BEG YOU, GUV, I GOTTA CALL MY BRIEF, I GOT COURT MONDAY!'

'They look quite good, actually, shall we get some next week?'

Bang bang bang. 'I NEED SOME FUCKING BURN!'

'Why don't you order a pack and I'll get some matches?'

Bang bang bang. 'I HAVEN'T HAD A SHOWER IN FOUR DAYS, YOU CUNTS!'

'I've been giving serious consideration to a tub of this chocolate spread.'

A lot of the guys on G Wing have hardly anything to spend, and some of their canteen orders are heartbreaking. One bag contains only a cheap 'I Love You' card; another has just a single lolly at the bottom. I'm extremely fortunate to have enough money to buy vital supplies each week, and a bit of me wants to donate something to beef up these orders.

We then go round the cells with an officer handing everything out. As each door is unlocked, we are hit by a wave of BO. Loads of prisoners beg to have a shower, but all are refused. Some inmates obsess over their canteen – they've made a careful note of exactly what was ordered, so we have to stand there while they tick off every last item. One guy explodes when a pack of Monster Munch turns out to be the wrong flavour, and insists we exchange it on the spot.

The officer sighs, 'Fill in a general app,' and slams the door shut.

I remember how infuriated I was on the other side of the door, and marvel at how quickly I've turned into the screws' bitch. Afterwards I ask the officer if I can get a positive IEP, and he promises to write me a glowing review.

22 August

One of our neighbours, a banker convicted of Libor rigging, gets shipped out to open prison. He is replaced by a belligerent ball of anger called Wayne, and the White Collar Club is up in arms. There are snooty complaints that this will lower the tone of the neighbourhood, and a lot of jokes about a dip in house prices. Wayne first blows his fuse while queuing up for lunch.

Dinner is served

The system for ordering and collecting our food was so convoluted that it could actually have been designed to incite violence. Each week we pre-ordered our meals from a daily selection of five options. The servery was down on the Ones, and at lunchtime we grabbed our plastic plates and queued up. At the front were seated several stoned prisoners who had somehow been selected to

---

manage the process. We'd call out our name, and the first inmate slowly checked our order from a huge handwritten spreadsheet, which was always covered in highlighter pen and Tippex. People moved cells a lot, so the information was often wrong. When he eventually found the right name, he shouted out our choice and the next prisoner handed us a plastic card. All the while an officer kept bawling, 'KEEP MOVING!' even though the line only moved as slowly as this elaborate system allowed.

Next we'd shuffle round to yet another prisoner, who took the plastic card right back off us and hopefully shouted out what was written on it. We'd then step up to the hotplate, behind which was a glassy-eyed lad in filthy chef's whites, who'd supposedly serve up whatever dish we'd selected. It was basically a long game of Chinese Whispers, where most of those whispering were illiterate and on drugs. It rarely, if ever, worked, and I soon stopped caring what meal I ended up with, given that it all tasted equally shit.

As I get my dinner, it becomes evident that our new neighbour has not received what he ordered and is taking a stand.

'I WANT A CHICKEN BURGER!' he bellows.

'You didn't order chicken burger,' sniggers the guy behind the servery.

'YES I DID! I WANT A FUCKING CHICKEN BURGER!'

'No chicken burger on today, bruv.'

'I DON'T CARE, I WANT A CHICKEN BURGER NOW!'

'Listen, fam just take whatever we've got. You can have beef pie, biryani or, er, the other thing. What do you want?'

'I WANT A CHICKEN BURGER!'

Two officers lead Wayne away. He's only voicing the frustration that is constantly bubbling within all of us. Somewhat predictably, he is swiftly nicknamed 'Chicken Burger'.

23 August

There's a lot in the news about Islamic extremism in prisons. Justice Secretary Liz Truss wants to set up specialist units to keep dangerous extremists away from other inmates, and stop the spread of poisonous ideologies.[9] I'd definitely agree that prisons are ideal places to exploit weak minds. I would have gladly joined the Islamic State to get out of my cell on K Wing. Prisons are so appalling that vulnerable inmates are going to be susceptible to anything promising to strike back against the state. The obvious way to prevent radicalisation is to improve conditions, but Truss's solution seems to be the exact opposite. She intends to separate and segregate those at risk, and quarantine the potential terrorists together. She's found a pot of money to tackle the spread of extremism, but not for easing general overcrowding.

From where I'm standing, I'd say that ISIS is the least of our worries. The five main wings remain on 23-hour bang-up, meaning that a thousand men are prevented from doing any work or education due to lack of staff. This was supposed to be a temporary measure, which the authorities had promised would end this week. Instead, a note comes under our doors announcing that the regime is going to get even worse. From now on, every wing will lose both S&Ds and exercise on a specified day of the week. Everyone will take it in turn to be stuck in their cells for 48 hours straight. This note triggers a small riot on B Wing and a fire on C Wing.

25 August

I keep hearing high-pitched screams just outside our door. I peer fearfully onto the landing, to discover it's just a group of young friends discussing their recent crimes. I find their volume astonishing; I'd have thought discretion was a virtue in their line of work.

I'm also struck by how many inmates have their hands thrust down the front of their trousers. This revolting habit is ubiquitous among prisoners of all ethnicities and ages. Some guys will cheerfully clasp their bollocks while talking to me, and yet I'm the one who gets embarrassed. The worst part is when I spot these same inmates serving lunch. I'm no stickler for health and safety, but I'm sure there are rules about genital contact prior to handling food.

27 August

Martyn and I now get plenty of unlock on weekdays, thanks to our burgeoning collection of prison jobs. But there's no freeflow at weekends, so we're always looking for a way to get out on Saturday and Sunday mornings. Today we spend 45 minutes pestering passing officers until one of them finally opens our door. As time goes on, we have quickly learnt which buttons to press with the various screws. Our favourite officer is Mr O'Reilly, who previously served 20 years in the army. He swears permanently, is always cracking filthy jokes, and has the best record for unlocking our cell at weekends. He opens us up at 9 a.m. sharp, calls us a couple of cunts, and goes for a fag in the laundry.

Once we're out, the trick is to stay out. I start instinctively grabbing my clipboard every time I leave the cell, as it's incredibly effective at convincing officers that I'm doing something important. Whenever a hostile screw appears, my tactic is to look busy and keep moving. If challenged, I'll ask a complicated question to try and throw them. This buys a few crucial seconds, during which something far more serious will hopefully grab their attention. I end up deploying much the same strategies that I used at school to avoid playing rugby.

When I return from delivering slips, I always drop by Lance and Scott's cell, keeping me out for another 20 minutes. This afternoon Lance is in the middle of a long anecdote when Officer Cox appears at the door and politely taps his watch. Lance waves haughtily, as if dismissing a flunkey, and continues with his story. We all find this hysterical, although Mr Cox looks mightily pissed off.

On Sunday morning Mr Cox is back on duty, and refuses to unlock any of us. Through our observation panel I watch the pantomime unfolding opposite. Lance and Scott refuse to accept their bang-up, and keep pressing their emergency button, making a little red light flash outside their cell. Mr Cox appears, engages in a heated discussion through their door, then angrily switches off the light and walks away. Five minutes later, the light goes on again and the whole rigmarole repeats. Scott and Lance then go into litigation mode and push a piece of paper under the door. After much debate, Mr Cox reluctantly signs the document and passes it back. I later see this hastily scrawled disclaimer, which absolves Scott and Lance from the dire consequences of them being unfairly banged up.

'I'm taking this all the way to the top,' Scott fumes. 'I *have* to get out every Saturday and Sunday morning to do my P2P work. Otherwise all hell will break loose.'

'What's P2P?' I ask.

'It's a prisoner-led initiative designed to facilitate the flow of new arrivals into their designated pathways while addressing the skills communication and employment aspects of their needs and opportunities.' This means nothing, but I instinctively feel that I should be part of it. I'm still desperate to get Enhanced so I can have more visits from Kit, and urgently need to prove my worth to the authorities.

Days later, Scott brandishes a letter signed by the head of Trinity, Governor Methi. It stipulates that his cell has to be unlocked every Saturday and Sunday at 9 a.m. so that he can carry out his P2P duties. Scott somehow makes a dozen photocopies, and ostentatiously tapes one to his door.

Power trip

Trinity was purportedly run by Governor Methi, something of a mythical figure, who seemed to avoid any contact with prisoners. Martyn finally pointed him out to me one afternoon while we were delivering canteen. I noted that he chose to walk the landings when 99% of inmates were banged up for canteen delivery. I christened him Governor Yeti, as no one ever saw him, and it quickly caught on.

I had always thought there was just one governor in each prison, but I soon discovered there were at least a dozen people in Wandsworth with the word in their job title: Trinity Governor, OMU Governor, Healthcare Governor. This ego fluffing enabled underachieving civil servants to feel important without costing any more money.

However, the real power on the wings resided with the officers, who worked in a quasi-military command structure:

Three stripe – custody managers (CMs), responsible for a whole section of the prison, and seemingly with a minimum weight requirement of 20 stone.

Two stripe – senior officers (SOs), who controlled each wing.

One stripe – wing staff, who prisoners dealt with day to day. These fell into three broad categories:

- Battleaxe matrons. The most fearsome example on Trinity was Miss Black. Inmates attributed her legendary temper to not having had a shag for years, and claimed that she got off on bossing men around. However, the regime was far more likely to run on time if she was on duty.
- Hard-bitten ex-soldiers. Terrifying at first, but actually the friendliest of the lot. They had usually been on the job for at least a decade, and quickly spotted which prisoners were going to be trouble. Thanks to Chris Grayling's reforms, however, these experienced hands were leaving en masse and being replaced by ...

- Rabbits in headlights. These younglings, often in their early twenties, tiptoed round the wing looking like they bitterly regretted switching jobs from PC World. They would struggle to maintain order in a school library, and locked everyone up at the first sign of trouble.

28 August

Chaplain Steve is on holiday, and this week's service is taken by a supply vicar called Eric. He's clearly being paid for the gig rather than by the hour, as he rattles along at breakneck speed. Marbles wobbles in late with his trousers round his ankles. Eric starts to wrap up, and asks the congregation, 'Do any of you have problems that need our prayers today?'

Marbles staggers to his feet and launches into a rambling account of a complex land dispute involving his Bangladeshi family. The details are sketchy, but it centres on an argument between Marbles' sisters and the tenants of some farmland owned by their late mother. Eric nods sympathetically, but is almost certainly thinking about his lunch. Marbles finally grinds to a halt, and Eric asks if anyone else is in need of prayers.

A hand goes up at the back. It's a small mixed-race lad with a shaved head and dark eyes. 'My son died six months ago. I'm really struggling to cope.'

We bow our heads in respect, recognising that our petty problems pale into insignificance next to such sadness. Marbles, however, not wanting to be upstaged, loudly embarks on part two of his sister's struggle with Bangladeshi land rights. Eric looks at his watch.

Lance, who is supposed to be the chaplaincy orderly, is noticeably absent from this shambles. He arrives at the end of the service, and just shakes everyone's hands as they leave. Later I chat to Hitchins, the chap who got 14 years from Judge Beddoe, and joke about Lance's lax attitude to his church duties.

Hitchins flies off the handle. 'I am fucking sick of all these idiots taking on too many jobs. They just do these gigs for the bloody unlock, and don't take their responsibilities seriously!' This starkly demonstrates the yawning gulf between prisoners – Lance and I can laugh our way through the next few months, until we escape to open prison. Hitchins has to serve seven years, and this place is his permanent home.

Some of our neighbours have acquired ostentatious door signs to broadcast their roles. To keep up with the Joneses, Martyn makes a batch of laminated signs stating our various jobs – *Education Orderly, Canteen Delivery, Slip Delivery* – and we spend considerable time fixing them to our door. I still feel embarrassingly short of prison duties and worry that I'm miles away from getting Enhanced.

Meanwhile, Martyn has started running the Alcoholics Anonymous meetings. He admits that he's not actually an alcoholic, but the job gets him out of the cell for an extra hour on Wednesday evenings.

He returns from his first session mildly miffed. 'The AA is full of Muslims, who are all teetotal anyway. They're just doing it for the bloody unlock.' He fails to notice the irony.

At the end of their first session, they're all given medals declaring how long they've been without a drink. Martyn proudly tacks his *3 Months Sober!* gong to the noticeboard. It seems like a hollow reward: it's impossible to get booze in Wandsworth, so nobody could fall off the wagon if they wanted to.

29 August

Scott appears outside our cell door first thing. 'They've asked me to do the bloody register. I'm far too busy, do you want to take it on?'

I can't help feeling that an officer should really undertake this task, but I still leap at the chance to shine. I'm given a printed list, and instructed to tick off the inmates' names as they pass through on freeflow. The centre gates soon open, and a marauding clump of G Wing residents surge towards me. Trying to find them on the sheet is harder than it sounds. A lot of them have limited English, and some are genuinely unsure how to spell their own names. The screws keep yelling at everyone to keep moving, and I'm jostled by the stampede.

In front of me, a Polish con with missing teeth grunts, 'KGZELYSKIN!'

'Right, OK, is that with a K or a—'

'KGZELYSKIN!'

'Sorry, I can't quite see where you are on my list ...'

'KGZELYSKIN!'

By process of elimination, I work out that his name begins with a U.

Doing the register means I get unlocked 10 minutes before everyone else, enabling me to call Kit before he goes to nursery. Another little piece of my brain starts to heal.

30 August

I've got another visit with Lottie and Kit. Getting across to the visit hall is always fraught, as we have to wait in our locked cells to be collected by an officer. This never happens on time, and I pace up and down impotently, increasingly fearful that I've been forgotten. The schedule frequently runs an hour late, so by the time I'm picked up, my blood pressure is through the roof. We're led across to the revolting waiting room, which actually provides a welcome buffer to calm down before the visit.

It's also a great spot to pick up prison gossip. Today I overhear Guvboy, the lad who's been coveting my slips, talking nervously about his ongoing trial. He's up for firearm possession, and is about to go into the witness box. One of his mates advises him to 'be a man' and 'stand tall' in front of the jury.

Before I can stop myself, I start giving him tips on cross-examination. 'You need to slow down, be respectful and think before you speak.'

Another of Guvboy's associates agrees. 'He's telling da truth, fam.'

Guvboy thanks me; his eyes indicate that I won't get any more hassle for my slips. I don't spoil the moment by adding that I fucked up my own cross-examination so much that I got five years, so I may not be the best authority on the subject.

We're called through to the visits hall, but I'm pulled aside by a stern female officer who admonishes me for wearing shorts. The temperature is in the thirties, and I've acquired a pair of blue prison shorts, which everyone is wearing on Trinity.

'You can't have a visit wearing gym kit!' she barks.

'It's shorts. In summer.'

'That's totally inappropriate dress.' She points to a sign on the wall listing the rules about clothing on visits. It looks as if it was written by Mary Whitehouse; even our guests are prohibited from wearing ripped jeans. I start pointing out that both my visitors have seen me in a lot less than this, but I'm interrupted by a Trinity officer, who offers to take me back to change.

I pull on my tracksuit bottoms – which haven't been washed for two months – then jog back looking like a hobo and smelling like a bin. The female officer nods approvingly, and I'm finally allowed through to see Kit, who is, obviously, wearing shorts.

31 August

Delivering the visit slips is rarely dull. G Wing is always locked down, so prisoners bombard me with requests as I walk past. Today one guy hisses at me, 'Bruvva! Bruvva!'

I'm not exactly pushed for time, so I stop to see what he wants.

'Do me this favour, I beg you!' Through the observation panel I watch him tear off some loo roll, which he twists into a wick. 'Take

85

this to the next cell, yeah, and get my brethren to spark it up.' He wants me to stuff this burning bog roll back under his door so that he can light a spliff. I politely decline on the grounds that:

1) The gap under the door is less than 2 mm, so his plan is doomed for practical reasons if nothing else.

2) Arson is the worst crime you can commit in prison, and can incur tougher penalties than murder.

He doesn't handle rejection very well, and screams as if he's falling down a well. I slip away and call home.

There's a widespread fear of catching germs from these communal phones, so the lad next to me has a large grey sock pulled over his handset. As he whispers loving platitudes to his missus, he looks like he's delivering an anonymous tip in a 1930s noir film. I suspect that he'll acquire more diseases from sticking a fiftieth-generation prison sock in his ear than from a plastic phone. I'm not exactly helping matters, as Kit is currently insisting that I blow raspberries every time I call. I always end up coating the receiver in dribble, so I'm probably responsible for half the phone germs on Trinity.

1 September

My first month sharing with Martyn has had a hugely positive impact on my outlook. We rub along remarkably well, and his upbeat and cheery manner is highly contagious. No matter what insanity we witness during the day, we are always giggling about it after bang-up. We become addicted to quick crosswords, and hours slip away while we argue about the correct spelling of rare plants. Martyn has an old radio, and we belt out Classic FM to drown out the mayhem outside. Each day is full of ridiculous challenges, but this actually helps us pass the time. We'll spend hours planning how to get a weekend shower, and when it works we're over the moon. I sometimes get the door unlocked but don't actually leave the cell; I just sit listening to the radio, blissfully content that I'm staying in through my own choice.

I am still fixated on getting Enhanced, as I can't handle waiting two weeks between visits. I have now amassed three positive IEPs, and fill out an Enhanced Application Form. It asks how I've been of benefit to the prison community, so I write a short essay about my tireless work issuing slips and delivering canteen. To win this level and get Enhanced, I need to confront the evil boss, aka SO Romley, who it transpires is the most loathed screw in the building.

As I approach the centre office gathering the courage to make my case, I channel my inner Delboy. 'He who dares, Rodders, he who dares,' I whisper to myself. Romley sits at a huge desk, looking like Robert Mugabe when he was at dictator school. My pitch is not a rip-roaring success. He quickly discovers that I haven't waited the requisite 12 weeks to get Enhanced, and chucks my application in the bin. I suffer a mild panic attack and stagger back to the cell. The mental floodgates open to all the negative thoughts that I've been holding back, and I get locked in a downward spiral, telling myself, 'I'm in prison! My career is in ruins! I can't see my son!' – repeated on a loop. It's as if I've been convicted all over again, and I curl up in my bed.

Lance chooses this moment to undertake one of his practical jokes. Like many prisoners, I've developed a Pavlovian response to anything coming under the door, as it's usually mail or a newspaper. Lance plays on this by sliding a crisp wrapper into the cell, and I jump up expectantly. He laughs himself silly at my reaction, and I go a bit Chicken Burger at him, screaming, 'Go fuck yourself!'

Immediately the larky schoolboy vanishes, and Lance calmly finds out what's wrong. I tearfully explain that my Enhanced application has been rejected, which will destroy my relationship with Kit.

'Romley is an awful cunt,' he agrees. 'Let me deal with it.'

Later on, we're called for exercise, and Lance grabs my shirt and makes a beeline for the SO's office. This time a reasonable-looking young woman is sitting at the desk. 'Alwight, Miss Sharp, you're looking bootiful today!' (For unknown reasons, Lance always uses a cod-cockney accent when addressing screws.) 'Atkins 'ere wants to see his kid more. Make him Enhanced, there's a love.'

She rolls her eyes. 'What's your prison number?'

'A8892DT,' I stammer.

She taps at her keyboard. 'Done.'

'Gawd bless yer, miss!' calls Lance. I walk out to the yard in a bit of a daze, and Lance flicks my ear. 'You owe me a pack of Haribo.'

We sit in the sunshine laughing at the madness of prison rules. Most officers find the IEP scheme completely baffling, making it ripe for exploitation by rogues like Lance. I call Lottie and tell her she can now book visits every week. The next canteen, I order a £1 pack of Haribo for Lance, in return for doubling the access I get to my son.

4

Goodfellas and Goldilocks

In which I start working on the inductions, and visit some serious gangsters in their private members club. Martyn joins the reform programme, which swiftly descends into abject chaos.

Things I learn:

1) How to build a drugs empire

2) Why the prison is falling down

3) Never borrow another prisoner's mug

The White Collar Club splinters, and I somehow get upgraded to the Executive Suite.

2 September

A note comes under the door congratulating Martyn on his appointment to the Reform Hub. This is a prestigious group of prisoners who will advise the executive governor, Ian Bickers, on improving conditions. The reform programme is now gathering pace, and in an interview for the *Wandsworth Guardian*, Bickers sets out his vision for turning the prison around. 'My aspiration is to increase the number of front-line staff who will be able to spend more time engaging with prisoners in our care and helping them to rehabilitate.'[1]

Since we became a reform prison, however, officer numbers have tanked. Bickers has succeeded in hiring more middle management, including a highly paid head of reform, a job that has echoes of BBC satire *W1A*. The position has been taken up by Cathy, who wears sharp power suits that look distinctly odd on a filthy prison wing. She's created a 'hub' of inmates to suggest ideas for bettering Wandsworth, and has hired Martyn and several other white-collar guys, but then panics that they don't remotely reflect the prison's population, and hurriedly brings in a couple of career criminals.

The Reform Hub gets off to a bumpy start, as none of the inmates are unlocked for the first meeting. Cathy tries to remedy this, but she doesn't know where any of them live. She finally tracks down Martyn, but can't get him out as she doesn't have a key. Their inaugural meeting has to be conducted by shouting at one another through four inches of steel. Cathy has written up some new initiatives, which she shoves under the door for Martyn's perusal. I have a flick through. The material is written in surreal corporate lingo: *Stop assuming that prisoners are liabilities, and start viewing them as assets!*

3 September

I'm definitely starting to outgrow dry lining. The ever-tightening regime means that the afternoon session is barely an hour long, so there's never enough time to do any work. We just sit around listening to Dylan chuntering about his criminal past. Today it emerges that he is currently inside for stealing tools, but has nonetheless been allocated to a workshop containing Stanley knives, pliers and saws.

There's a pile of mugs and an urn for us to use, so I fix myself a coffee and sit quietly reading the *Guardian*. Another inmate looks at me in horror. 'That's Alan's mug!'

I don't treat this with the seriousness it deserves. 'The mugs are all identical, and there are plenty more there.'

A hulking heap of tattoos and biceps appears, grunting, 'Who's been drinking out of MY mug?' like a grotesque penal Goldilocks. I clearly haven't learnt my lesson from the Scottish towel incident, and I apologise profusely and scrub Alan's mug clean.

Nigel later pulls me aside. 'You need to be careful. These guys have been inside for years, and latch onto any possessions to retain a sense of identity.'

I start plotting ways to escape dry lining. Martyn's elevation to the Reform Hub means that he has to quit being education orderly. The job involves inducting new prisoners on E Wing, and testing their English and maths. It sounds pretty interesting, so I offer to fill Martyn's shoes. He suggests that I just turn up and introduce myself to Danielle, the staff member who manages the inductions.

5 September

I embark on my new career as education orderly. In the morning, I join the other Trinity prisoners who work on the 'mains' – which refers to the six main wings. Trinity and the mains are completely separate buildings, so we have to walk through the open air to cross over. I can't get over just how massive this place is; someone points out that Wandsworth is the largest prison in the UK.[2] We go in through a side door, and then up a spiral staircase to the massive centre.

As I pass through the gate into E Wing, it strikes me that this is the exact spot where I first tumbled into Wandsworth. It feels like returning to the scene of a crime. The Twos landing is still awash with severely mentally ill prisoners. These characters absolutely terrified me two months ago, but now I'm completely relaxed in their presence. I head up to the classroom where I sat my own education tests, and meet Danielle. She's in her mid forties, and very smartly dressed.

'Hi, I'm Chris, Martyn's replacement.'

She's pretty dismissive. 'I don't know if we need another orderly.'

I've obviously been quite presumptuous by just turning up, and I get paranoid that I'll have to crawl back to dry lining. Another orderly slouches in, and I realise we probably are a bit overmanned, as only three prisoners are unlocked to do the inductions. Fortunately, the other orderly, Connor, is happy to sit around and gossip, so I get stuck in and show off my diligence.

Danielle nips out to do some errands, and Connor gives me a wink. 'Don't worry about Danielle. She's always frosty with new people, but she'll soon warm to you.' Connor is from Brighton, and has a mischievous twinkle in his eye. He's on remand facing a dizzying array of drugs charges, and has already decided to plead guilty.

'How long are you looking at?' I ask.

'If I can walk out that courtroom with a twelve, I'll give the judge sexual favours.'

Later, Danielle walks me back to Trinity. As we say goodbye, she smiles for the first time. 'You did well today. Do come back tomorrow.'

6 September

My second day working on E Wing is a lot more eventful, as utter carnage unfolds on the landing outside. When things kick off, a screw calls for assistance by blowing a whistle, and a load of officers come running. The younger, fitter screws are the first to arrive, followed by the former soldiers. Eventually an obese three-stripe officer wheezes along, by which time the excitement is over. I'm initially shocked by the constant violence, but it quickly fades into the background.

The induction job lets me briefly meet most of the new arrivals in Wandsworth and get a fascinating insight into how everyone else has fucked up their lives. A young lad slouches in boasting that this is his sixteenth conviction and his eighth time in prison. I take his date of birth and realise he's only 19. One guy is shaking with fear and shock, and I assume he's received a life sentence. He tearfully explains that he's got 10 weeks for a driving offence. Another bloke is joking around as if he hasn't a care in the world. It turns out he's just been handed an 18 stretch, and it hasn't hit him yet.

Inductrination

My job entailed encouraging newly arrived prisoners to do their education tests. Most of the incoming inmates were desperate for phone calls, showers and visits, but the best we could give them was an English assessment. First the courts deprived them of their liberty, then Wandsworth reception robbed them of their dignity, and finally we popped up to criticise their spelling.

Once the tests were finished, Connor and I quickly marked the papers. At first I was gobsmacked at how many inmates were functionally illiterate. I'd never previously understood why criminals walked out of prison and immediately committed more crimes. Seeing the appalling levels of literacy made it patently obvious why the cycle of reoffending perpetuated. Many of these guys simply couldn't operate in normal society. There was a steady influx of eastern European drug dealers, and it was a damning indictment of the British education system that they could frequently read and write better than our home-grown criminals.

We then explained what courses were on offer: basic IT, hairdressing, art, building work and bike repairs. We'd allocate everyone to a course, which was fairly pointless as most Wandsworth inmates could not physically attend. Freeflow remained cancelled across all the main wings for most of my time there, so only Trinity prisoners could actually get unlocked for classes.

Danielle asks if I can pick up some paperwork from the hairdressing classroom on Trinity, so after lunch I make my way to the grubby salon where convicts learn basic barbering skills. I knock on the door, and a thin-faced woman lifts her head up from a magazine. I request the paperwork as instructed.

'Why are you asking *me* for this?' she snaps. Talking to prisoners is evidently outside her job description.

'It's for Danielle in Education.'

'I CAN'T comply until I've had instructions from my manager.'

I beat a hasty retreat. Some staff automatically treat all prisoners like dirt, which doesn't do much for anyone's self-esteem. Danielle has also given me a list of Trinity prisoners who missed their initial inductions, and I go round G Wing making some enquiries.

'Hello, Mr, er, Gnhebdbi. Would you be interested in doing any courses during your stay?'

'GIMME BURN, PLEASE, I BEG YOU!'

Not for the first time, I'm thankful that the door is safely locked. 'I don't actually smoke, but if you have a look at this leaflet—'

'GO NUMBER 3-16, MAN OWES ME EIGHT-BALL, INNIT. GET IT FOR ME, BRUV!'

'I'm not allowed to pass things between cells.'

'GET THAT FUCKING RICE OR I'LL FUCK YOU UP, YOU GET ME!'

I suddenly realise that my job has a small degree of power. 'Have you thought about learning hairdressing?' I say. 'You'll score loads of spice there.' I swiftly enrol the horrible inmate on the barbering course, thus getting my revenge on the hairdressing tutor who chewed me out earlier.

7 September

I'm doing my rounds for Danielle when I accidentally discover a library at the top of K Wing. It's gone to some effort to avoid drawing attention to itself, as I lived an entire week on this landing and was completely oblivious to its existence. It's the same size as my parents' living room, but contains significantly fewer books. Behind a desk sits an elderly prisoner librarian. Next to him is a magazine rack, which is completely empty except for an old issue of the *Economist*.

'Is this all there is?' I ask.

'That never gets nicked, as it doesn't have a TV guide,' he replies.

Another prisoner enters behind me, sweating buckets. He inspects some non-fiction titles while grunting darkly to himself.

'Where are the books on DRUGS?' he barks suddenly.

The old librarian sighs wearily. 'I'm sorry, we don't have any books on drugs.'

The customer isn't satisfied with this. 'Have you CHECKED?'

To be fair to the librarian, there isn't an awful lot to check. 'I'm certain.'

The guy harrumphs and turns his attention to the fiction shelf. 'Hey! HEY! Where are the books on WITCHCRAFT?'

The librarian rolls his eyes. 'We don't stock any books on witchcraft either, I'm afraid.'

The guy is furious. 'What kind of library *is* this?' he yells, and storms out. I have to say I agree with him. This *Economist* is pre-Brexit, and painfully out of date.

The library is extremely peaceful compared to the rest of Trinity. I start slipping over here more often, and make friends with the staff member in charge, an affable Italian called Federico. I decide that he's Wandsworth's most inept employee, in the face of considerable competition. He usually arrives several hours late, can't read his own handwriting, and often loses his keys, which is not best practice in a high-security prison.

8 September

Martyn is getting steadily disillusioned with the Reform Hub. Cathy is harnessing his City experience to produce glossy presentations about the upcoming reform revolution. He shows me his latest work, entitled 'Reform Vision/Objective'. Some of the material is unintentionally hilarious: 'To provide every man with the opportunity to engage in education and work which increases their life chances. The Wandsworth staff are committed to creating a learning community where the men are empowered to make decisions about their own development.' This is light years away from reality, where 80% of the inmates are trapped in their cells all day.

Within hours of me reading this, the entire prison goes into crisis lockdown, as too many staff call in sick. Martyn and I eventually wrangle ourselves out to deliver the visit slips. I've never seen G Wing this bad. On one landing every single emergency light is flashing. It's oddly reminiscent of Oxford Street at Christmas. The sound of door-kicking and screaming is so loud it drowns out my attempts to notify the residents of forthcoming visits. I call Lottie, and whisper that I'm the only prisoner out of his cell in the whole place, then quickly hang up. She must think I've gone completely crackers.

During the night, one guy on K Wing becomes empowered to make decisions about his own development. He repeatedly complains of chest pains, and eventually a screw opens the door. The prisoner barrels out onto the landing and climbs up into the rafters, just to get a bit of time out of his cell. They call in a Tornado team, who inflate a giant bouncy-castle-style cushion on the Twos. It takes four hours to get the prisoner down.

9 September

I try to get out into the exercise yard every day, even if it's only for 10 minutes. The fresh air works wonders, and it's a good place to meet new people. Today I'm chatting to a cheerful drug dealer called

Andre, who's doing five years for dealing coke. He's fascinated by my work in film and has his own ideas for the big screen.

'You could do a film about me, couldn't you?' he suggests hopefully. We walk a few more steps. 'Might be a pretty shit one, though,' he adds.

He's not wrong. Over the coming months, dozens of criminals suggest I make a film about their lives. These stories would mostly adhere to the classic three-act structure: man buys drugs; man gets caught; man goes to prison. On the up side, these franchises would have an inexhaustible supply of sequels.

Uncontrolled substances

It quickly became clear to me that a large proportion of Wandsworth's inmates were in prison because of drugs. The direct crimes involved possession and supply, but drugs were also behind many burglaries, muggings and violent offences. Despite the increasingly tougher penalties, there was no shortage of men desperate to enter the narcotics trade, attracted by the potentially vast profits. The wholesale dealers were often well educated, and mingled easily with the white-collar fraternity.

Connor, my friend who assisted on the inductions, previously ran one of London's busiest cocaine delivery services. He started out on his own, with just a moped and a mobile phone, and worked the gay scene and City bankers. He knew that most dealers were pretty flaky, so ensured that his 'ticket line' was always slick and reliable. The fleet swelled to 20 couriers, and the money rolled in, allowing him to live the high life. He was spending £2,500 a month on trainers, and took over a Marbella club for his thirtieth birthday. Occasionally a courier was caught, but they simply claimed the drugs were for personal use, and received a suspended sentence.

> Things started to unravel when Connor made a bulk purchase
> from a European supplier who was being watched by the National
> Crime Agency. The cops started following his team day and night,
> tracing calls and photographing their exchanges. The NCA swooped
> mob-handed, and the whole gang were charged and remanded.

10 September

Martyn has just gone under 24 months to serve. This means that he's now eligible for Category D status, which is the magic ticket to open prison. Categorisations are dealt with by the Offender Management Unit (OMU), and Martyn has wrangled a slot on this week's OMU 'surgery'. In preparation, he writes extensive notes about his positive contribution to Wandsworth, and why he'll rehabilitate more effectively at HMP Ford. I wish him luck, but the prospect of his departure makes me deeply anxious. I've barely recovered from living with Romanian Dan, and I'm extremely paranoid about sharing with another nutjob.

I needn't have worried, as Martyn returns from his OMU meeting in bits. 'They're keeping me here until Christmas!'

He asked to have his security status lowered, but was told that he isn't due to be recategorised for another three months. Every inmate is randomly allocated a recategorisation date by NOMIS, the prison's ancient IT system. Martyn's next review isn't until November, even though he's eligible for Cat D now. He asked if they could assess him sooner, as he's been a model prisoner, but computer says no.

Quite aside from the arbitrary unfairness, this process is extremely wasteful. It costs thousands more to house prisoners here than in open prison. Wandsworth has been shamed as the second most overcrowded prison in the country,[3] and the management are all scratching their heads and wondering why.

11 September

I naïvely assumed that I'd be given my Cat D the moment I became eligible in January. Following Martyn's disastrous OMU meeting, I'm now desperate to know when my own recategorisation date is. This means engaging with Tracey, the Trinity admin assistant, who is unlikely to win 'Most Productive Employee in Wandsworth' any time soon. My extended sobriety has made me highly attuned to the smell of alcohol, and I'm in no doubt that she likes a drink.

I stick my head round her office door. 'Hi, Tracey. Could I possibly have a slot on the next OMU surgery?'

She flails around as though this is an impossible demand. 'OMU are *extremely* busy right now!' However, I've learned that the only way to get anything done in prison is through polite persistence, and eventually Tracey gives me an appointment in three weeks' time.

Later, I ask Officer O'Reilly to check my visits allocation on NOMIS. Looking at the screen, I notice that my recat date is actually displayed at the top of the page: *Next recategorisation: 11/1/17*. This is perfect timing, as it's only 10 days after I'm eligible for Cat D at the start of 2017. When I tell Martyn, he is furious. I offer him my OMU appointment to argue his case, which he gratefully accepts. When I ask Tracey to switch the slots, she goes berserk.

'You're on the list now!' she wails.

'My enquiry has been resolved, and my cellmate desperately needs the meeting.'

'I can't take you off the list just like that!'

I've seen this list; it's just a handful of names scribbled in her 2014 diary. Changing it will take five seconds.

'What if you're being bullied to give up your appointment?' she demands.

'I promise I'm not under any duress.'

'Well you have to prove that you're acting of your own free will.'

I don't point out that this challenge has evaded the finest philosophers for centuries, and give up.

Wandsworth's archaic bureaucracy adores paperwork and abhors IT. I've come from a world of instant messaging, clouds and artificial intelligence, run by Bill Gates and Mark Zuckerberg. Now I'm up against slips, lists and general apps, run by Tracey and a leaky biro.

One list I cannot get on is the one for family days. Once a month there are special extended visits, where prisoners can spend five hours with their kids. None of the officers have a clue how I sign up, so I start submitting a general app every three days.

12 September

Today's *Times* has an article about HMP Wandsworth: 'Prison staff refused to accept more inmates into a jail because of the poor state of the cells … Damaged cells have been unusable for weeks, food serveries closed and windows left broken because of serious failings by Carillion, the construction and facilities management company.'[4]

These issues are all on E Wing, where I work every day doing the inductions. I feel oddly proud that my home is now so dangerous that it's made the national press.

Castles in the air

Wandsworth was over 160 years old, and falling apart. It was designed to house 963 inmates, but held over 1,500. The infrastructure and repairs were supposedly maintained by the construction firm Carillion, who won the contract in 2012 from … drum roll … Justice Secretary Chris Grayling. It later emerged that they underbid by £15 million, and the government admitted that 'what Carillion was proposing to us was completely unsustainable in terms of their finances'.[5] Carillion collapsed in 2017, and the head of the Prison Governors Association said, 'These contracts have failed in their entirety, leaving accommodation and maintenance in a far worse state than when governors owned their own works departments.'[6]

At one point it was announced that construction work had been approved for the H Wing shower room. This was initially greeted with some jubilation, until it transpired that they were only going to install a cage over the doorway. The officers were concerned that prisoners were still showering off-schedule, and wanted to limit access. No one with a functioning sense of smell would ever complain that Trinity residents were washing too frequently, but nonetheless a secure gate was ordered by the finance department. Thankfully, this project was entrusted to Carillion, and didn't even get started before the end of my sentence.

There was a thriving compensation culture, as inmates were quick to sue for even the slightest injury. In 2016, the MoJ paid out £28.3 million in prisoner compensation,[7] much of it for entirely preventable incidents stemming from the collapsing infrastructure.

13 September

A slip of a boy tiptoes into our induction classroom, and words explode out of him. 'I'm on remand for ABH but I've got court on Friday and I reckon they'll lay extra charges on me for GBH, you get me. What happened was, I stabbed a couple boys who were fucking my girlfriend, swear down, I got back to her flat, yeah, she'd told me she was at work, so I got back early and there were all these shoes outside, so I'm banging on the door and she opens up and won't let me in, so I push past her and there are two guys in her bed, so I heard these voices in my head, 'cos I'm psychotic and that, and these voices are telling me to knife them, and even though I know I shouldn't do it, the voices just got louder, so I get my knife out and stabbed them, and my girlfriend is screaming at me to stop, so I slapped her as well, so they'll probably charge me for bashing her and all.'

I sit digesting his story for a moment, then say, 'OK, great. Do you want to do this maths test?'

Wandsworth takes a lot of remand prisoners directly from police stations. Many are 'clucking' – going through drug withdrawal – but some are still high off their last fix. One guy staggers in gurning his face off, and tries to chat up Danielle.

'Why don't you come back to my cell for some champagne, dancing and cocaine?'

She fixes him with a steely glare. 'Why don't you sit down and do your English assessment?'

He continues to invade her space. My instinct is to step in, but he is completely steaming. Getting into a scrap could put a black mark against my name and keep me in Wandsworth even longer. To be fair to Danielle, she doesn't need much help.

'You have five seconds to leave,' she says as her hand moves to a large green button on the wall. 'Or I will call the officers.'

The creep snaps to his senses and flies out of the room. Danielle isn't ruffled in the slightest, and carries on telling us about her son's latest rugby match.

14 September

Now that I'm Enhanced, my weekly canteen spends have gone up to £37, and I celebrate by ordering a duvet and a bag of nuts. Some anthropologists argue that human luxuries become necessities over time, and this is certainly true in prison. The novelty of the duvet soon wears off, and I long for my Sports Direct tracksuit, so I can join the upper echelons of prison society. I am now entitled to wear my own clothes, but these are stuck in my prop box, which is held in reception. This is strictly off limits to normal inmates, and can only be accessed by Fenton, the property orderly, a scarily thin former lawyer who has been in Wandsworth for years. I ask him to retrieve my clothing.

'No problem,' he replies confidently. 'I'll put you on the list.'

15 September

I'm chatting with Lance in his outsized pad when Officer O'Reilly runs in. 'We've just found a noose in some idiot's cell. Can you come and talk to him?'

In his role as a Listener, Lance is on call 24/7 to deal with prisoners who are suicidal or self-harming. Scott is the head Listener in Wandsworth, and he takes it really seriously.

'It's the only worthwhile thing I've done inside. This place is full of hopeless guys who have nowhere else to turn. Sometimes we can make a real difference.' An epidemic of mental illness and endless bang-up is fuelling a steep rise in self-harm and suicide attempts. The Listeners are a vital safety net, and every few months the Samaritans visit Wandsworth to train new recruits. Scott encourages me to sign up. 'The training takes a few weeks, and then you'll be out on the wings. It's pretty fucking full-on.'

'I really want to do something positive while I'm here,' I tell him.

'It will make a big difference to you as well,' says Scott. 'It'll definitely change the way you look at the world.' He motions round at his palatial cell. 'And you'll pick up some *serious* perks.'

I tell him to put my name down.

16 September

I'm getting increasingly friendly with Connor, the affable drug lord who helps run the inductions. He never seems remotely bothered about being in prison, despite facing a double-digit sentence. His quick wit and warm manner is a welcome contrast to the desperately wretched souls who stumble into our classroom every morning. Today he invites me down to his cell in the Annexe, which is an exclusive corner of the E Wing basement. I had no idea this place even existed when I lived on this wing. It's the Wandsworth equivalent of a members' club, and even has a private door to keep out the riff-raff. Seated round a table are several hoods playing poker in their dressing gowns; it reminds me of the Mafia's prison lair in *Goodfellas*.

I start popping down here more often, and discover their den is replete with all mod cons, including a toaster, sandwich maker and even a George Foreman grill. On the wall is a large flat-screen telly, and they're always watching the latest series and movies. The prison's TV system has only a handful of freeview channels, so these lads are obviously downloading illicit content from somewhere. They are surprisingly open about their suspicious viewing habits. While chatting with an officer, one of Connor's crew merrily discusses the new series of *Game of Thrones*, which is only available on Sky. The dense screw doesn't twig that the Annexe must have an illegitimate streaming service, and instead chips in with his own opinion: 'I prefer the Lannisters' storyline; that dwarf is bloody funny.'

17 September

Liz Truss, the new Justice Secretary, has just made her first appearance in the House of Commons. A friend sends me a scathing report from politics.co.uk: 'Prison reform looks dead in the water under Liz Truss ... She waffled and giggled but rarely got close to answering the question. It was painful to watch ... Asked whether there are too many or too few people sent to prison, Truss's eyes widened like a scared rabbit ... What about prisoners – as at HMP Wandsworth – spending up to 23 hours a day locked idle in their cells? Well, obviously they shouldn't be wasting their time ... The best Ms Truss could do was a platitude about prisoners "getting the reform they need".[8] Living in Truss's flagship prison, I have a unique window into whether the inmates are indeed getting the reform they need. The latest initiative is the complete rebrand of the jail's population. It's been decreed that inmates will no longer be called 'prisoners', but will henceforth be referred to as 'men'. This tactic is straight out of a 1990s management consultants' handbook. Similar wordplay attracted ridicule elsewhere in the public sector, when dustmen were renamed 'waste management operatives'. The 1990s is, however, cutting-edge for Wandsworth, and the authorities feel that calling us 'men' will somehow reduce reoffending. We all agree that this rebrand will go down a storm on G Wing, where most of the 'men' haven't showered for five days.

Martyn provides highly entertaining updates on the Reform Hub. Attention is currently focused on uniforms, as management are keen that the members of the Hub have matching outfits. There's been much debate over the colour scheme; a grey and orange combi is currently the favourite, but yellow and black is a close second. A measuring session is booked for next week, and there's been a lively discussion about how the uniforms can be ironed.

The vital importance of the Reform Hub is not always acknowledged by the officers. One lunchtime Martyn doesn't appear after freeflow, and the screws can't complete their noon count. An exasperated Officer Lilley appears outside our door.

'Where's your cellmate?' he shouts.

'No idea!' I shout back.

Five minutes later, Lilley reappears asking the same question (despite the door remaining locked), eliciting exactly the same response. We go through this routine a couple more times, as though the repetition will make Martyn magically pop out of the toilet. The screws then initiate a search by standing at the bottom of the wing and shouting for Martyn as if they've lost a dog: 'DODGSON! ... DODGSON! ... DODGSON!' When Dodgson does not come to heel, Lilley returns to the cell.

'Where does Dodgson work?'

'The Reform Hub.'

'What's the Reform Hub?'

'Good question. Basically it's a project to advise on the strategy and implementation of the new autonomous process—'

'Where is it?'

'Up on the Fours, I think.'

Lilley pounds up the stairs. Five minutes later, he reappears with Martyn and angrily bangs him up. Apparently Martyn was in the Reform Hub office giving a presentation to several middle managers when Lilley stormed in and snapped, 'Do you know what time it is?'

Martyn's response was perfect. 'No, I don't. Your colleagues confiscated my watch when I arrived because it had a stopwatch.'

18 September

The visits orderly breathlessly announces a new edict: 'They're going to ban any physical contact during visits!' This tips me into a massive depression. Kit is too young to understand why he can't sit on my knee, and will think it's because I don't love him. I curl up in bed and weep at the thought of my son drifting further away from me. The next day the orderly sheepishly admits that the edict has been rescinded. 'Someone got confused about prison rules.'

Loose lips sink ships

During my time inside, prison communications were a nightmare, and nonsense rumours were a painful part of our lives. The authorities kept inmates perpetually in the dark, so the information vacuum was filled with guesses and half-truths. Official announcements were often wildly inaccurate, and based on how things should be rather than how they really were. A major source of misinformation was Radio Wanno, the prison's internal radio station, which specialised in completely misleading official bulletins. During September, for example, it kept running an old announcement promising that the emergency summer lockdown would end in August, even though the main wings remained on 23-hour bang-up.

Another source of fake news was Tracey, the Trinity admin assistant. She frequently wrote baffling and incorrect signs on the whiteboard by the centre office. One week she scrawled a terrifying note: *THERE IS CURRENTLY A SIX-MONTH WAITING LIST TO GET INTO ALL OPEN PRISONS.* This sent shock waves through H Wing, where most of us were counting the days until we got made Cat D. It was a very dark time, and lots of people were inconsolable. The following week, a bus shipped five prisoners to HMP Ford, and the sign was quietly wiped off the board.

The officers frequently added to the confusion. A screw would walk onto a noisy wing and shout out, 'LAST CALL SHOWERS!' or 'KIT CHANGE CANCELLED!' Unfortunately, the structure of the wing amplified and echoed every noise, so these instructions became mangled with the din of a hundred babbling prisoners. Lance often goaded me into adding our own official announcements. We'd yell, 'GYM CANCELLED!' or 'LAST CALL EXERCISE!' and then giggle hysterically at the ensuing anarchy.

Younger prisoners often adopted the same inefficient means of communication. If a lad wanted to attract the attention of a friend at the other end of the wing, he'd simply scream his name, cranking up volume, pitch and duration until he was noticed. With both officers and prisoners bellowing increasingly loudly to be heard, the air was permanently filled with a cacophony of deafening gibberish.

19 September

Our sink taps suddenly stop working, and the toilet won't flush. The water has been accidentally turned off across Trinity, which triggers a dark and primal fear on the wings. A nervous screw goes round saying, 'All we can do is notify Carillion.' Just mentioning Carillion is enough to tip some prisoners into a demonic rage, and several officers are assaulted because of the drought.

Meanwhile, someone in authority decides that it's an excellent time to initiate a 'dignity check'. Martyn is asked to ascertain which cells are missing crucial items such as privacy curtains, pillows and loo seats. He heads over to G Wing, and I tag along for moral support. Most of our enquiries go as follows:

'We're doing a dignity check. Is there anything missing in your cell?'

'THERE'S NO FUCKING WATER AND I CAN'T TAKE MY MEDS!'

'We can't help with the water, I'm afraid, but do you have enough towels?'

'FUCK THE TOWELS, WE NEED WATER! MY PADMATE'S DONE A SHIT AND IT WON'T FLUSH!'

'So sorry, but the water isn't our department. Have you both got chairs?'

'I'M GOING TO DIE IN HERE!'

By dinner time, the taps are still dry, and there are no additional drinks with the meal. I corner an officer and suggest that someone visits a nearby supermarket and buys a stack of Evian.

'That's completely impossible,' he replies tersely.

When we turn in for the evening, the sound of screaming and kicked doors is horrendous. I turn up the TV volume to drown out the noise. BBC2 is showing a documentary about the Mojave Desert, one of the hottest places on earth. It's probably not the best choice of viewing, as we sit completely parched watching stories of explorers dying of thirst. Martyn and I then have a serious discussion about boiling the water out of the loo. This has to be the most undignified I've felt in my entire life; we are now truly subhuman. I go to sleep trying not to dream of the desert. The next morning, the water is back on.

20 September

I get a note saying that I've been accepted on the next family day. I'm choked up, mainly at the thought of spending five hours with Kit, but I'm also overwhelmed that somebody has actually read my general apps.

I am loath to attend wearing my horrible tatty rags, but Fenton, the property orderly, has failed to secure my clothing. I pull him to one side.

'My son is coming in on my first family day, and I refuse to see him dressed like this.'

He promises to deliver my Sports Direct tracksuit.

21 September

During the inductions, a young lad saunters in and sits down moodily.

'How good is your maths?' Danielle asks brightly.

He sucks his teeth. 'Good enough to count money, innit.'

I was brought up believing that it's vulgar to discuss money, but I'm definitely in a minority inside. This is starkly evidenced one afternoon when I swing by the new Vocalise course, which teaches verbal communication skills. The lags are asked to stand up in turn, give their name and tell the class a bit about themselves. A huge Arab drug dealer clears his throat and announces, 'My name is Ali and I like money.' Satisfied that this gives a rounded picture of his personality, he sits back down.

Show me the money

Everyone in prison was obsessed with wealth; they just lacked the means to accumulate it honestly. Ted was no exception, and once ranted about a newspaper article on Ernest Hemingway receiving $35,000 for winning the Nobel Prize in 1953.[9] It was unclear

---

whether he was upset at the size of the sum, or whether he thought Hemingway was undeserving of the award on the grounds of literary merit. He later became enraged by a TV report on the disappearance of the toddler Ben Needham, who went missing in Greece in the 1990s. A new British police inquiry had started searching for his remains, and Ted loudly condemned the operation as 'a fucking waste of public money'. Bone fragments were then discovered near an archaeological dig,[10] but still he was unmoved. 'Of course there are bleeding bones there, it's the remains of an ancient civilisation, isn't it!'

Whatever crime people had been convicted of, the real motive was usually greed. My outside friends were often surprised to learn that the most prevalent magazine in prison was *GQ*. It was far more popular than sporting or pornographic publications, as it played directly to the inmates' capitalist lust. Prisoners drooled endlessly over Orlando Bloom's watch or David Beckham's shoes, believing they too could possess these luxuries if they sold enough drugs. Prison is what lies behind the mirror of consumer capitalism, the unseen consequence of telling everyone that they can have whatever they want.

22 September

I'm hanging out in the Annexe more and more, essentially pretending to be a high-rolling gangster. Today we're chatting about how best to track the passage of time. One of Connor's associates admits that he ticks off every hour until he's released. He even counts how many meals he's consumed, as it makes him feel like he's constantly moving towards the door. Several other guys refuse to count the days, which is unsurprising given the length of their sentences. Personally I find it impossible to comprehend the total time remaining, so I start creating milestones in the near future – for instance that in three days I'll have completed 10% of my total time inside – which gives me a more manageable target to aim for, rather than drowning under the full sentence. However, when I hit these markers I always suffer an emotional dip, as it doesn't bring any tangible change to my circumstances.

While the 27 months in front of me seems insurmountable, the time I've already served has flown by. Many inmates believe that the dysfunctional anarchy in Wandsworth actually helps the weeks pass quicker. One of the Annexe crew asked to be transferred here just to make his sentence go faster.

23 September

As I'm ambling through G Wing, I catch something oddly familiar in the shouting. I listen again, but all I can hear is the usual *bang bang bang*, 'GUV, I GOT GO SHOWER!' I carry on walking and suddenly hear, 'Why can't they have a fucking *English* weather girl?'

I gleefully yell, 'TED!' and run about trying to find the old bastard.

He shouts back, 'CHRIS!' and I hone in on his cell. The door is locked, so we have a reunion through the observation panel. My letter to him took a month to leave Wandsworth and come right back in again. He moved to Trinity a few days ago, and they dumped him on G Wing.

'This is worse than the black hole of Cal-fucking-cutta, I'm telling you.'

I promise to get him onto H Wing as soon as possible. 'It'll help if you start on a course. I should be able to get you on dry lining.'

'What's that, teaching you to snort coke?' Ted moves away from the glass to write down his prison number. I can now see into the rest of his cell, and I'm taken aback by the sight of a man praying behind him. Ted is obviously now sharing with a devout Muslim, and I smile inwardly at the irony.

24 September

I constantly fear that my brain will degenerate without decent stimulation. I'm now doing five prison jobs, none of which are remotely mentally taxing. I see a sign advertising Open University courses, and go to a meeting in the K Wing library. The OU has been running degrees in prisons for years, and the idea is immediately appealing. The one thing I'm not short of is time, and this extended break is offering me the chance to learn something entirely new. As I go through the prospectus, I am strongly drawn towards psychology, a subject I've long been fascinated by.

Distance learning in Wandsworth is managed by Linda, a brash Scotswoman who does her job with an efficiency so rare that it's almost sinister. I ask to start a psychology module, and Linda gets me enrolled in a week – which is a fraction of the time it currently takes to send a letter. I soon receive an exciting cardboard box from the OU containing several thick study guides, four psychology textbooks and a DVD. This last item is a bit of a problem, as I have no way of playing it.

25 September

Fenton has finally gained access to my prop box, and hands over my clothes. I toss aside my fetid prison tracksuit, like the blind beggar in the Bible casting off his cloak, and slip into my brand-new Sports Direct tracksuit. I feel like Hugh Hefner in his trademark silk pyjamas.

26 September

It emerges that the only DVD player is in the main library, which is strictly off limits to Trinity residents. This doesn't stop Lance from spending most of his mornings there, abusing his position as a Red Band. These are allegedly the most trusted prisoners in the jail. They actually get a red band of fabric to hang round their necks, enabling them to move around the prison unhindered. As the chaplaincy Red Band, Lance is supposed to be doing God's work on the wings, but he usually bunks off to the library instead.

I join Lance as he heads through the main wings, his red band magically opening every gate without question. I get a similar feeling of power when I'm out filming, as most people blindly accept that you can go wherever you want. We climb the steps to the library, and I mentally cross off another hitherto restricted part of the jail. The room is easily ten times the size of the miserable dump on K Wing, but similarly bereft of inmates. The only prisoners present are two library orderlies trying not to look underworked. One pretends to dust the bookshelves; the other slowly moves books from one pile to another. Federico, the chronically relaxed staff librarian, flicks through the DVD collection. The head of the library, Christine, is ensconced in the office, necking tea and chomping biscuits. For the whole morning Lance and I are the only visitors.

I pluck up the courage to approach Federico. 'Sorry to disturb, but could I possibly watch my Open University DVD on the library player?'

He looks at me with his sad Italian eyes. 'Chris, it's impossible. Prisoners – sorry, men – cannot use the DVD player.'

'Why's that?'

'It's a new rule, to stop Islamic radicalisation.'

27 September

The family day is up in the visits hall. My expectations have been pretty low, but the officers have gone to considerable effort to jolly the place up. They've cleared away all the tables, put down mats and set out lots of games and toys. We are spared the horrible bibs, and the officers wear their own clothes and keep a low profile. During normal visits we have to stay seated, but today we are free to roam about. Kit and I had a very physical relationship, so it's wonderful to roll around on the floor again. For the next five hours I forget that we are in prison.

Looking round the room, I'm touched to see several grizzled cons playing with their young kids. I recognise Mike, the massive inmate from A Wing who procured our kettle. He's pulling faces at a gorgeous 18-month-old boy who he's bouncing on his knee. Later on, Kit accidentally bashes Mike's son, who promptly screams blue murder. Mike lumbers over to his howling child and demands to know who was responsible, but thankfully the kid hasn't got the language skills to grass us up. And I thought playground politics were intense in Hampstead.

At the end of the day, the officers all line up and perform the Macarena. Anywhere else I'd be ridiculing their efforts, but in this bleak and soulless place their dancing brings a tear to my eye. Kit is distinctly underwhelmed, and sits colouring in his *Paw Patrol* magazine.

Spending this extended time with my son reminds me who I am again. It's like suddenly mainlining on my old life, and helps me see tiny specks of light at the end of a very long dark tunnel.

28 September

Scott and Lance hand in their notice at the Reform Hub. They've previously weathered several similar initiatives, and could see the writing on the wall. Martyn has clung on, hoping that his efforts will convince the authorities to expedite his recategorisation. Cathy asks him to write a report on the negative impact of Wandsworth's incessant bang-up. She's delighted with his work, and arranges for him to present it to the senior management. When the time comes, she heads up to the Reform Hub office, but discovers that Martyn is stuck in his cell. He shouts through his door that he's unable to present his study on the consequences of being locked in a cell all day, as he's been locked in a cell all day. He then tenders his resignation.

The Hub goes down to just one member, a career criminal called Arnold, whose contribution to the reform process has been limited since he was put on Basic for threatening to murder an officer.

The day after Martyn's departure, the uniforms finally arrive. The Hub sinks without trace, but this doesn't remotely dent official enthusiasm for the reform programme itself.

29 September

Martyn and I are still fiercely competitive in terms of prison jobs and our 5K times, but we continue to get on extremely well. Despite the ridiculously cramped living conditions, we have yet to have an argument. We spend hours chatting about our kids, and fantasising about what lies ahead in open prison. I develop a false sense of security, which is shattered when our neighbour Hitchins is told that he's moving to HMP Coldingley. I like Hitchins a lot; he was very good to me when I first landed, and he's given me plenty of support and advice. He's initially reluctant to leave, but is soon swayed by glowing reports of Coldingley, which has mostly single cells, en suite showers and nice gardens.

His departure has a seismic impact on the White Collar Club. Hitchins was a Listener, and lived in the big cell next door with Nigel, my friend from dry lining. Nigel isn't a Listener, but Hitchins wielded enough power to get him into the Listener cell. Now that Hitchins has gone, Nigel needs a new padmate, and asks Martyn to move in with him. Martyn is torn, but I tell him to go with my blessing. It's a bit emotional saying goodbye, even though he's only moving four feet to the right.

I now desperately need to find someone to move in with me, otherwise the officers will allocate someone at random. Fortunately Ted's efforts at multiculturalism on G Wing have not been a success. He's desperate to get away from 'that fucking suicide bomber', and jumps at the chance to bunk up again. I speak to the movements officer, who agrees the switch, and I help Ted lug his stuff over.

These new living arrangements last less than 24 hours. I'm playing backgammon in Scott's cell when Martyn staggers in white-faced.

'We're being thrown out!' he gasps. 'The SO has just told us to pack our bags!' Apparently the other Listeners were furious that Hitchins' old cell had been annexed by two outsiders, and complained to the SO.

Martyn and Nigel are unceremoniously banished to a normal cell on the Threes. To add insult to injury, they are put next door to Samuels, the loudest spice addict on H Wing. It's like being evicted from Mayfair and exiled to Southend. As they mournfully carry their stuff up the stairs, the whole wing bears witness to their humiliation. There is considerable Schadenfreude at the sight of two members of the White Collar Club finally getting their comeuppance.

I feel awful for Martyn, as none of this was his fault. Several people point the finger at Nigel, suggesting that this is exactly the kind of behaviour that got him into trouble in the first place: having it pretty damn good, but still pushing his luck that little bit too far.

1 October

Living with Ted again is like moving back in with my parents. He still spends most of his time shouting at the TV, and I'm shocked at how intolerant prison is making me. The news has an item on rising street crime, and Ted starts ranting about Romanians being thieving toerags. Rather than squirming as before, I now find myself nodding along (as a consequence of my time with Romanian Dan) before realising what I'm doing. Another report investigates how illegal immigrants are crossing into the UK in the back of trucks.

'They should chain the doors shut!' yells Ted.

I can't let this one slide. 'When you absconded, you bunked off to Spain in the back of a lorry. Doesn't this make you an illegal immigrant as well?'

Such challenges usually trigger a pointless half-hour argument, after which Ted always claims victory because 'we won Brexit'. The banter is mostly good-humoured, but I get annoyed when he slags off our neighbour, 'China', a Chinese computer hacker with the most unimaginative nickname in Wandsworth, making a barbed comment about him being stupid and untrustworthy.

'China is doing four years for rewriting a highly complex stock-market algorithm,' I point out. 'So he must be reasonably intelligent.'

'Yeah,' snorts Ted, before landing the killer blow. 'But only in Chinese.'

I huff in silence and try to do the *Guardian* crossword. It just isn't the same without Martyn.

3 October

Scott asks me for a quiet word in his cell. 'Lance is leaving for Ford tomorrow. That's market-sensitive information, so keep it to yourself.'

This is very sad news. Lance has given me many desperately needed laughs, and H Wing will be a darker place without him.

Scott leans in and whispers, 'There's a place going in the Executive Suite. Wanna get bumped up to club class?'

This knocks me sideways, as Scott's pad is the most sought-after cell in Wandsworth. I'm instinctively cautious, though, as it's only days since Martyn and Nigel's failed annexation of the other big Listener cell.

'What about the rest of the Listeners?' I ask.

Scott laughs loudly. 'Listen, Tiger, I'm the fucking Listener *coordinator*. Nobody is getting bounced out of my crib.' I agree to move in on the spot.

The difficult bit is breaking the news to Ted. He's furious that I'm abandoning him 'for the second fucking time', and is paranoid that he'll have to share with 'another inbred foreigner'. He needs to find a replacement sharpish, or he'll wake up sharing with someone from G Wing.

Lance soon vanishes to Ford, and I lug my stuff across the landing to Scott's room. It's basically two cells knocked together, though with only one loo and sink, so it's more than double the floor area of a normal cell. I find the difference in size pretty disconcerting. I've got used to conversing with cellmates who are no more than three feet away, and I struggle to focus on Scott at the other end of the room. I pace around trying to adapt to the space, until it all gets too much and I have to sit rocking gently for a bit.

Scott finds my discomfort highly amusing. 'You'd better get your shit together. Things'll go up a gear now you're rolling with the big guns. The Listening will kick off soon, and you'll see things that'll turn your piss pink.'

I settle down for the night, and discover that Lance has obtained an extra mattress for my new bed. It's luxuriously soft, and I drift off with dots jumping in front of my eyes. Even a positive change in prison is highly destabilising.

5

Biohazard and Back Rubs

In which Scott introduces me to a dark new underside of Wandsworth. We cross swords with the evil Officer Moss, who puts my cell upgrade in immediate jeopardy.

Things I learn:

1) How environment conditions behaviour

2) The mental health risks facing the officers

3) How to sew 18,000 pairs of pants by hand

I eventually make it onto Listener training, securing my place in the Executive Suite.

4 October

Moving in with Scott triggers a significant shift in how I'm treated. Officer O'Reilly calls me Chris for the first time, while gangsters who've previously ignored me now give a friendly grunt and even the occasional fist bump. Scott seems to know everyone in the prison, and doesn't care who crosses our threshold. Our cell is widely viewed as the H Wing common room, and I have to get used to undressing surrounded by gossiping criminals.

Over the road, Ted is struggling to find a decent cellmate. He doesn't know many people on Trinity, as he hasn't been here long and spends most of his time shouting at the TV. I ask around on H Wing, trying to sell him as a great person to live with. However, I have to disclose that I've just moved out, so my pitch falls pretty flat. I don't get any takers, so I decide to look elsewhere and head across to G Wing. I knock on a few locked doors trying to find possible candidates, but they mostly just glare at me with spice-glazed eyes. I want to do right by Ted; if I field someone unsuitable, I'll never hear the end of it.

The clear favourite is a young Liverpudlian called Gary. When I tap on the glass, he bounces up to the door with a desperation I remember all too well. He's spent a year in an Irish jail for smuggling cannabis, and was repatriated to the UK a month ago.

'How are you finding Wandsworth?' I ask.

'This wing is total minge. I can't handle all this bang-up.'

Gary ticks all the relevant boxes: he's smart and spice-free, and relaxed enough to put up with Ted's eccentricities. When I suggest he takes my old pad, he immediately agrees, without even asking who he'll be sharing with. It's like selling rotting food to the starving. He moves in with Ted the next day, and they get on like a house on fire.

7 October

My honeymoon in the Executive Suite doesn't last long. Today's visit slips don't arrive until after bang-up, and the envelope is just shoved under our door. I'm keen to get out and deliver the slips, otherwise prisoners will think their visits aren't happening.

'Hit the cell bell,' instructs Scott.

'Er, are you sure? They keep warning us against improper use.'

'Don't be such a pussy,' he admonishes, and presses the button on the wall.

Unfortunately, the wing officer turns out to be Officer Moss.

Mildly obese, and with a short fuse, he screeches at prisoners from dawn till dusk and is widely despised.

'What's your emergency?' he barks unhelpfully.

'I need to quickly nip out and deliver these visit slips.'

'Not now, you can't. You should have done it before bang-up.'

'The slips didn't arrive until after bang-up.'

'Tough!' Moss slams the flap shut in my face and flounces off. There's nothing I can do until the next day.

8 October

Saturday morning our door swings open at 9 a.m. Scott has a magic letter from Governor Yeti, which gets him unlocked on weekend mornings for his P2P work. I run round delivering the slips, but several inmates have already left the wing, and they subsequently miss their visits. The knock-on effect sends the afternoon's visiting schedule into meltdown. I'm supposed to have a visit at 2 p.m. with Lottie's mother Debby and Kit. I'm not picked up until after 3, at which point I'm climbing the walls. By the time I get to the hall, I'm in a right state, and the visit is quite hard going. Two of my friends have come to visit as well, and I find it difficult juggling my attention between them and Kit. I feel that I'm short-changing everyone.

After 45 minutes, an officer thumps our table. 'Time to wrap things up!'

This makes my blood pressure skyrocket. 'We haven't had the full hour!'

'We're way behind, so you have to finish early.'

I turn to call Kit from the play area without realising he's standing right behind me, and accidentally elbow him in the head. He bursts into tears, and I scoop him up and hug him tight. The screw orders me to cease contact. Kit screams, 'I WANT DADDY!' and the officer starts pulling him off me. Both Kit and I are now in floods of tears, and Debby leads him away. Several other families are similarly distraught. I want to tell someone that this chaos stems from Moss refusing to let me deliver the visit slips, but nobody would give a damn.

9 October

On Sunday morning, the situation goes nuclear. We're unlocked at 8.30 a.m. Scott goes out for a shower, and I sit reading the paper. Officer Moss suddenly appears and starts to close our cell door.

I try to protest. 'Erm, we're to be left open on Sunday mornings so Scott can do his P2P work.'

'You haven't been unlocked for that yet!' Moss shouts. 'I've only opened you up for church, and now I'm banging you up again.' I haven't been to church for weeks, but I've remained on the list. I'm probably still on it to the present day.

'Scott's in the shower,' I blurt out.

'But he's not allowed out until nine!' Moss screams.

I try to point out that it is in fact now nine o'clock, but the door is slammed shut in my face.

Moments later, Scott appears outside with wet hair. 'Why are we banged up?'

I struggle to explain. 'Moss unlocked us for church and not for P2P, even though it's actually gone nine—'

Out of nowhere, Moss suddenly pounces on Scott. 'What are you doing out of your cell?'

'I was having a shower,' Scott replies bluntly.

Moss is standing right next to him, but still bawls every word. 'You didn't get my permission for a shower!'

He opens the cell door, and starts to push Scott inside. Scott mounts a spirited defence.

'We get unlocked on Sunday mornings for P2P. I have a signed letter from the governor.' He deftly plucks a photocopied letter from a pile he keeps by the door.

Moss goes ballistic. 'Right, you're nicked for being outside your cell without permission! I'm giving you a negative IEP!' He bangs us up and storms off. Five minutes later, he reappears, unlocks our door again and screams, 'Right, *now* I'm opening you for P2P!'

I feel responsible for this bizarre contretemps. Scott has survived two years in Wandsworth without incident, but four days of living with me has landed him with his first negative IEP.

He doesn't seem remotely worried, however. 'We can't give a fucking inch on this. We *have* to be out in the mornings at weekends, or the whole P2P process is sunk.'

I still have no idea what P2P actually is. Scott fixes us both an exceptionally strong coffee and lets me into some company secrets. 'P2P is anything we want it to be. My kids are in Australia, and I used to have a nightmare calling home because of the time difference. I was only getting out to use the phone in S and Ds, which was in the middle of the night in Melbourne. So I invented a prisoner support scheme. Since Trinity is full of guys who can't even spell their own names, I offered to go round G and K wings and help inmates fill in general apps. Crucially, I said that we had to do it at weekends. I called it Peer to Peer, or P2P, gave it a crappy logo and pitched it to Governor Yeti. He bought into it completely.'

Scott now has bulletproof permission to get unlocked on weekend mornings, when the rest of Trinity is banged up. He always knocks on a few doors and fills out a couple of apps, just to keep the cover going. 'Every month Yeti asks me for an update. I give him a full presentation, using a load of bullshit management terms, and he laps it up. That guy is such an underachiever.'

The entire facade exists purely so that Scott can call his two children, his wife, and whichever lawyers he isn't currently suing. Lance's departure means there is a space on the P2P board, and I join up immediately. I walk round the empty wings making calls, flushed with the knowledge that my unlock is protected by the

Trinity governor. Martyn and Nigel are still banged up, and I swing by their pad to flaunt the fact that I'm out. I later learn that they've uncharitably rechristened P2P 'Phone to Phone'.

10 October

Officer Moss does not succeed in giving Scott a negative IEP. These demerits need to be signed off by a senior officer, and none of the SOs will support giving Scott such a petty punishment. Moss doesn't take this humiliation lying down, and we hear that he'll soon retaliate with an excess kit check. There are strict limits on the number of prison-issue items we can all have, and officers sporadically inspect cells to confiscate surplus gear. Our pad has some hot property that could get us into trouble, including several additional towels, food that has blatantly been swiped from the kitchen, and a spare kettle that we use for cooking.

Scott is unfazed, and stuffs everything into a huge orange plastic bag marked *DANGER! BIOHAZARD WASTE*. 'No screw is ever going to put their hand in here,' he assures me. In addition to being the Listener coordinator and running P2P, Scott is also a biohazard cleaner. The job entails mopping up bodily fluids after self-harming, dirty protests and other mishaps. The salary is £35 a week, making it the best-paid gig in Wandsworth. It also provides unlimited cleaning products, including these large waste bags. 'It's the perfect hiding place,' he insists. 'The screws are all scared shitless of catching hepatitis and AIDS.'

I return a few hours later to find that the kettle, towels and food have all survived the search. However, most of my clothes have been taken instead. Under my bed were my precious tracksuits, which have now vanished. I assume these items were mistaken for prison-issue garments, but Scott is convinced that Moss confiscated them out of spite.

The second we're unlocked, I sprint outside looking for the laundry, which I eventually find behind the workshops. It's a decrepit corrugated-iron shed covered in pigeon crap, and would be vastly improved by a friendly bomb. I explain that my own clothes were accidentally taken in the kit check, and am directed to a towering metal cage stuffed with unwashed rags. I'm so desperate to avoid wearing prison-issue clothes that I clamber into the steaming pile, gagging from the stench of a hundred inmates' armpits. At the end of *The Shawshank Redemption* Tim Robbins swims through a mile of his fellow prisoners' turds. I feel that I'm now sharing a similar experience. My survival instincts kick in, sharpening the senses, and I catch a flash of my grey tracksuit. I crawl out of the cage with my cherished clothes held high, smelling like an autopsy gone wrong.

The kit check also confiscated my additional mattress. Sleeping on just one mattress again is horrible, and I get a trapped nerve in my back. I'm warned by other prisoners that osteopaths are unavailable in Wandsworth. All I can expect is a four-week wait to see a doctor, who will only prescribe paracetamol if I'm lucky.

11 October

Nigel pops by with distressing news. 'Officer Moss has been dragging your name through the gutter. He was mouthing off that you don't deserve to be in this cell as you aren't a qualified Listener.' Moss is unfortunately right. I am on the list to start the Listener training, but until then I am technically interloping. I don't know how much I trust Nigel as a source, given his history of being thrown out of Listener cells. I later discuss the issue with Scott, who admits that this could be a real problem.

'The most important thing is to make sure you actually get accepted into the Listener training. As long as you make it onto the programme, you should be OK.' This doesn't exactly calm my nerves. I'd assumed the Samaritans would roll out the red carpet for me, but apparently there is a rigorous selection process and lots of people get rejected. If I fail to make the grade, Moss will take great pleasure in ejecting me into the nearest cesspit.

12 October

I'm introduced to a former sports physiotherapist called Bloom. He's a hulking great Irishman with ginger hair down to his waist, and he offers to give me a massage in exchange for a pack of burn. I strip to the waist and sit on a chair while he rubs baby oil into my back.

Scott watches keenly from the sidelines. 'How long have you got to serve?' he asks Bloom. This is a standard conversation opener; a way of gently probing what someone's crime is.

'I'm a lifer,' admits Bloom cheerfully, which means that he's almost certainly been convicted of murder. In future I'm going to check if my physiotherapist has killed anyone *before* they start groping me. 'I have a few anger-management issues,' he adds as he kneads my skin with his enormous hands. 'One of my neighbours insulted the missus, and things escalated pretty quickly. I stabbed him fifty times, cleaned the knife and went back to work.'

Apparently nobody realised anything was amiss until they saw that Bloom's shoes were covered in blood. He pleaded guilty, served his minimum tariff and was released on a 99-year licence. Lifers never come off parole, so any slip-ups mean they'll be back behind bars.[1] A few months ago, Bloom was recalled to prison having been arrested for assault. 'My wife punched herself in the face and then blamed it on me.' I don't dare question this unusual scenario, and instead cluck sympathetically. Bloom is now stuck inside until he can convince the parole board that he is fit for release.

Despite being a murderer and a probable wife-beater, Bloom nonetheless does a pretty good job on my back. Scott announces that he too has a few twinges, and Bloom happily gives him a once-over.

126

13 October

Scott is widely accepted as an expert on Wandsworth's labyrinthine bureaucracy, and there are always visitors seeking his counsel. Today he is helping Mustafa from the kitchens, who is applying for home detention curfew. This allows prisoners on short sentences to spend their last few months at home wearing an electronic tag,[2] also known as a 'chav nav' or 'Peckham Rolex'. Mustafa's HDC application has been rejected due to a restraining order from his wife, so Scott makes detailed notes and promises to write his appeal. He never asks for payment, but we still receive a variety of random gifts. Hours later, Mustafa suddenly beckons me to our door, thrusts several chicken thighs into my hands and disappears without saying a word.

Scott rarely visits the servery, and instead cooks every evening. He starts prepping about 7 p.m., chopping onions, garlic and peppers, which he fries in the spare kettle. This isn't as disgusting as it sounds, as prison kettles have a flat metal surface that is pretty good for frying. He adds chicken, tinned tomatoes and chickpeas, throwing in some couscous after an hour to thicken the sauce. These concoctions always taste delicious; Scott somehow produces better cuisine out of a small kettle than comes out of Wandsworth's industrial kitchen.

He is constantly teaching me how to buck the system. 'The secret to survival is bulk theft. If you're caught swiping a bag of oats, you're fucked. But if you pick up a whole box, the screws will hold the gate open.'

I feel like Luke Skywalker under the tutelage of wise Yoda, and Scott is quick to rebuke me when I stray from the path. The laundry is taken over by a giant with a sinister stoop who is immediately christened Lurch. One afternoon Lurch advises that my clothes will come to no harm in return for a tin of tuna. I acquiesce to this mild protection racket, but when I tell Scott, he goes nuts.

'You're creating wage inflation, you fucking idiot! It'll undermine the whole wing economy!'

I try to point out that it's only a tin of tuna, but he just starts banging on about the failure of Keynesian economics.

14 October

My psychology studies are completely engrossing, and are providing unexpected insights into the prison experience. I'm currently studying Milgram's classic 1963 experiment into obedience. Milgram recruited 40 volunteers and told them to deliver increasingly severe electric shocks to someone in the next room. What they didn't know was that the person screaming next door was only an actor, who never actually felt any pain. Over half the participants administered potentially lethal voltages simply because they were instructed to do so by a man in a white coat. The experiment revealed how environment can powerfully affect behaviour, and that most people will mindlessly follow authority even if it causes great harm.[3] From where I'm sitting, it explains why certain screws are unnecessarily vile to prisoners on an hourly basis. Officer Moss may well be a decent and caring man outside Wandsworth, but inside these walls he has been conditioned to brutalise others without question.

The only problem with my OU course is finding quiet time to study. The Executive Suite has a nice big table, but Scott and I spend most of our time having heated discussions and playing backgammon. Linda, the sweary Scot who runs distance learning, suggests that I try working in the education department, which is a large prefab building next to Trinity. I head over and discover that it's full of empty classrooms. The quietness is like a warm sponge, and I get out my textbooks and dive in. Prior to prison, I was pathetically easy to distract – I had screens all over my desk, and I'd waste hours on Twitter. Now I'm hermetically sealed from all diversions, and my productivity soars.

Out of the window looms B Wing. I feel guilty having a whole classroom to myself, while hundreds of men remain trapped in their cells. The summer lockdown on the mains shows no signs of ending, which means that teachers are being paid to twiddle their thumbs.

I slowly explore the rest of this building, and discover a vast textile workshop with rows of ancient sewing machines. Prisons aren't allowed to exploit cheap labour to compete on the open market, but they can make products for other jails. Wandsworth's textile operation is supposed to manufacture clothing for the entire prison estate. Up on a big blackboard is an order for 18,000 pairs of boxer shorts. Sitting in front of it are three glum Latvians, painstakingly sewing these pants one at a time by hand.

16 October

I'm sitting in the visits hall with Lottie and Kit when Governor Bickers unexpectedly strides in. This is the first time I've seen him in the flesh, and he's being papped by a young assistant. Bickers approaches a nearby table where a prisoner is enjoying some precious time with his wife and kids, and sits down with the family, who duly engage him in conversation while the flunkey buzzes around taking pictures. When they're satisfied that they've nailed the shot, he sweeps back out.

Say cheese!

Cameras are banned in prisons, which makes the environment very far removed from the selfie-obsessed world outside. I brought in about 30 photos of Kit, which became my most treasured possessions. One of my favourite shots was from a visit to Peppa Pig World, of the two of us sitting on a tiny roller coaster and howling with laughter. If I hadn't come inside, this wonderful image would have been buried under terabytes of other barely viewed photos. Instead, it turned into a central part of my life. I'd often gaze at these pictures, trying to remember what those days were like. Was I

---

happy? Did I spend too much time checking my phone? Did I spend too much time taking pictures?

Lottie discovered an app called Touchnote, which allowed her to turn photos into postcards. She sent me one every week, and I put them up on the wall by the table. They became a window into a parallel universe, charting the life I could have led if I'd been found not guilty. My collage soon came to the attention of Officer Moss.

'ATKINS!' he screeched from the doorway. 'Take those photos down immediately!'

'Er, why?'

'They could be covering up an escape hole.'

Wandsworth was evidently using *The Shawshank Redemption* as a training film. I tried to explain that the cards were adorning an internal wall, so any obscured hole would just burrow further into the prison. Moss just repeated his original order at an increasing volume until I started removing the postcards. As an act of quiet rebellion, I put them up again by my bed, where they couldn't be seen from the door.

18 October

I return from exercise to find our cell full of prisoners I've never met, happily making themselves at home. They have presumably been invited by Scott, who has since buggered off to do something else. My first three months in Wandsworth were beset by a desperation to get my door open. Now that dozens of inmates view my cell as a common room, I sometimes wish we could be banged up more often. The Executive Suite has the only comfy chairs on the wing, another perk of living in the big Listener cell, but our plush furniture inevitably attracts unwanted company. Random prisoners just float in uninvited and break out into spontaneous moaning. Sometimes, just before the end of S&Ds, Scott will actually ask the screws to bang us up. 'It helps me sleep at night knowing that the door is locked through my own choice.'

Living with Scott is certainly exposing me to a hitherto unseen side of Wandsworth. One afternoon, Officer O'Reilly walks into our cell and barks, 'Excess kit check!' I panic, as the spare kettle hasn't been stowed in the biohazard bag. Scott produces a small ashtray and says, 'Smoke 'em if you got 'em,' whereupon they both spark roll-ups and start gossiping. Officers aren't allowed to smoke on the wings, so it's been tacitly agreed that O'Reilly can puff in our cell instead of doing any searching. He's far more human in this environment, and has an infinite supply of prison anecdotes.

'I was doing the visits run last week, and opened up a cell on K Wing. I said to the guy, "I guess you know why I'm here?" The stupid fucker reached into his pocket and handed me an iPhone. I was only picking him up for a visit, but I ended up taking him down the block.'

O'Reilly also told us how a few years ago, a prisoner with Asperger's was assaulted by his cellmate. The victim immediately told the officers everything, which is practically unheard of in prison. The screws realised that they'd struck gold and started quizzing him about what else was happening on the wing. This vulnerable inmate was tricked into being an unwitting informer, who then suffered relentless abuse for being a grass.

19 October

At 8 a.m., Officer Monaghan informs us that freeflow has been cancelled. The reason is unclear; his thick Irish accent is incomprehensible through our metal door. I turn on Radio 4 and learn that an inmate has been murdered at HMP Pentonville,[4] which is probably why we've been locked down. The *Today* programme interviews Andrew Selous, a former prisons minister, who denies that his swingeing cuts to officer numbers are connected to the rise in violence. He claims that 'there is a huge amount of work being done to reduce violence',[5] implying that prisons are effectively transforming violent convicts into employable citizens. His description is ludicrously removed from reality, but goes completely unchallenged.

The ex-minister does eventually acknowledge that locking prisoners up for 23 hours a day can lead to trouble. As the day wears on, we learn that afternoon freeflow is cancelled as well. Wandsworth has reacted to the Pentonville stabbing by deploying the very tactic that causes unrest: bang-up leads to violence, leads to bang-up, leads to violence, repeat to fade …

We finally get out at the end of the day, and I run into a dozen agitated prisoners who have just arrived from Pentonville. Some of them were connected to the stabbing, and have been transferred to Wandsworth to separate them from a rival gang.

'Cheers, Pentonville, keep 'em coming!' I whisper to myself. I can't wait to do their English and maths tests.

20 October

An unidentified Wandsworth officer has hanged himself at home. I later learn the identity of the dead officer and it's not someone I know well. Apparently he had gambling debts and suffered from depression, and his body stayed undiscovered for three days.

I discuss the death with a long-serving prisoner, who shakes his head saying, 'Tragedy. Fucking tragedy.' I'm touched that he's set aside the usual inmate/officer animosity, but he soon puts me straight. 'Total nightmare. Every time a screw dies, we have an all-day lockdown for the bleedin' funeral.'

21 October

The selection for Listener training is in a week's time. I'm getting extremely anxious about being accepted, not just because the programme's extremely worthwhile, but because otherwise Officer Moss will have me evicted. The Samaritans drop round some literature for me to read: 'The Listener scheme is a peer support service which aims to reduce suicide and self-harm in prisons. Samaritans volunteers select, train and support prisoners to become Listeners. Listeners provide confidential emotional support to their fellow inmates who are struggling to cope.'[7]

Scott suggests I sit in on one of his Listener sessions to get my feet wet. I hope he doesn't mean this too literally – apparently self-harming can be pretty gruesome. I'm not very good with blood; I even get squeamish watching *Casualty*.

After lunch, an officer knocks on our door. 'Samuels wants a Listener.'

'He's a regular customer; can you bring him down to the cell?' asks Scott.

I'd normally cross the wing to avoid Samuels, as he has regular spice attacks and is constantly fighting the screws. He's about 50, and is surprisingly ripped for someone who's spent most of their life on crack. He slopes into our cell talking 19 to the dozen, blurring the line between words, groaning and laughing.

'Man got *mad* debts, innit. Big man on da Fours gonna fuck me up, you get me.'

Samuels is heavily indebted to a spice dealer, and the interest is accruing faster than a payday loan. He has no means to pay, but the dealer keeps supplying more drugs on tick. Things have now come to a head, as a screw has just found a phone in the dealer's cell. The dealer will have to appear before an adjudicator – a visiting magistrate who rules on serious offences – and the punishment is likely to be an extra month on his sentence. The dealer has instructed Samuels to take the heat for the phone, in lieu of the debt. This explains why Samuels has been kept strung out on free gear, as he's been primed to take the fall whenever things come unstuck. It's actually a very effective form of business insurance.

Scott is very different during this encounter, his usual brash arrogance replaced by sympathy and kindness. They talk it all through, and despite not finding any solution, Samuels calms down considerably. I don't say anything, just try to take it all in. The conversation comes to a natural close, and I call the officer to escort Samuels back to his cell. It's quite humbling trying to help someone I've previously written off as a total lowlife.

22 October

BBC News does a report on the drugs epidemic in prisons. It includes some dramatic CCTV footage from Wandsworth. A drone buzzes over the fence and hovers next to A Wing with a large package dangling underneath. Seconds later, a stick emerges and pulls the contraband inside.[8] Watching my home on TV triggers a peculiar feeling of pride, like seeing my old flat on the coverage of the London Marathon.

Hours later, we're visited by a rat-faced Geordie dealer called Tommy, who has cropped hair and wild eyes. It transpires that he ran a thriving drugs empire from the Executive Suite on a previous sentence.

'This was a ferocious pad, I'm telling ya. We had four-foot-high speakers in the corner, Xbox, PlayStation. We had a drone coming in every night.' He was raking in several grand a week, until the security department spun his cell. 'Got busted with an ounce of crack and an ounce of heroin. I only got six months extra time, total result. On road I'd be looking at eight years.'

Tommy slipped through a legal loophole that gives dealers lighter punishments if they're caught in prison. Governors often opt to handle drug offences internally, rather than charging the perpetrators in court. Sending Tommy to trial would have meant a much longer sentence, but would also have drawn public attention to the rampant drugs trade in Wandsworth. He was instead put on an internal adjudication, which kept the matter under wraps.

I enquire further about his current operation. Drones are out of fashion following a nasty incident outside Wandsworth. A local gang were piloting in a drone laden with drugs when they were disturbed by the police. A high-speed car chase ensued, and the gang's vehicle crashed, killing a female passenger.[9] Tommy has since reverted to a more traditional approach. He moved into a cell overlooking the exercise yard, and immediately kicked out the window glass. The next stage involved making a rope from a torn bedsheet and tying a bar of soap to the end. He demonstrates how he sprints down the length of the cell and hurls the soap out of the window.

'Forget soap on a rope, this is dope on a rope!' he chortles. I suspect he's told this joke before. The makeshift rope is received by his associate on the other side of the fence, and parcels are then hauled in.

The number of banned items brought into London prisons is up by 400%, and the steepest rise is in Wandsworth.[10] Tommy's rope strategy is high-volume, high-profit, but has a long lead time. Smaller drops are made by his missus in the visits hall.

'She sticks an ounce up her snatch, gets past security, then goes to the loo and whips it out. At the end of the visit we hug and she passes it over.'

'How do you get it back to the wing?' I ask naïvely.

'I bank it, of course.' This refers to hiding contraband up one's anus. Before the visit, Tommy liberally applies Vaseline to his arse to facilitate a smooth insertion. He has a pair of underpants stitched into his boxer shorts in case the contents get dislodged during transit. He proudly insists that his banking capacity is at least two ounces. 'You gotta do what you gotta do.'

23 October

Scott is embroiled in a long-running feud with Sally in Activities, who has banned him from all IT access in Wandsworth. This is a bit of a problem, as he is fighting a bruising appeal. He has engaged the services of Fenton, the rake-thin former lawyer, and together they write out reams of legal statements by hand. I am soon press-ganged into becoming Scott's legal secretary, as I have now wrangled access to the PCs in the main library. I head over to the library and sit in the corner, theatrically reading my psychology textbook. After 20 minutes, Federico starts dozing in the corner, so I quietly pull out Scott's hand-written notes and surreptitiously type everything up. I do a spell check, then send the document to the printer, whisking the pages out before anyone can read them. I smuggle it all back to the wing, and Scott sends the papers to the court the next day.

H Wing is full of people losing confiscation battles. Will is an irascible Essex boy who was convicted of running a boiler room fraud. 'It was like *The Wolf of Wall Street*, but in Chigwell,' he boasts in our cell. 'Those CPS cunts are forcing me to sell my house so they can seize the remaining equity.' He has a cunning plan, and intends to sell the property at an artificially low price to a friend, who will then pay back £100K 'on the tangle'. He does a funny twisty hand move as he says this, like a drunk fish swimming. There is a murmur of approval from the surrounding acolytes.

I've been quietly washing up in the corner, but I snap at this point. 'If you hadn't noticed, we're in a high-security prison having all been convicted of serious financial crimes. Have you considered that we aren't particularly good at it? Isn't it time to play with a straight bat?'

Ted is also going through the confiscation wringer, but is much more circumspect. He's been threatened with an additional three and a half years if he doesn't stump up. I get out a calculator, and we work out that he will effectively be 'paid' £1,000 a day to stay in prison.

'I'm fucked if I can earn a grand a day on the outside. I'll be better off serving the extra time,' he concludes. I can't imagine that this is what the legislators had in mind when they brought in the Proceeds of Crime Act.

Empty gesture

A 2013 National Audit Office report concluded that Proceeds of Crime confiscation orders were not proving to be value for money: 'Only about 26p in every £100 of criminal proceeds was actually confiscated in 2012-13.'[11] This was in keeping with the stories I kept hearing about how the confiscation system was completely broken.

Kane was a prisoner with Asperger's who was the undisputed Scrabble champion on H Wing. He had completed half his sentence for VAT fraud, but his release was blocked by the CPS, who had been doggedly pursuing £120K of his assets. He had long maintained that he was penniless, but under the Proceeds of Crime Act, he had to prove that he didn't have the money. As I found with my missing canteen, it's very hard to prove a negative. Kane was unable to demonstrate that he didn't have the funds, and was given an additional two years inside.

He then proposed an ingenious solution. He asked to be released on a heavily restricted licence, so he could work off the debt. He'd been offered a City job earning £150K a year, which would clear the confiscation bill in 12 months. The CPS rejected this proposal out of hand. This is what my mother would call 'cutting your nose off to spite your face'. If Kane served the two years, he wouldn't have to pay the government anything and it would cost nearly £100K to keep him locked up. The dispute went back to court, where the judge was baffled that the CPS were actually refusing £120K. Kane won the day and went home shortly afterwards.

24 October

Body-worn cameras are being introduced in Wandsworth, and rolled out across prisons nationally.[12] I'd assumed that officers would be issued with the same high-tech devices worn by the police. Today I see one of these new cameras, which looks as if it's come out of a Christmas cracker. It's basically a cheap GoPro on a bit of string round the screw's neck.

'Congratulations on your new surveillance equipment, miss.'

She doesn't seem very familiar with the device. 'Do you think it's switched on?' she asks. The officer is only five foot two, so even if the camera is filming, all it will get is a nice shot of my chest.

25 October

Ted pops in for a coffee. He quietly observes that I've been looking darkly troubled recently, and wants to know if I'm OK. There's no denying that I'm still struggling to come to terms with being inside. Some days I'll bounce down the wing cracking jokes with everyone, feeling that I can breeze through prison. An hour later I'll slide into a vortex of despair, unable to face the next 24 hours, let alone the next two years. Wandsworth is so unbelievably strange that it's still hard to accept I'm really here. I'll suddenly snap my head back, open-eyed, a voice in my head shouting, 'I'm in FUCKING PRISON! My life is FUCKED!' I'm also deeply anxious about the upcoming Listener selection. If I don't qualify, I'll probably get thrown out of this cell.

Writing my diary helps immeasurably. I've now scrawled hundreds of pages about my Wandsworth experiences, and I've yet to confront a traumatic event that hasn't been eased by writing about it afterwards. On the outside I'd deal with upsetting situations by pointing a camera at them; now I'm doing much the same with a pen and paper.

26 October

I'm delivering the canteen with Officer Marchbanks. He's not the fastest screw around, and by the time we get to the bottom landing, we're an hour behind. The Ones on G Wing are home to the servery workers, so Marchbanks opens them up for work while we finish our deliveries. The lads pile out and jump in the shower, and the atmosphere is fairly jolly, right up until a mobile phone starts ringing in one of the cells. I haven't heard a phone ring for several months, so it takes me a few seconds to grasp what the noise actually is.

Nobody moves. The phone's owner has clearly realised that if he runs to switch it off, he will be as good as admitting guilt. It's like a saloon shootout scene in a western, when the piano stops playing and everyone freezes. Everyone except for Mr Marchbanks, who carries on delivering the canteen, oblivious to the electronic chirping. The poor man is so stupid he hasn't registered the significance of the ringing. God knows what they teach them in training. It seems to last forever, but eventually the phone goes quiet. The saloon piano starts playing, and we all carry on as before.

Wake-up call

I was probably one of the few prisoners in Wandsworth who didn't own an iPhone. The prohibition on mobiles worked about as well as the ban on drugs – there may as well have been a Phones4U popup in the servery. The demand for illicit phones was heavily driven by the drug trade.[13] Calls on the prison phones were recorded, so a thriving spice market required secure communications. Dealers needed at least one smartphone, also known as a 'moody phone', to call their external suppliers and arrange deliveries. Mobiles were also vital to sell spice on the wings. Cash rarely changed hands inside the jail; instead, payments were made via bank transfer to a designated account. Dealers needed mobiles to lend to their customers, who then called their loved ones and coerced them to pay for the next score.

Many prisoners used mobiles for everyday contact with friends and family. Thanks to my multiple jobs, I was able to call home twice a day, but the majority of Wandsworth residents rarely left their cells. Several wings had S&Ds in the mornings when kids were at school, so a mobile was the only way that some inmates could keep in contact.

Another driver was cost. Calling out from prison phones was extortionate; it cost 37p per minute to call an external mobile.[14] Many inmates were unable to do paid prison work, and didn't have any money coming in, so they couldn't put funds on their phone account. On the outside, mobiles were being practically given away with unlimited minutes, so it was obvious why they were being smuggled in. Demand was fuelled even further because new prisoners had to wait weeks for their phone pins to be activated. One morning I was doing the inductions, and a middle-aged man started crying into his maths test.

'I can't call home, and my family have no idea where I am.' When he arrived, he was given the standard £2 emergency phone credit, which only lasted for 24 hours. He was then banged up for two days straight, and when he finally got out, the pin had stopped working. He had no means of contacting his wife and children, who didn't even know that he'd been arrested.

I told the tearful prisoner to keep filling in phone pin applications, which should activate his numbers in a couple of weeks. This just made him wail even louder.

I leant in and whispered, 'There's a spice dealer down the other end of the landing. He'll probably lend you his phone in return for your smoker's pack.'

The most popular model of mobile phone was the 'Beat the Boss'. They were the size of a thumb and had no metal parts, therefore eluding detection by the chair-shaped sit-down metal detector known as 'the Boss'. Many prisoners kept their mobiles hidden all day, and only used them at night. If a call had to be made in the daytime, it was deemed a good idea to pretend to have a dump and phone from behind the privacy curtain. Even the most belligerent screw would allow prisoners time to make themselves decent, buying a few crucial seconds to flush the mobile down the pan.

One prisoner famously called home while on the convenience and was rudely disturbed when his door banged open. The guy panicked and chucked the phone in the khazi. It turned out the intruder was just a friend mucking about.

27 October

Today is the selection for Listener training. There are six of us from Trinity on the shortlist, and we're all escorted to the chapel in the mains. This is a proper church, and is far more grandiose than the tiny room on K Wing. I join 25 other wannabe Listeners in the pews, where we are addressed by the head of the local Samaritans branch, a genteel man in his sixties called Arthur.

'Prison suicides are now at an all-time high, and Wandsworth is going through a self-harm epidemic. Most of the inmates you'll deal with will have some form of mental illness. It is very challenging work, but I think you'll also find it highly rewarding.'

We are then called up to be interviewed, and I'm quite unsettled waiting for my turn. When I finally sit down with Arthur, he asks me why I want to be a Listener.

'It's the only humane response to the agony and heartbreak on my doorstep. I feel compelled to help.' I don't mention that I'm already living in the big Listener cell and will be hoofed out if today goes badly.

'Do you have any personal issues we should know about?'

I haven't really thought about this, and blurt out that my teenage cousin hanged himself eight years ago. 'I don't think I've ever got over it.' Saying this out loud makes me realise why I've been so uncomfortable today.

Arthur nods reassuringly. 'That won't be a problem, but it's good that you raised it.'

Back in the cell, Scott tells me that I've easily made the grade. 'We just have that session to weed out the undesirables.' Apparently one of the candidates said that he'd make a good Listener because 'I'm a face, you get me? I'm a face on wing, an' I got respect, innit.' Scott concluded that he'd abuse the position to sell spice, and binned him off.

I well up with joy that I've finally secured my rightful place in the Executive Suite. Little do I know that becoming a Listener will bring me into contact with far more misery than if I'd flunked out.

6

Suicide and Sellotape

In which I get thrown into Listening at the deep end, and witness unparalleled human suffering. The reform revolution flounders, and I join the Purple Army to steady the ship.

Things I learn:

1) How to break out of Pentonville

2) The problems of multi-faith worship

3) How to describe an abstract concept

I befriend a veteran Listener who's losing his mind, and he becomes a dark portent of my own future.

28 October

The Listener training takes place in the main chapel. Arthur starts off with some case studies, and we listen to the harrowing stories of several 'contacts' – the term for prisoners who've requested a Listener. Contrary to popular belief, Listeners are not supposed to talk their contacts out of killing themselves. It's often counterproductive to try to convince suicidal people that life is worth living. If someone is so desperate that they've called a Listener, they have probably heard the 'think of your children' arguments already. They might be facing any manner of complex problems, and we won't know nearly enough about their situation to provide a quick fix. Listeners have to resist the temptation to find solutions, and instead ask open-ended questions. The central goal is to get the contact verbalising their darkest fears.

'Steer into the pain,' Arthur tells us again and again. 'Simply getting your contact to talk about their distress can pull them back from the brink.' It's a lot to take in. Everything else I've encountered in Wandsworth has been banal and inconsequential, but the Listening is suddenly deadly serious.

29 October

A few doors down from us lives an elderly prisoner called Clenshaw. He has severe arthritis, and is rudely ungrateful to anyone giving him assistance. This morning he sticks his wizened head around our door.

'They've just made me Equalities Red Band. What the fuck did they go and do that for?'

This is quite a privileged position, requiring Clenshaw to go round the whole prison helping victims of discrimination. Racism, homophobia and Islamophobia are rife in Wandsworth, and have long been swept under the carpet. Inmates seldom report abuse to staff, but are more willing to engage with other prisoners. The authorities presumably assumed that Clenshaw was ideal for the Equalities job as he's disabled himself and will have first-hand experience of discrimination. There are, however, two key problems with this appointment:

1) He is so incapacitated that he can barely get out of bed unaided. This may hamper his ability to circulate all eight wings, which have four flights of stairs apiece.

2) He is also notoriously racist, sexist and homophobic, so may struggle to protect minorities from this very abuse.

I'm now getting so busy that I try to shed some of my prison duties. I attempt to quit taking the morning register, but the officers beg me to continue. The job really stretches my patience, and I frequently turn into Basil Fawlty.

'Name?'

'A739—'

'No, that's your prison number, what's your name?'

'G2-07.'

'That's your room number; I really need to know your name.'

'I go hairdressing.'

'HOW HARD CAN IT BE TO KNOW YOUR OWN SODDING NAME?'

'Paul.'

I often do the register alongside Mr Mendes, one of the more affable screws, who doesn't take the task particularly seriously. He mostly flirts with the female officers while ticking off every prisoner's name without even looking at whoever is filing past.

Dead-end jobs

Prison jobs were allocated by the activities department, which was run by the mighty Sally. She was said to eat inmates for breakfast, not just because she was tough to work with, but because she was also spectacularly obese. Sally kept trying to 'save' wayward prisoners by giving them wholly unsuitable roles. When Lurch left the laundry, she gave the job to a young lad with strange tufts of hair on his head resembling horns, who was swiftly nicknamed 'Mr Tumnus'. The new laundryman rarely, if ever, did any washing, and instead used the laundry as a base for his spice operation. I kept visiting to sniff my bag of clothes, trying to deduce if they had actually been washed or just taken out for some fresh air. Mr Tumnus' incompetence actually worked in his favour; as inmates became increasingly concerned at the hopeless service, his fee swiftly rose to three tins of tuna per wash, though it brought no noticeable increase in standards. Much like Britain in the 1970s, the laundry's productivity plummeted, costs skyrocketed, and Scott's fears of wage inflation started to come true.

30 October

Listener training continues, and we start doing role play in pairs. One of us pretends to be a suicidal prisoner, while the other encourages them to open up. The exercises are really helpful, but obviously a far cry from the real thing. Scott soon suggests that I join him when he's next on duty. He does two 24-hour shifts a week, and he soon gets his first call-out.

We head along to the H Wing Listener Suite, which is where Scott sees most of his contacts. It's a stark, grimy double cell further down the Twos, which is completely empty except for three horrible plastic chairs. It stinks of cigarette smoke and is lit by two harsh strip lights. There we meet a young Lithuanian called Miko, who sits hunched and sweating in the cold air.

'My cellmate, he's driving me nuts. He plays music all night, really loud. All day he lies in bed watching TV.' Miko hasn't slept for days, but is terrified of confronting his tormentor. I instinctively want to share my experiences with Romanian Dan, but we've been taught to avoid introducing our own problems, as it shifts attention away from the contact. I leave the talking to Scott, who gently probes Miko's fears.

'Have you got any other problems?' he asks. This seems like an odd question, given that Miko is at the end of his tether with his cellmate. But apart from living with a total arsehole, he seems otherwise OK. Scott excuses himself, and I'm left alone with Miko. I'm initially a bit tongue-tied, but then ask him about his family, which seems a fairly safe topic. Miko is extremely tense, twitching at the slightest noise, and he scratches his arms continuously.

Scott soon returns with good news. 'I just spoke to the SO. He's gonna move you to another cell.' Miko is overcome with relief, and goes off to pack his things. We aren't supposed to get involved with our contacts' problems, but Scott will always help out if he can.

'This happens all the time; these poor guys get forced to share with complete fuckbastards. Couple of years back, someone stabbed their cellmate to death. I get on pretty well with most of the SOs, and they'll usually sort it if you ask nicely.'

Our next contact is Ali, a small Asian guy in his twenties. He shakes our hands, sits down and says that he's feeling suicidal. The mother of his young son has just been arrested for stealing clothes, and he is terrified that their child will go into care. The prospect of never seeing the boy again is causing him to have extreme panic attacks. I find it really difficult to talk about this, and have an instinctive urge to change the subject, but Scott is utterly unfazed.

'So have you actually attempted suicide?' he asks. Ali admits that he has tried to hang himself; he still has ligature marks around his neck. He talks lucidly about his suicidal inclinations, which are exacerbated by his mental health problems. I desperately want to find some positives in his situation, but Scott does the opposite and pushes the conversation further into the darkness. After an hour, Ali looks visibly relieved to have unloaded everything.

Our final contact is a young tearaway who is spiced out of his tree. He keeps rapping, quite badly if my judgement is anything to go by, and makes an ill-advised attempt at break-dancing. There doesn't seem to be anything wrong with him that abstinence won't fix.

Seeing these three contacts back to back leaves me deeply unsettled. I thought I had Wandsworth figured out, but the Listening has opened up a whole new dimension of wrong. It seems unconscionable that the authorities would deal with some of these vulnerable people by simply locking them up all day. I'm also starting to get extremely worried at the thought of having to deal with similar inmates myself.

'You'll get used to it,' Scott reassures me. 'You have to walk that thin line between getting too emotionally involved and pissing yourself laughing.'

1 November

I've signed up to a creative writing course. This afternoon I go to the first class, which is held in the tiny K Wing library. We're taught by a Canadian novelist called Sarah Leipciger. She's sharp and warm, and endeavours to stir our creative juices. Unfortunately, the lesson is also attended by Clenshaw, the racist equalities rep. He talks like Blakey from the seventies sitcom *On the Buses*, and continually derails the class with his dull-headed contributions.

'I want everyone to think of an abstract concept,' says Sarah.

Clenshaw looks puzzled. 'What's an abstract concept when it's at home, miss?'

'It's something you can't picture, like fear, or happiness.'

'Like an angel?'

'Angels aren't really abstract,' persists Sarah, 'as we can visualise them. I'm thinking more like joy, intelligence.'

Clenshaw isn't letting go. 'But angels are intelligent.'

'Yes, but they're not—'

'Or are you saying all angels are stupid?'

'No, but they aren't an abstract concept.' Sarah desperately tries to keep the momentum going. 'What I'm looking for is a recipe. We're going to cook something abstract, so we need to find the ingredients.'

Clenshaw is aghast. 'You want me to cook an angel?'

I soon quit the course.

2 November

I've become quite friendly with Les, who is the only competent barber on the wing. He is quite erratic; one minute he'll engage in a sensible conversation, and the next he'll come out with something utterly ludicrous. He is also a long-serving Listener, and today he staggers into our cell in quite a state. 'Just had someone cut up in front of me. Poor fucker nearly died.' He had been called to attend a young Latvian who's fighting extradition. The prisoner immediately produced a razor blade and opened his wrists, losing several pints of blood. It's part of a worrying trend among eastern Europeans, who keep self-harming to avoid deportation.

Scott is called on to do a biohazard clean, and I help him carry the gear to K Wing. I nearly throw up when I see the cell. It's like an abattoir at the end of a shift. There's blood on the floor, the walls and the ceiling. It's even spilled into the corridor, and I manage to get some on my shoes despite not setting foot in the cell. It takes Scott three hours to clean it up.

Later on, I check in on the Latvian, who is now occupying the observation cell. It's where they put prisoners at high risk of suicide, and it's shielded by a cage and a Perspex window. The wretched guy just sits there motionless, with bandages all up his arms. I can't think of what to say, so I quietly slope off, furious at myself for not engaging with him. Days later, he tears into his arms once more. This time he's rushed to hospital and we never see him again.

3 November

After a month of terrible headlines about the prison crisis, Liz Truss tries to take back the initiative. She makes a big announcement about her reform programme, telling the media that prisons are going to get the 'biggest overhaul in a generation.'[1] This is promptly upstaged by the Prison Officers Association, who simultaneously announce that conditions are so lawless they'll have to seize control of failing prisons. The head of the POA, Mike Rolfe, claims that UK prisons are a 'bloodbath', and threatens to take over every jail in the country.[2]

It's little more than a stunt, but the POA's announcement dominates the news agenda and ruins Truss's big day. BBC News eventually cuts to her standing in front of a cheap purple *REFORM* sign, looking exceptionally miffed. She sets out her plans for tackling the stubbornly high rates of reoffending, which cost the taxpayer approximately £15 billion a year. 'We will give governors the tools they need to drive forward improvements. We will push decision-making authority and budgets ... down to governors, whether that is education, family services or how they run their regime.'[3] She is adamant that the only way to solve the crisis is to turn every jail into a reform prison like Wandsworth.

Down on the ground, her cherished reform programme is steadily gaining momentum. This week our glossy internal newsletter, *The Reform Chronicles*, breaks a major scoop: 'You will see some of the old and irrelevant signs coming down, and new ones going up.' Signs saying *Wandsworth Prison* are to be changed to *Wandsworth Reform Prison*. The other exciting measure is the planned replacement of several hundred windows.[4] Someone has probably read that fixing broken windows in 1980s New York was believed to have reduced the crime rate.[5] It's a shame they didn't read the later research, which attributed the falling crime to the legalisation of abortion.[6]

The news about the windows emerged in the recent Trinity rep meeting, where Scott and other selected prisoners put their concerns to Governor Yeti. Given that conditions are so bad that even the officers are killing themselves, Scott couldn't help thinking there were better places to spend the money. He suggested they focus on the inhumane living conditions, and pointed out that most wings were still on 23-hour bang-up, which was causing terrible mental health problems among the prisoners. Apparently Yeti just turned round to him and sniffed, 'It's *men*, not prisoners.'

I tell Scott that I *have* to go to one of these meetings.

4 November

Liz Truss finally announces a genuinely positive measure – prisons in England and Wales are to get 2,500 extra staff. This reportedly includes 400 emergency new staff for the 10 'most challenging' jails.[7]

I read the list and am amazed that Wandsworth isn't on there. Christ knows how bad things are in the other prisons that they deserve more reinforcements.

Bottom of the barrel

Staff levels were at a record low in Wandsworth. The prison had dozens of staff vacancies, and the authorities were desperate to attract more applicants. Things got so bad that Radio Wanno started asking its audience to encourage people to apply, even though the station was exclusively targeted at convicted criminals. Nationally the recruitment crisis led to entry requirements being quietly lowered, just to get more boots on the landings. According to former prison governor John Podmore: 'New recruits must be found for £9 per hour, and then there's the training, which at 10 weeks is the shortest of any jurisdiction across the world, with entry requiring no basic minimum qualifications.'[8]

The recruitment crisis led to the rise of Operational Support Grades (OSGs).[9] These were the prison equivalent of Police Community Support Officers, also known as 'no stripe' officers, or 'basic screws'. They had limited powers and no cell keys, and it was a wonder that some of them could even fill in the application form. One afternoon I was escorted the back way to the education offices by a very young OSG. He was unable to get through the final door, and flapped that 'I don't have the right key.' We banged on the door for 10 minutes, eventually attracting Linda, the head of distance learning. She turned the handle and let us in, revealing that the door wasn't even locked.

---

5 November

Wandsworth's executive governor, Ian Bickers, has come up with a bold solution to address the officer shortages. New signs go up round the wings: *There is an army of peer advisers working in every area of the prison, running information desks on the wings, supporting newly arrived prisoners. They will be wearing purple shirts.* This causes some confusion, as nobody has ever seen a purple-shirted adviser, or indeed any information desks.

The 'Purple Army' turns out to be the centrepiece of Bickers' reform revolution. He plans to train up 60 trusted prisoners, giving them a City & Guilds qualification in advice and guidance. They will then undertake basic admin tasks, alleviating pressure on the officers, who'll have more time to unlock inmates.[10] It's basically an official version of P2P, Scott's elaborate cover story for getting out at weekends, and actually sounds like a really good idea.

I fill in an application form to join up. It's been a long time since I formally applied for a job, and I struggle not to sound like an arrogant prick. 'STRENGTHS: studied maths and physics at Oxford University, 3 BAFTA nominations. WEAKNESSES: convicted fraudster.'

We are soon called to arms, and six of us assemble in a Trinity classroom. My fellow conscripts include Fenton the property orderly, and Clenshaw the racist equalities rep. We are greeted by Ruben, who is running the peer advice scheme. He produces a box of garish purple shirts, which are quickly snapped up. We were initially going to be branded in orange, until someone pointed out the disturbing connotations with Guantanamo Bay.

The first lesson is on the Equalities Act. Ruben, who is openly gay, walks us through the protected characteristics, telling us that the law prohibits discrimination on the grounds of religion, sexuality and gender reassignment.

This last one throws Clenshaw. 'What's gender reassignment when it's at home?'

Fenton explains.

Clenshaw is appalled. 'You mean they mutilate themselves? That's revolting.'

Ruben winces, and moves on to the landmark case involving two gay men being refused entry to a B&B.

'Quite right too,' growls Clenshaw.

Ruben looks as if he might cry.

I can't contain myself. 'Clenshaw, you do know that you're the Equalities Red Band?'

'I know, it's a total joke. It takes me half an hour to walk to E Wing, and by the time I get there, I need to come back for the toilet. If I do ever speak to prisoners, the conversation starts and ends with me asking them for a cigarette.'

Par for the coarse

It's something of an understatement to note that Wandsworth was not a very politically correct environment. This was a consequence of the entire culture being stuck in a bizarre time warp. The admin, work practices and most of the furniture were straight out of the 1970s, so it was hardly surprising that the language was pretty filthy. This permeated both prisoners and officers, and I'll admit that I also became fairly uncouth over time. I haven't tried to hide this, as I want the book to show the reality of the effect of prison, even on a screaming liberal like myself. I apologise for any offence caused by some of my crude comments, and chalk this up as yet another reason for urgent prison reform.

---

6 November

More details emerge of Liz Truss's new reform plans. She wants to publish the English and maths scores of newly inducted prisoners and create prison league tables.[11] This is another trick borrowed from Tony Blair, who introduced league tables in the nineties to shame failing schools and hospitals. The idea was that stakeholders would vote with their feet and drive up standards. The efficacy of such tables has long been questioned, but I fail to see how they can possibly work in prisons. Convicts can hardly choose which establishment they end up in.

7 November

Things are going from bad to worse on E Wing, and the trouble is being exacerbated by the new SO. He's an old-fashioned bully, who is obsessed with keeping everyone locked up. This is causing serious problems for Connor and his associates in the Annexe. The SO thinks that these lads have life too easy, and has drastically reduced their unlock time. While the Annexe crew do enjoy certain luxuries, they also cover all the orderly jobs on E Wing.

Today Connor turns up half an hour late to do the inductions. 'Sorry, Danielle, that arsehole SO has had us banged up all morning.' The schedule runs 90 minutes late, and eventually a handful of inmates are unlocked for their education assessments. We are soon joined by two women from the Rehabilitation of Addicted Prisoners Trust (RAPt), which manages drug and alcohol prevention in Wandsworth. They're supposed to give new prisoners a substance misuse screening on arrival, but these have all been missed due to the regime problems. It's been decided that the inmates should instead be interviewed while they're doing their education tests.

The two women strut round the classroom asking, 'Do you have any problems with alcohol or drugs?' in full earshot of everyone else. This is a blatant breach of the Data Protection Act, as medical information should only be discussed in private.

One guy is desperate to avoid the Substance Recovery Unit on D Wing. 'I was there on my last sentence, when I was on heroin. I'm clean now, and I can't go back to the rehab wing as it's full of junkies and drugs. I'll end up using again.'

The RAPt worker is unmoved. 'You've had drug issues in the past, so the system has put you on D Wing.'

This is a common complaint. The very wing where inmates are supposed to get clean is also the easiest place to obtain drugs. One time I'm called into the Listener Suite to talk to Jack, who has recently escaped from the rehab unit. 'I was hooked on Subutex, and it nearly killed me,' he says.

Subutex is an opioid prescribed to ease heroin withdrawal. It's also quite addictive in its own right, and is in high demand on the black market. The addicts undergoing treatment are supposed to swallow the tablets in front of the medical staff, but they often hide them under their tongue, then sell them on to other prisoners. Jack was a cleaner, and hung round the meds hatch picking up second-hand tablets. He proudly kept his landings spotless, as he was permanently wired on Subutex, but the drug also gave him intense mood swings. One day he climbed up to the rafters and nearly jumped to his death.

Induction crunch

When I arrived in July 2016, 49% of new arrivals went through induction and took the English and maths tests. In the four months after Wandsworth became a reform prison, this tanked to 21%, as officers simply weren't unlocking new prisoners for their inductions.[12] Since four out of five inmates weren't even taking the education assessments, publishing the results would be utterly meaningless. 80% of new inmates weren't being told the basics of how the prison worked. This sharply fuelled the levels of stress and anxiety across the wings. I ended up seeing dozens of Listener contacts who were stressing over simple admin issues like phone calls, visits and post that should have been addressed during induction.

8 November

BBC Breakfast reports that two inmates have escaped from HMP Pentonville. The news flashes up the prisoners' mug shots, and they don't exactly look like criminal masterminds. They apparently sawed through metal bars, clambered over roofs and slid down a pole on a sheet.[13] Beforehand they'd stuffed pillows into their beds, and the prison didn't sound the alarm for 15 hours.[14] The authorities are apparently baffled that it took so long to notice they were two men short. I am reminded of how Officer Mendes does the morning register, ticking off every name without looking at the prisoners, and I'm actually surprised that Pentonville discovered the escape as quickly as they did.

These escapes have a disastrous impact on Wandsworth. The officers go on high alert, and start doing counts on the hour through the night. This is a nightmare, as they switch on the cell light each time they check we're present. It only takes a second in a normal cell, but the beds in the Executive Suite are much further from the door, so they keep our light on for ages. I get woken up every time they do a count, and Scott's coping strategy doesn't help. I'm roused at 5 a.m. by him standing in his pants bellowing, 'Can you fuck off with your checks? We are *Listeners*! On call twenty-four-fucking-seven, saving lives!'

The next morning Officer Mendes is noticeably more diligent while taking the H Wing register.

9 November

Donald Trump has won the US presidential election. It's the inevitable next chapter for the parallel universe that was formed following my conviction and the Brexit vote. I can't help feeling that if I'd done a better job in the witness box, Hillary Clinton would now be in the White House. I pop over to Ted's cell so that he can bask in his right-wing triumph. Gary, the young Scouser who replaced me, is sitting on his own.

'Ted's gone to Bristol for his confiscation hearing. They came for him at six a.m.'

It's eerily bizarre to have a friend simply vanish in the night. There's now no trace that Ted was ever here. It's like Soviet East Germany, where people would just disappear from the streets. Prison mostly feels scarily permanent, punctuated by these unexpected moments of instability.

10 November

The SO on E Wing has responded to the Pentonville escapes by tightening the regime even further. Newly arrived prisoners are now only allowed out once, for a phone call and shower; after that they're on full 24-hour lockdown. This flies directly against prison rules, which guarantee everyone half an hour's daily exercise. E Wing residents are only getting out for a few minutes to collect their food, and I watch some of them queuing up for lunch. They look like abandoned puppies in an RSPCA advert. One guy gets overly excited by the brief freedom and hops onto the netting that stretches between landings. The whistle goes, and five screws dive over the handrail after him. Their combined weight causes the netting's supports to come loose, and there's a collective shout of 'GET OFF!' The screws scramble back onto the landing as if they're in a penal version of Cirque du Soleil. The constant bang-up is most evident when I walk into the induction classroom and am overpowered by the stench of body odour. Danielle brings over half a dozen cans of air freshener just to get us through the morning.

Days later, an E Wing resident decides, quite literally, to take matters into his own hands. He diligently collects his own turds in a bin, and when the door is finally opened, he hurls them at the nearest officer. Serendipitously, this turns out be the SO responsible for the barbaric regime. The flung dung goes into the screw's eyes, ears, mouth and nose, like a faecal rendition of 'Heads, Shoulders, Knees and Toes'.

11 November

Channel 4 has been heavily trailing tonight's documentary, *The Secret Life of Prisons*. It promises to give 'a sickening insight into the world behind bars, where inmates regularly take drugs, brutal beatings are a daily occurrence and guards are terrified of their wards'.[15] Most of it has been filmed by prisoners on mobile phones. The most shocking footage is of a lad with learning difficulties who gets repeatedly punched to obtain more spice. I'm horrified by what these addicts will do to get their next fix. That said, I'd have gladly taken a belt in the chops for a glass of Sauvignon Blanc when I first arrived.

The film cuts to some aerial shots of Wandsworth, which the narrator describes as 'one of the most dangerous prisons in Britain'. H Wing explodes with celebratory door-kicking. I kick our door for the very first time, and it feels awesome.

There's an interview with a woman who specialises in smuggling contraband into prisons. She visits 10 jails a week, and demonstrates how she hides tiny mobile phones inside Mars bars. Her antics make a total mockery of prison security; Liz Truss must be going bananas right now. The film is a powerful watch, but it only focuses on drugs and violence, and avoids the more complex problems. There's no mention of the archaic processes and chronic mismanagement, though these are obviously less captivating issues for a wider audience.

The documentary has an explosive effect on Wandsworth. The next day our security department shuts the door well after the horse has bolted, and gives all incoming staff a prolonged frisking. Even the rabbi gets strip-searched. Our cells are unlocked for freeflow, but half the screws are still stuck in security. The gates off the wing stay shut, so dozens of prisoners bottleneck on the Twos, creating a serious crush risk. We're all free but no flow.

Two different SOs keep walking onto the wing and yelling completely contradictory instructions. I watch an exasperated officer going down the Fours unlocking all the prisoners, and another screw following him a minute later locking everyone back up again. Governor Yeti flaps up to me and demands, 'Why isn't anyone going to work?' This is a whole new level of madness – a governor asking prisoners why his own wing has ground to a halt.

Arthur scoops up the rookie Listeners and takes us across for training. We have to wait in the main centre for ages. Several senior figures pace about looking as if they've just been bollocked by the MoJ. Three security officers and a sniffer dog come off A Wing with a massive evidence bag. They look delighted with their haul, despite it containing a derisory quantity of drugs. Samuels, H Wing's resident spice addict, easily smokes more gear than that while he's watching *X Factor*.

Never wrong for long

Prisons are extremely sensitive to negative press. The Pentonville breakout sent the Wandsworth authorities into a complete tizz over potential escapes. The Channel 4 documentary abruptly switched the focus onto smuggled contraband instead. Everyone immediately forgot about breakouts, the night checks stopped and the authorities started panicking about smuggled phones. Mars bars vanished from the visits cafeteria, but quietly reappeared several weeks later.

Shortly afterwards, I was waiting for a visit when we were given a stern lecture from the SO. 'All right, lads, we've had to tighten things up a bit. You're still allowed physical contact with your kids, but there's no kissing your female guests.' Another prisoner became highly agitated, presumably as his missus was currently loading up a gobful of spice ready for oral transfer. He stamped his foot, snarling, 'What kind of gay visit is this?' as though it was pointless spending an hour with his child if he couldn't bank a bag of drugs.

13 November

Scott comes in looking extremely glum. 'There's been another suicide on the mains.' Details are thin, but apparently it was a Lithuanian teenager who had severe mental health problems. He was on remand for shoplifting sweets, and had been sent to the segregation block. Two nights ago he was found hanging in his cell after his emergency bell had gone unanswered. Apparently some of the Listeners on the mains sat with the victim before he died, and they're in a pretty bad way. My knees go weak when I hear this, and I'm suddenly hit by the grim reality of what I'm going to be dealing with in the near future.

14 November

I'm doing the inductions when an exasperated officer walks into the classroom.

'We've got a Bulgarian downstairs who's just had a stroke. Nobody understands him, and we can't explain what's going on. Can you come and translate?'

I have no idea why she thinks I can speak Bulgarian. 'Sorry, miss, I studied French for eight years and still can't ask the way to the beach.'

The officer doesn't find this funny and leaves. There are dozens of Bulgarians on the wings who would happily translate, but only the screws know where they are. Wandsworth has a high turnover of foreign nationals, but there's no internal translation system. Osvaldas Pagirys, the Lithuanian teenager who just took his own life, barely spoke any English. Days before his death he was assessed by a mental health nurse but wasn't allowed an interpreter. She couldn't understand what he was saying, and decided that he was safe to go to the block.[16]

In the evening, rumours swirl that something big is going down tomorrow. I instinctively grab a shower, assuming that whatever is coming will involve excessive bang-up.

15 November

Morning freeflow is cancelled. I turn on the TV news and see some familiar screws standing outside Wandsworth waving placards. The Prison Officers Association has gone on strike for the very first time, despite being legally banned from industrial action. Steve Gillan, its general secretary, tells the press: 'Every prison officer in England is commencing a protest outside their establishment against the disregard for health and safety of our prison officers and prisoners.'[17]

Gillan is later interviewed on the radio and challenged over whether deserting the wings to go on strike will make conditions even worse. He replies that prisons are actually safer today, as all the inmates are locked behind their doors.

This is a dangerous fiction. Wandsworth is presently being managed by some well-meaning but inexperienced volunteers. Food is delivered several hours late, someone nearly dies from self-harming, and an inmate climbs into the rafters for several hours.

Liz Truss takes the POA to court, where the judge rules that the strike is breaking the law.[18] This doesn't seem like a very good example to be setting us criminals.

16 November

I run into a nervous clump of new screws. They're being given a tour of the wings, and have the air of tourists who've visited a prison by mistake. The bar for entry is definitely being lowered, quite literally, as one newbie is barely five foot tall. She looks like a child who's dressed up as a prison officer for Halloween.

This pint-sized officer soon starts working on Trinity. She has a gigantic afro and a rasping Brummie accent, and is immediately christened 'Mini Me'. One afternoon I'm circulating G Wing when Mini Me pelts past shouting, 'Spice attack on the Fours!'

This is such a regular occurrence that it barely registers, and I call a friend for a catch-up. Minutes later, Mini Me reappears with the Wandsworth duty nurse and they peg it back up the stairs. Unfortunately she has now forgotten where the victim lives. As they go from cell to cell, the nurse keeps rebuking her for losing a patient, and eventually the diminutive screw snaps, 'I'll fucking lamp you if you spark off again!'

Some more officers arrive and the spice cadet is soon located and brought back to consciousness.

17 November

Every month the entire prison goes into a blanket lockdown for staff training. Martyn and I always plot a way to get out of this, which usually involves joining a focus group. Today some European academics are visiting Wandsworth to discuss rehabilitation, and we spend the afternoon chatting to Scandinavian professors.

One of the visitors, a Dane, remarks to Martyn that the landings are extremely quiet. 'Where are all the prisoners?'

'Banged up,' replies Martyn.

The professor is perplexed. 'What is this "banged up" you speak of?'

'It's where the cells are locked all day.'

'So where are the prisoners if the cells are locked?'

'In their cells.'

'But how do they go to classes and workshops?'

'They don't.'

'So how do they rehabilitate? What do they do all day?'

'Smoke spice and watch *Cash in the Attic*.'

The academic is struggling to understand our regime. The Danes have a highly progressive attitude towards incarceration, focusing on education and training rather than punishment. Subsequently only 27% of Danish prisoners go on to reoffend,[19] compared to 48% in the UK.[20]

Executive governor Ian Bickers turns up half an hour late, which seems a bit rude, given that his guests have travelled across Europe and still managed to get here on time. Since they hark from countries with far lower recidivism rates than Britain, I imagine that he will want to learn all he can from them. Instead he gives a long speech about his vision for a reformed Wandsworth.

I start to wonder if he thinks he's running an entirely different prison. He keeps referring to the Purple Army as though it actually exists. 'We now have fifty qualified peer advisers, who are prisoners trained to do basic administrative tasks. This takes vital pressure off the officers and is helping turn the prison around.' In reality, the Purple Army exists only in Governor Bickers' head, as an exercise in desperate wishful thinking. The scheme has died completely on the mains, where none of the recruits have even been unlocked for training, let alone done any work.

Things aren't much better on Trinity. There are now only four of us in training, and the classes keep veering into outright farce. In our next peer advice lesson, Ruben introduces us to the concept of client confidentiality.

'This can be broken in certain circumstances,' he tells us. 'So if you hear anyone discussing criminality, it has to be reported to the authorities.'

I raise a hand. 'Given that we live in a Category B prison, we constantly overhear talk of law-breaking. If we follow your instructions, we'll spend every waking hour grassing up our neighbours.'

It later emerges that the Purple Army is being sabotaged by the Prison Officers Association, who are unkindly calling us the Purple Helmets. The screws' union is fiercely resistant to prisoners taking work from officers, fearing that it will threaten their members' jobs. This is a remarkably blinkered position, as officers don't have time to do low-level admin work anyway, which is why Wandsworth is such a dysfunctional mess. Learning this makes me suddenly feel sorry for Governor Bickers. He's actually attempting some radical reforms, but is being blocked by a union stuck in the 1970s.

18 November

It's Children in Need night on the BBC. It includes a brutal documentary about kids with parents in prison.[21] The film follows two youngsters whose father is doing a 10 stretch in Manchester, and the interviews are gut-wrenching. The kids tearfully explain that this isn't the first time their dad has gone away. When he was released from his previous sentence, he swore he'd never get in trouble again. He subsequently did another drug deal, and has now gone back inside. It is this betrayal that hurts them the most. Watching this film makes me feel like the world's biggest lowlife for abandoning Kit. It should be compulsory viewing for everyone about to leave prison.

Unhappy families

Barnardo's estimates that at any given time there are 200,000 children in England and Wales who have a parent behind bars.[22] This fact is rarely mentioned in the reporting on prisons. It's easy to dismiss the vile conditions of British jails by blaming everything on the prisoners. 'If you can't do the time, don't do the crime!' is the predictable response to stories on the prison crisis. Focusing on innocent children doesn't fit that narrative, so they just get ignored. The consequences for these kids can be dire. Children with a parent in prison are twice as likely to experience mental health problems, and three times as likely to be involved in crime: 65% of boys with a convicted father will go on to offend themselves.[23]

By far the worst part of my incarceration was the separation from Kit. Lottie remained unswervingly supportive throughout my sentence, and brought him in to visit every week. He'd stand waiting as I came into the visits hall, and bounded up to me like a puppy, completely unfazed by the grim surroundings. There's a consensus that kids under five won't register the brutality of closed

---

165

prisons, but those over six might find visiting really upsetting.

Lottie referred to Wandsworth as 'the building' to avoid using the word 'prison', but otherwise didn't shield Kit from the reality of where I was. Other inmates maintained highly elaborate cover stories to prevent their kids learning that they were in jail. Scott's biohazard colleague Howard had three children back in Nigeria. He'd told them he was in London on business and didn't have time to come home. This might have worked on a short sentence, but Howard was doing 13 years for drug smuggling. It would just take one of his children to google their dad, and the game would be up.

19 November

I do another Listener shift with Scott, and we're soon called to meet an enormous African guy called Booker. He gives me an elaborate handshake that goes on for well over a minute.

'I hear voices,' he informs us. 'They talk to me all the time. They scare me. They tell me to do bad, *bad* things.'

I strongly suspect these voices are more terrified of him than the other way round. At one point he suddenly puts his head under the cold tap in the corner, before continuing his rant where he left off. He claims to be simultaneously Catholic, Protestant and Muslim. As the meeting ends, he insists that we hold hands in prayer, during which he pecks me on the cheek and pinches my bum.

I'm pretty unnerved by this encounter, and have a sneaking feeling that Booker was overplaying his madness. Days later, he makes unwanted advances towards a female officer, and is brutally restrained by several screws.

Beggars belief

Religion was a big deal inside. The adherence to multiple faiths was fairly common, as many inmates pursued religion purely to get out of their cells. As the bang-up increased, so did the number of prisoners demanding their right to worship. It was rumoured that the various faith leaders were paid according to attendance at their services. The Catholics, Protestants, Muslims and Hindus all welcomed newcomers with open arms. The Jews, however, were more discerning. Before supposedly Jewish prisoners were allowed to worship, they were grilled by the rabbi about their lineage.

The different faiths were quite happy to share their congregations, but the rampant polytheism eventually came under official scrutiny. The SO told Martyn that henceforth prisoners could only follow one religion each. Martyn bravely tried to engage the screw in a metaphysical debate about multi-faith worship, and posited the classic polytheistic view that all Gods may in fact be the same God.

The officer countered with a novel theological argument: 'There's only one religious option allowed on NOMIS.'

20 November

I'm pottering about G Wing when I'm beckoned over by Les the barber. He whispers that he's 'dropping a Listen', and that I should watch the master at work. Les's contact is French, so their discussion is being translated by his cellmate and then yelled through a steel door. Les loudly queries how many times the Frenchman has self-harmed, while giving me a running commentary on what a brilliant job he's doing. I later discover that three of his contacts have self-harmed in the last week alone. Scott darkly suspects that they've

167

been cutting up because of his unorthodox counselling methods. Witnessing such trauma is taking its toll on Les, and he is clearly starting to unravel.

He is not the only one finding this work extremely draining. Leroy is a ripped south London hood who has been Listening on the mains for years. He was called to see Osvaldas Pagirys on the night before the Lithuanian killed himself. Leroy reveals that Osvaldas was desperate to speak to his family, but that the screws refused to unlock him for a phone call. Twenty-four hours later, the teenager was dead, and Leroy is racked with guilt that he couldn't do more to save him. It's only now that I grasp the real risks of becoming a Listener. Wandsworth is full of desperately lost souls, and sharing their pain is likely to have a profoundly harrowing effect.

21 November

I packed my bang-up bag in July, and didn't think to include any warm clothes. The temperature is now approaching freezing, so I try to get some warmer garments sent in. The property rules have been tightened once again, in a vain effort to curtail the flow of spice into the jail. A mystifying notice appears, which could have come straight out of a *Monty Python* sketch: *Clothing can only be handed in by named contacts of Enhanced prisoners who can only drop off approved items when not coming on a visit between the hours of 10.45 –11.30 on Tuesday and Thursday, but ONLY if the prisoner has filled out a new property form which needs to be completed IN ADVANCE to specify date of drop-off and EXACTLY what is being dropped off (colour, make, size, etc.) and by whom (name, address, DOB). Property form must be signed by wing staff BEFORE it is sent to property clerk for approval and slip returned to prisoner BEFORE anything is handed in.*

This sign baffles even Fenton the property orderly, and he has two law degrees. I submit numerous apps begging to get some jumpers sent in, but none are answered. I ask Fenton why I've been knocked back.

'Not sure, though you do receive a lot of books,' he notes. 'They've probably decided that you've had enough property this year.'

I had no idea that being well read would negate my right to warm clothing. Tramps sometimes stuff newspaper into their clothes to make an insulating layer, so maybe this is what I'm expected to do with my burgeoning book collection.

Hot property

The IEP system was supposed to incentivise good conduct by giving property privileges to those who behaved well. Enhanced prisoners were allowed to order in additional clothing, stereos and PlayStations as a reward.[24] But the property department was so defective that these items were impossible to access. Therefore the system just punished people who followed the rules, and encouraged rampant corruption. Lots of prisoners acquired legitimate items on the sly, as it was impossible to get anything through the proper channels. It was reminiscent of the factories in communist Russia, which had similarly absurd bureaucracy and regulations. Everyone quickly ignored the rules and the black market thrived.

I did mostly toe the line, but sporadically picked up a few things to make life a bit more comfortable. I gave up dealing with the property department, and tracked down the orderly who worked in the stores. After some negotiation, we exchanged a pack of Jaffa cakes for a prison-issue coat. The jacket was orange and grey, and would definitely go down a storm in Shoreditch, but it soon provoked undisguised jealousy from fellow prisoners. I was preparing the inductions in the E Wing classroom when a mean-looking prisoner barged in.

'Bruv, you got Rizla for me?'

'I don't smoke.'

He spied my swanky coat on the back of a chair. 'I need a jacket, bruv. Lemme have that coat.'

'Sorry, dude, this one's mine.' I sat down on the chair to make the point.

The guy refused to leave. 'How can I get one like that?'

'Go to the laundry and speak to Al. Tell him I sent you.' He grunted appreciatively and cleared off. He was going to struggle speaking to Al in the E Wing laundry, as there wasn't a laundry on E Wing. Telling the truth in prison could sometimes be extremely dangerous.

22 November

The lens of my glasses keeps popping out. The only way I can screw the frame back together is with a biro top, which is extremely time-consuming. I decide that a razor blade will do the job far better, and start to pull apart one of the prison razors. This fucks up completely, and I slice my finger open. I fly into a panic, terrified of being classified as a self-harmer and/or catching hepatitis. I call the night screw and show him my bloody hand.

He peers in through the observation panel. 'I'll go and see if there's a plaster in the first aid kit.' He returns half an hour later. 'Bad news. We don't even have a first aid kit.'

I take stock of the situation: I can't see, I'm losing blood, and I am down to just one hand. Scott, who has been watching me floundering with some amusement, finally takes charge. He rummages around in a biohazard waste bag and produces a thick roll of Sellotape. 'This will solve almost any problem in prison. Give me your hand.' He fashions a makeshift bandage out of loo roll, and expertly tapes it onto my finger. Next he cuts some Sellotape into strips and painstakingly secures my lens back into the frame.

I put the glasses on, and Scott admires his handiwork. 'You totally look like a nonce.' This is not the best look to have in prison, but I've long since given up hope of seeing an optician. Kane, an extremely eccentric prisoner who spends too much time in our cell, is similarly short-sighted. He has now acquired two different pairs of glasses, neither of which matches his prescription, but which work perfectly when worn together. They also double the size of his eyeballs, which doesn't help his already strange appearance.

I'm extremely fortunate never to have needed serious medical treatment in Wandsworth. At one point both Scott and I catch man flu, and I head to the Trinity meds hatch. I wait patiently while the recovering addicts are given their medication, and finally reach the front of the queue.

'I've got the flu, can I have some paracetamol?' I ask.

The nurse shakes her head. 'We can't dispense paracetamol after four p.m.'

'Why not?'

'Those are the rules.'

'But you've just handed out some weapons-grade meds to those guys from G Wing. I only need something for a cold.'

'Not after four o'clock.'

'I work for the education department and don't get back to Trinity until half four.'

The nurse shrugs and walks away.

The next morning, Scott marches up to the meds hatch and is told they can't hand out cold medication before 8.30 a.m. He points out that he has to start Listener training at 8, but this cuts no ice. If we wanted spice, heroin, coke, weed, speed, skunk or crack, we could source it in seconds, but we aren't allowed paracetamol because we've elected to work. The flip side is that people suffering far more serious physical and mental problems are increasingly using illegal drugs to self-medicate.

171

24 November

Martyn finally gets his Cat D. This is what he's been dreaming about for months: a few clicks on the OMU computer, and a pass to open prison. Cat D prisoners are usually sent to HMP Ford, which is down on the south coast. Friends who've gone on ahead have written back reporting that the food is immeasurably better, the visits are two hours long, and there's not a screaming screw in sight. Martyn is now on the Ford transfer list, and should get shipped out in the next couple of weeks.

My own recategorisation date is now just seven weeks away. I'm desperate to confirm that I will actually be made Cat D, and I've got a slot on this week's OMU surgery. Eight of us stand waiting outside the office of Governor Daniels, the head of OMU, who is a notorious hard-arse. Every prisoner who goes in front of me has their Cat D refused. The last guy storms out shouting, 'Chattin' shit, bruv!' and kicks a chair. I enter the office and sit down cautiously.

'How can I help?' Daniels asks.

'I have a recategorisation coming up. I'm *quite* keen to get made Cat D and move to pastures new.'

He looks at my file, contemplating my future like a Roman emperor at a gladiator contest. Am I getting a thumbs-up or a thumbs-down?

'Doesn't look impossible.'

I start breathing quickly.

'Have you got your certificates?'

I'm not ready for this. 'Er, certificates?'

'I'll need to see what courses and jobs you've done.'

This is my chance to shine. 'Well, I'm working as a Listener, I'm in the Purple Army, I'm on the board of P2P, I'm the senior education orderly, I tick off the morning register, and I deliver visit slips and canteen.'

He looks utterly underwhelmed. 'None of that appears on your NOMIS file. Get me written proof, and you should have your Cat D in January.'

I have no idea how to do that. 'You'll have it by the end of the week.'

Papa's got a brand-new tag

The security categorisation was only one of the ways we prisoners were classified by the system. As well as our IEP level – Enhanced, Standard or Basic – determining what privileges we could access,[25] there were also risk ratings of how dangerous we were, and violent offenders were further labelled by Multi-Agency Public Protection Arrangements (MAPPA).[26] In case that wasn't enough, we all got a score from the Offender Assessment System (OASys) predicting how likely we were to reoffend.[27] This sea of acronyms and conflicting classifications was introduced by successive government ministers, all trying to fix the system by making it more complicated.

One afternoon a nervous young man approached me. 'Mr Atkins? I'm from Probation, I need to do your OASys report.' Most of the assessment was rudimentary box-ticking, typical of the 'one size fits all' tests that proliferate in the prison system. He then asked how I felt about my crime. The words came tumbling out, and I expressed my deep regret, mainly for the suffering I inflicted on those closest to me. I was later told by other prisoners that you would win points for showing contrition, which improved your chances of getting to open prison. As it happened, my remorse was genuine, but offenders could easily trot out a load of insincere crap and the system would be none the wiser.

The probation officer closed his folder. 'By the way, I just wanted to say that I'm a big fan of *Taking Liberties*.' This was the documentary I made just before *Starsuckers*. 'You should really do a film about how terrible the prison system is.' I was unsure of how to react to this. The whole point of the exercise was to lower my risk of reoffending, and it was my obsession with film-making that got me into trouble in the first place.

25 November

I've developed an odd sense of anticipation about who will walk through the door of the Listener Suite. Waiting for our contact is like a penal version of *Stars in their Eyes*: 'Today, Matthew, we will be talking to … Mitz! A man with danger in his eyes and blood on his arms.'

Mitz is pretty terrifying. One minute he's calm and lucid, the next he's screaming blue murder. He constantly hears voices instructing him to self-harm, and usually keeps the TV on permanently to drown them out. Right now, he is apoplectic as his TV has been confiscated, apparently by a vindictive screw. As he tells the story, Mitz portrays himself as the innocent victim of officer brutality. What he doesn't know is that I actually witnessed this altercation, and have a very different recollection. Mitz was blatantly hustling spice on a landing, and the officer politely asked him to get behind his door. Mitz told the screw to 'suck your fucking dick, you fucking pussyhole', and then everything kicked off.

I daren't reveal my inside knowledge, and just nod sagely while Mitz vents. After an hour, he starts to calm down, and I realise that we don't need to believe our contacts in order to help them. We shake hands, and an officer leads Mitz away.

Back in our cell, I turn into a gibbering wreck. For some reason I crave salt, and start stuffing handfuls of peanuts into my mouth.

'That man should be treated in a secure mental health unit,' I rant at Scott. 'Not counselled by amateurs!'

'Sorry to butt in there, Tiger,' interrupts Scott. 'But you've just shaken hands with a guy covered in his own blood. You might want some of this industrial antibac before you eat any more of those nuts.'

26 November

The Listener training comes to an end and the stabilisers are about to come off: for the next week, I'll still do sessions with Scott, but then I'll start seeing contacts on my own. The trainees have a group chat about everything we've learned, and what lies ahead. It's oddly moving to hear all these hardened cons sharing their feelings. Arthur gives us a sobering pep talk.

'It's really important to look after yourselves and each other. There have been physical attacks on Listeners, and the job is emotionally very draining. Someone from Samaritans will visit you all each week and check that you're coping. If it gets too much, you have to take a break.'

If anyone needs to stand down, it's Les, who's behaving increasingly erratically. Later on, we talk in his cell. 'I've been Listening for two years, and it's fucking me up. Sometimes I can't sleep at night; all I can see is their blood.' He rolls what looks like a spice joint, and I leave him to it. I desperately hope this isn't what I'll turn into.

7

Spinsters and Spiceheads

In which I start Listening on my own, and struggle to remain emotionally detached. I finally enter the observation cell, and meet a suicidal teenager on the verge of starvation.

Things I learn:

1) How to eavesdrop on other prisoners' correspondence

2) The difficulties in reducing reoffending

3) How to rig an election

Just as I get to grips with Listening, my mentor disappears, leaving me to fill his shoes.

28 November

It's the day of the Trinity information fair. Becoming a reform prison has given Governor Bickers control over much of the prison's budget. He is a big fan of courses that promise to tackle reoffending, and has invited the providers of these programmes to Trinity. K Wing is decked out in cheap bunting, as if a crack den is celebrating a royal wedding. Trestle tables are laid out, and the wing fills with voluntary types brandishing leaflets.

Rehabilitate this

There were well over a hundred rehabilitation courses accredited by the government,[1] and many were on offer at Wandsworth. Some were quite fluffy, involving dance, gardening and meditation. A lot of them had an exclamation mark in the title, like 'Getting it Right!'[2] or 'Be a Hero!'[3] Most had brightly coloured promotional material, as if they were aimed at small children. The blurb for 'Man Up!' promised 'a group-work programme designed to support men and young men to explore the ways in which the concept of masculinity contributes to shaping individual identity'.[4] It claimed to show wayward prisoners how to be modern men, even though the course was taught exclusively by women. It was a bold aim, given that the programme consisted of just six afternoon sessions. The literature was full of glowing quotes from anonymous offenders, but there was no hard evidence that the scheme had any impact on reoffending.[5] This was a common theme; these courses all sounded like they *should* reduce crime, but there was scant proof that any of them were effective.

There was stiff competition among the providers of such programmes. Courses often changed their name to make them sound like the next exciting thing, just to attract further funding. It was astonishing that cash was available for these questionable programmes, but there was not enough funding for the mental health services that actually saved lives.

Most of the visitors to the information fair are women, so Martyn and I start chalking up as many flirty conversations as possible. In retrospect, any flirtation probably existed on only our side of these encounters. A rumour circulates about refreshments in the chapel, so we storm in and fill our pockets with Bourbon biscuits.

177

Sally, the obese woman who runs the activities department, scowls murderously while guarding the cake.

The day's highlight is a performance from the Liberty Choir, who regularly visit Wandsworth to rehabilitate prisoners through the medium of song. An electric piano blasts into life, and they launch into an ungodly rendition of 'Price Tag' by Jessie J. I'm struck by the unintentional irony of the lyrics – 'It's not about the money, money, money' – being chanted by inmates in prison for stealing money to fund their habits. Anywhere else the choir would be a laughing stock – out of tune, out of time and mostly out of their minds. But right now, as we stand in this apex of human misery, their vocal enthusiasm grabs our souls, and a wave of humanity bursts forth. Suddenly we're no longer prisoners, staff and visitors, but warm friends swaying and humming together. Officer Moss starts throwing shapes and waving his jazz hands. I can't stand the man, but I have to admit he's got some mean moves.

The song ends and Governor Yeti calls it a day. Officer Moss suddenly changes character, like a pound-shop Incredible Hulk, and screams, 'EVERYONE AWAY NOW!' Our visitors, who perhaps assumed that we sang gentle raps every afternoon, look on horrified.

29 November

I've developed a complex filing system to process my hefty incoming correspondence. Everything is read immediately a couple of times to raise my spirits, and to check if it contains anything urgent. News of a death or a break-up gets escalated for an immediate reply, while everything else is filed in reverse order. I then endeavour to respond within 28 days of the person's last correspondence, as some people send me a second email before I've replied to the first.

Scott is not impressed. 'You're being fucking anally retentive. Be warned, your post will drop off over time.' He has been inside two years, and now receives more letters from other prisoners than from friends on the outside.

At one point I accidentally receive some emails addressed to other inmates. Someone has printed them double-sided to save paper, but accidentally printed other people's messages on the back of mine. I read these random emails far more avidly than I do my own. Some are painfully mundane, moaning about the gas bill and the latest series of *TOWIE*. Others are more juicy: *I tell you what tho, my Kitty Cat is missing you cooooolllll, just know that when you come home it's going to be peak for you coolllll xxx*

I feel mildly guilty snooping on this private correspondence. In my defence, I have no idea who these people are, and I assume that my emails are being read by other prisoners as well.

30 November

There is a Listeners' meeting every week in the main chapel. Thirty of us sit in a huge circle, and it has a vaguely Masonic feel. Arthur asks each of the newly qualified Listeners how many contacts we've attended. Rookies need to accompany experienced Listeners a few times before we can work on our own. I've already been out on a dozen occasions with Scott, but none of the guys on the main wings have attended a single contact. This is part of a wider problem, where the officers on the mains aren't unlocking the Listeners at all. Some contacts have been sitting in their cells for hours, desperately waiting to speak to someone.

Three weeks ago, Osvaldas Pagirys died while waiting for his bell to be answered, so it's beyond negligent that these alarms are still being ignored. Arthur assures us that he'll raise it at the next Safer Custody meeting. This is a monthly gathering of the prison's senior management and the Samaritans, where they address the risks of suicide and self-harm.

'I'll definitely tell the security governor what's going on,' he promises.

It later emerges that the December Safer Custody meeting has been cancelled.

As we return from the mains, Scott announces that I should start seeing Listener contacts on my own. 'We'll still work together after seven p.m., but you can fly solo in the daytime. It'll toughen you up.' This is pretty scary. I have been getting more confident interacting with contacts, but only while Scott is in the room. I quietly pray that my first outing will be with someone relatively calm.

I'm soon called into the Listener Suite and introduced to Ben. He's about 25 and sports a fine handlebar moustache.

'How can I help?' I ask.

'I was on the drug rehab wing, but it was doing my head in. I've just moved to Trinity to get clean.'

'How's that working out for you?'

By way of an answer, Ben tips some coffee granules out onto a wooden shelf, then produces a prison ID card and starts chopping them as if they're cocaine. Tearing a page out of a dictionary, he rolls it up and snorts a fat line of coffee. Then he leans his head back and barks, like Al Pacino in *Scarface*. I've seen a lot of drug-taking in Wandsworth but have never witnessed anything so preposterous. I start giggling uncontrollably, all these weeks of keeping a straight face finally bursting out of me. Thankfully he doesn't mind my laughter, and even offers me a line.

Ben was recently convicted of GBH. 'Some prick had a go at my missus in the pub. We had a right tear-up.' He starts acting out the ensuing fight, and while he's head-butting an imaginary assailant, I see a trickle of blood coming out of his nose.

'I hate to interrupt, but it looks like you're having a nosebleed.'

He looks down, wipes off the blood and gives it a taste – 'It's only coffee and snot. Happy days' – then continues his performance with such enthusiasm that I feel I should give him a few quid.

Ben is unrepentant about his actions, and believes that the violence was completely justified.

'I didn't *want* to fill the guy in. But he'd slagged off my girl, so what else could I do?'

Guilt trip

Remorse was in short supply inside. Prisoners often presented noble and honourable reasons for breaking the law. A classic was: 'I only pleaded guilty to stop them prosecuting my wife.' This excuse always struck me as fairly dubious, as the CPS rarely plea-bargain like their American counterparts. It was usually just an attempt to reframe their personal narrative. 'Bravely took the rap to spare the wife' sounded a lot better than 'Stole money that I blew on drugs'.

Sometimes I'd be shocked by the severity of a contact's sentence, but I was rarely hearing the whole story. I once met a prisoner who complained that he'd got eight months for driving without insurance. I was initially appalled, but later discovered that he was also driving a stolen car and ran someone over.

It was less common for inmates to simply admit that they'd fucked up and take responsibility for their imprisonment. I personally found that 'fessing up felt a lot better than claiming victimhood, and quickly neutralised any feelings of self-pity. Whenever I was sucked into a 'poor me' mental whirlpool, simply saying 'Fuck it, Atkins, you did do it' immediately collapsed the vortex, and allowed me to think about something else.

1 December

I'm spending more time in the education department, working through my psychology course. I also drink a lot of tea in the admin office with Martyn and Gary. The affable Scouser who replaced me in Ted's cell has slipped effortlessly into the white-collar clique, and his boyish charms are very popular with the female staff.

Danielle and Linda treat us with a rare dignity and respect, and I'm always keen to repay their kindness. This morning Linda asks me if I will help teach today's ESOL class – English Speaking for Other Languages. 'This new teacher Winston is a bit of a spanner,' she adds, 'and I could use an extra pair of hands.'

I head down to the classroom, and we're soon joined by a dozen eastern Europeans. Winston spends 45 minutes getting them to fill in forms, which is quite challenging as none of them can write English. Eventually the lesson gets under way, and he asks a Bulgarian guy to list the days of the week.

'Monday, Tuesday, Wednesday, Tursday—'

Winston interrupts. 'Ah, right, it's actually Thursday.'

The Bulgarian tries again: 'Tursday.'

Winston impatiently repeats, 'Thursday.'

I feel compelled to point out that the man is mispronouncing the word due to his missing front teeth.

Winston then initiates a word game called What Am I Thinking? 'I'm going to choose a word, and you have to guess it by asking me questions.'

It takes only two attempts to deduce that Winston's word is the highly unoriginal 'classroom'. He then tells a Romanian to stand up and think of a word. The poor guy doesn't understand the game, and instead starts ranting about his deportation proceedings.

'The lady said I must have ID, but my passport in Bucharest ...'

Winston doesn't spot the confusion, and assumes that the Romanian is giving clues to a fiendishly difficult word. 'Ah, right, so it's a form of ID, but not a passport. Is it a driver's licence?'

'I am inside a month but I still not got lawyer, and my mother cannot send money ...'

'Blimey, this one's hard,' ponders Winston. 'Is it a social worker?'

I meet the eyes of a bald Ukrainian with a vocabulary of 50 English words, and even he has realised that they're talking at cross-purposes. I quietly pull out my book.

Days later, the education department is invaded by Larry, a swarthy

Welsh inmate who's been assigned to clean the admin offices. He immediately proceeds to remove everything that isn't nailed down, and empties the fridge with such ruthless efficiency that I'm surprised he doesn't take the shelves as well. The admin staff are struggling to hang their Christmas decorations, and Larry bounds in to help. The women are so impressed with his manly assistance that they don't notice him snaffling two tins of ravioli, a pair of headphones and a hole-punch. He bundles his swag into a bin liner and nonchalantly carries it away as though he's helpfully taking out the rubbish.

3 December

Les asks me to help with a letter he's writing to his judge. He's currently serving a five stretch, but is now facing new charges. This happens quite a lot: people will be convicted of one offence, and then more skeletons emerge once they're inside. Les is being prosecuted over a dodgy share-selling scheme, and is sensibly pleading guilty. He's due to be sentenced in a few weeks, and is terrified of being given a consecutive sentence, which would get added to his existing term.

He has, quite proudly, never read a book in his life, which is painfully apparent when I read his letter. It's riddled with grammatical errors and spelling mistakes, and some of it makes no sense whatsoever. I start a new draft from scratch, and wax lyrical about how prison has transformed him into an upstanding citizen.

A week later, he shows me an updated version. It transpires that I'm not the only scribe on the payroll; Les has also crowdsourced input from Scott, Martyn, Fenton, Nigel and Pops, an elderly Greek prisoner on the Ones. I've always hated collaborating, and I'm particularly resistant to sharing the billing with Pops. He's a kind and generous man, but he's half blind and barely speaks English. The latest draft ends with 'Given my exemplary behaviour in prison, it would serve great purpose to society if I was handed a consecutive sentence.'

I suggest that Les might want to insert a 'no' in there somewhere. He just nods absently and heads off to find another ghost-writer.

4 December

Some contacts are so agitated that they aren't allowed out of their cells, so we have to talk through their doors. I'm called to G Wing to see Dex, who has been cutting up every day. The last effort tapped an artery, and his blood went all over the walls. He was moved to another cell, which he immediately trashed. He was then shifted to a third pad, which was also promptly demolished. This was all in the space of 24 hours. I walk up to the Fours landing to see that he has thrown all his cell debris out onto the netting. Given that he's constantly banged up, this is no mean feat; I simply cannot fathom how he's shoved an entire bed through his observation panel.

Dex is stuck in a chilling Catch-22. He's too disturbed to conform to the prison's regime, but isn't deemed mad enough to be committed to a psychiatric unit. I often wonder just how insane you have to be to get sectioned in Wandsworth. His trail of destruction is obviously caused by his mental health problems, but the system treats his antics as bad behaviour that deserves punishment. He keeps being sent for adjudications, which pile extra days onto his sentence. These recent cell trashings will land him with an additional 60 days. Like something out of a Kafka novel, he is accruing time faster than he can serve it, and at this rate it's quite possible that he'll never leave at all. The obvious injustice makes me desperately want to help this poor wretch, but there is simply nothing I can do to ease his awful suffering.

Dex isn't the only prisoner stuck in this dark vortex. In 2016/2017, the Wandsworth authorities handed out a total of 10,345 additional days,[6] often to prisoners with mental health problems. Nationally, the number of punishment days has doubled in five years.[7]

6 December

Welsh Larry continues his kleptomaniac rampage through the education department. Danielle's suspicions are raised when three bottles of her balsamic vinegar vanish in as many weeks. Larry also steals a clock, and switches it with an older one he finds in a cupboard. Unfortunately the replacement clock doesn't actually work, and his heist is swiftly uncovered. The officers spin his cell, where the cretin has proudly displayed the clock on his wall. The pilfered food is neatly lined up on his window ledge, including three bottles of vinegar marked *DANIELLE*.

7 December

We're opened at 8 a.m. by Officer Marchbanks.

'Scott, why haven't you packed your stuff? You're shipping out.'

We assume that it's a wind-up, but Marchbanks insists that Scott is being transferred today.

'I am not fucking going,' spits Scott. 'I'm balls deep in my appeal.'

I'm hoofed out of the cell while Scott remains banged up; prisoners being transferred have to stay isolated, in case they arrange an escape. He starts summoning increasingly senior officers to the door, subjecting them to an onslaught of persuasion.

'I'm running the Listener operation; if you transfer me, it'll jeopardise the safety of the entire prison ... I'm the only qualified biohazard cleaner on Trinity, so you're risking an outbreak of syphilis ...'

Governor Yeti appears and meekly insists that his hands are tied. The MoJ wants all foreign inmates sent to Huntercombe, which is a designated foreign national prison. Scott is Australian, so he has to go. When he starts ranting about the negative impact on P2P, I realise that all hope is lost. I wave goodbye and go off to do the inductions.

His sudden departure leaves me quite shaken. My immediate problem is finding a sensible replacement for the Executive Suite.

Martyn is due to go to Ford any day, and most of the original White Collar Club have moved on. I should really share with another Listener, but the pickings are quite slim: Lunn is a charming ex-accountant in his seventies, but I've heard that he snores like a cement mixer. I do have a soft spot for Les the barber, but he is quite, quite mad. The only other Listener on H Wing is Mus, a likeable Algerian, who has phones coming out of his arse (quite literally, I'm told).

I ruminate on this dilemma all morning, and return to the wing with a heavy heart. I do a double-take when I see Scott seated at our table, grinning inanely.

'I beat the bus, mate. They won't get me to Huntercombe in this lifetime.'

He managed to send word to Arthur at the Samaritans, who promptly nobbled the security governor. It was made clear that Scott was integral to the Listener scheme, and the transfer was cancelled. This elevates Scott's wing status into the stratosphere. Prisoners love it when someone bucks the system, and he's inundated with congratulations. Later on, we're paid a visit by Romley, the senior officer who looks like a young Robert Mugabe.

'Next time you on transfer list, you fucking go. I'll bend you up and kick you on fucking bus myself, innit.'

SO Romley actively cultivates his reputation as an inhumane sadist. Lunn tells me of a recent Listener contact who was gay and being bullied. The lad had started to self-harm, and any other senior officer would have immediately moved him off the wing. Unfortunately the SO on duty was Romley, who is openly homophobic. He refused to intervene unless the victim named the bullies. The prisoner refused to grass, so Romley left him to his nightmare.

8 December

The most influential prisoner on Trinity is Carlos the Greek. He's been in Wandsworth for five years, and occupies the best single cell on the Ones. His door is rarely locked, a fact that he flaunts by never showering with other prisoners and only using the phone after everyone else is banged up. These are perks of his job as Trinity number one, which mainly involves making tea for the officers and laughing at their jokes. Scott doesn't trust him an inch. 'That Greek runt is a fucking sniffer.' We christen him 'Teasnitch', which we only say out loud when our door is safely locked.

This afternoon Teasnitch asks me for a quiet word.

'We could do with some help on the Prison Employee Awards.' I struggle to take this seriously, but it's apparently a real event, just before Christmas. Prisoners get to vote for their favourite officer, and Teasnitch wants to stack the deck for Miss Taylor, an attractive young officer on K Wing. I daren't ask why; I suspect it's a bold attempt to get into her knickers. I agree to help in return for some evening unlock.

I take a stack of voting slips to G Wing, where it's fair to say the electorate is not very politically motivated. Most of the residents haven't phoned home or exercised in days, so suggesting they reward the screws responsible does not go down well. Lots of ballots are obscenely defaced, several are flushed down the loo, and at least one is set on fire.

I return to H Wing, and coerce Scott into helping formulate an alternative strategy. He produces the prisoner movement sheets, which list every inmate on the unit. I dig out some coloured pens, and we forge 200 votes for Miss Taylor. The only worry is that some prisoners will actually mark their own ballots, which might produce more votes than there are inmates on Trinity.

9 December

Lottie, Kit and my parents are coming in to visit. I walk into the hall and see my mother sitting on her own, looking bewildered. Lottie and Kit are queuing for coffee, and I realise that my father isn't here.

Lottie is pretty exasperated. 'These officers are complete cunts.'

Apparently my dad's name wasn't on the list at the gate, and his path was blocked by a security officer. Lottie showed them an email confirming that he had been approved for this visit. The screw kept repeating that his name wasn't on the list, and made my father wait outside. Then the scanner didn't recognise my mother's fingerprints, and an officer asked for her date of birth. My mum sometimes loses her memory, which gets worse with stress, and she forgot her birth date. The screw leapt on this and claimed that she wasn't really my mother. Quite why a 72-year-old woman would enter this shithole for any other reason than visiting her son is beyond me. Lottie thankfully intervened and convinced them to let my mum through. This is not uncommon behaviour from the screws, who often treat relatives as if they're criminals as well – as indeed they sometimes are.

Lottie and my mum are quite shaken, and for the very briefest moment they've experienced how we're treated 24/7. Kit realises something is wrong and sits quietly holding my hand. I only get this one precious hour with him all week, but our time is completely poisoned by how my mother has been treated.

At the end of the visit, I'm pulled aside for a strip search. I don't object, as I've got nothing to hide and no privacy left. As I'm taking my clothes off, a passing SO recognises me from Listener work.

'Hey, don't waste your time with him,' he says. 'He's sound.'

The visits officer stands firm. 'I have to fill the quota. It doesn't matter which arseholes I look at.'

I'm unsure if 'arsehole' is being used in the literal or figurative sense. I stand with my trousers round my ankles while they argue about me as if I'm not there.

'Honestly, guv, I don't mind being searched,' I interject. 'I actually get a mild thrill from exposing myself to authority figures.'

The visits screw tells me to put my clothes back on.

10 December

Lunn, the sprightly septuagenarian accountant, is unquestionably the most upbeat person on the wing, and today he drops by with interesting news.

'I've just disturbed Governor Yeti poking around my cell. He muttered that he was making sure I had everything and then scuttled away.' This excuse is highly implausible. Dozens of Trinity cells are in a shamefully dilapidated state, missing privacy curtains, loo seats, kettles, taps and lights. The notion that the governor is concerned about our fittings is as improbable as the idea of him monitoring our cholesterol.

The real reason is revealed in our next Purple Army training session. Just as we're wrapping up, Ruben makes an announcement.

'We have a special guest visiting tomorrow, and Governor Bickers wants to show her the Purple Army in action. Can everyone come to the Trinity centre at two p.m., and make sure you're wearing your purple shirts.'

Ruben initially refuses to identify the VIP, but accidentally reveals that it's the Justice Secretary, Liz Truss. This is deeply thrilling news. I often feel mystically linked to Truss, as we both embarked on our unlikely prison journey at the same time. The Purple Army is integral to Bickers' reform plans, and he's keen to parade the troops on manoeuvres. The only problem is that no qualified peer advisers actually exist to do any peer advising. Nonetheless, Ruben wants us to put on a good show.

'Just make it look like you're doing something useful.' This is a brutal illustration of how far I have fallen – I used to be a director of dramatic fiction, now I'm just a mere extra.

Truss will also probably want to see a prison cell, which could be problematic as most of them would be condemned by the RSPCA. Lunn doesn't smoke or do spice, and his cell is always spotless, so he has presumably been selected to give the best possible impression of Wandsworth's living conditions.

11 December

It's the day of Liz Truss's visit. I'm woken at 6 a.m. by a special cleaning detail banging about the wing. On freeflow I'm surprised to see twice the normal number of screws on duty. The male officers have brutally shaven faces and slicked-back hair, the women wear too much perfume and make-up. A gym session is called for the first time in weeks, I suspect to prevent Truss visiting an empty gym. I go over to E Wing, which is alive with prisoners feverishly scrubbing the floors. It's like the Sorcerer's Apprentice scene in *Fantasia*, but with Latvian drug dealers instead of dancing broomsticks.

Up in our induction classroom, things are not going according to plan. Thirty prisoners have arrived in the last 24 hours, but only two of them are unlocked for induction. One is a gigantic Irish Traveller, who lumbers in covered in cuts and bruises. He's wearing an ill-fitting suit and stinks of booze. I'm now getting quite good at guessing what people are in for.

'I don't suppose you were arrested for fighting at a wedding?' I hazard.

He eyes me suspiciously. 'How do ye know dat?'

'Lucky guess.'

The Traveller reluctantly takes the literacy and numeracy tests, and scores lower than the Albanian in the corner.

'Can I sign you up to some education?' I ask.

He looks at me blankly. 'What's dat den?'

I don't think I've ever been asked this before. 'Well, er, we could teach you how to read and write.'

'No tanks,' he replies firmly. 'Me mam loves me just the way I am.'

Back on Trinity, preparations for the Justice Secretary's visit have reached fever pitch. Governor Yeti has winched himself into a grey flannel suit, which he wears as awkwardly as the wedding guest on E Wing. I change into my Purple Army uniform and muster with the rest of the troops in the centre. We stand around pretending to advise our peers, clutching clipboards for dramatic effect. I'm reminded of the infamous Ghost Army in the Second World War, which fooled the Germans with inflatable tanks and rubber aircraft.

Ruben suddenly appears looking distraught. 'I've just heard that Liz Truss isn't visiting Trinity. She isn't even meeting any prisoners.' Looking round at this shower, I can't say I entirely blame her. I remove my purple shirt and join the other Listeners going to the weekly meeting.

We're led to the mains and briefly locked in a pen by the centre. I've never seen the place so deserted; it's as if all the inmates have been dissolved in bleach. Governor Bickers and Liz Truss suddenly appear behind us, and I jump back in surprise. The visitors seem equally shocked at encountering some real prisoners, and Bickers hustles them away. Truss is a lot shorter in real life, and her nose is constantly elevated as if she's visiting a sewage plant. Bickers is looking peculiarly Dickensian, with a waistcoat and dicky bow. He talks incessantly, like an estate agent who doesn't want to give prospective buyers an opportunity to ask about the damp. They stand with their backs to us looking down completely empty wings, and I can overhear snippets of his spiel.

'Reform … turning a corner … Purple Army.'

Truss appears to be counting the seconds until her ministerial car whisks her north of the river.

We're soon led away and taken through the drug rehab unit on D Wing. I walk past one of the female screws and get a whiff of a strong fragrance.

'Lovely perfume you're wearing today, miss.'

She looks at me blankly. 'That's the smell of burning heroin.'

Back on Trinity, there is an air of bleak disappointment at Truss's no-show. Governor Yeti looks like he's been stood up on prom night, and mopes off to change out of his flannel suit.

12 December

I'm asked to see a lad called Dean, who is on a monitoring programme for prisoners at high risk of suicide.[8] He has tried to hang himself several times, and has been placed in K Wing's observation cell. I walk past this cell every day, but this is the first time I've actually been inside. The walls are bloodstained, and there is barely any furniture. The bed is just a rectangular piece of foam, as even a standard prison mattress is deemed to be too dangerous. A TV sits on a plastic chair in the corner. There's no privacy curtain, no toilet seat, and nowhere to put toiletries, which Dean has arranged on the rim of the loo.

The cell has a thick sheet of Perspex in place of a door, and its occupant is watched constantly by a health worker sitting outside. The obs cell is situated on the main thoroughfare through Trinity, so hundreds of prisoners pass by every day and have a good gawp inside. This shaming of the mentally ill is reminiscent of putting lunatics in stocks in the village square. It's probably the most depressing place I've seen, and if I spent more than an hour in here I'd want to kill myself as well.

Dean is only 19, almost the same age as Osvaldas Pagyris, the Lithuanian lad who recently killed himself. It's really difficult engaging him in conversation. He is desperately lonely, but also deeply paranoid; he's clearly suffering from acute schizophrenia and thinks there's a giant conspiracy out to get him. I avoid challenging his delusions, and offer some magazines that I've brought along. He mournfully admits that he can't read. He shows me a book he's been given by the Shannon Trust, a charity that teaches literacy in prisons. He's working to the same level as Kit, and we sit on his bed going through the 'A is for Apple' exercises.

Dean is wasting away. He hasn't eaten anything for two days except for razor blades, and won't touch prison food as he is convinced he's being poisoned. I offer to bring him something to eat and promise not to poison him. He thinks for a minute and mumbles, 'Noodles.' I tell him I'll be right back.

As I walk away, I start to consider the pitfalls of giving Dean a meal containing boiling water. I worry that he might inflict more harm on himself, so decide to ask the SO for permission. I stop by the centre office, and realise too late that it contains SO Romley.

'Guv, Dean in the obs cell is suffering from malnutrition. Can I make him some noodles?'

'He'll eat servery food or nothing!' barks Romley, and slams the door.

I try to break the news to Dean, but the K Wing gate is now locked. I go back to H Wing utterly dejected. Lunn asks what's troubling me. I explain how I've just joined the long list of people who have let Dean down. Lunn is sympathetic, but warns me against taking on everyone's problems, 'otherwise you'll end up like Les'.

After bang-up, our cell door is unexpectedly opened by Mini Me, the pint-sized new screw.

'Can you make some noodles for Dean?' she asks.

'I've been banned by Mr Romley,' I reply.

'That horrible bastard has fucked off home. I'm not standing in a coroner's court and telling Dean's mum that her son starved to death on my watch. Put the kettle on.'

I break out the curry Pot Noodles, the finest the canteen has to offer. Mini Me escorts me back to K Wing, and I hand Dean his supper. He nods with gratitude and gives me a weak fist bump.

Around this time we learn that Chaplain Steve has handed in his notice. Even God is leaving Wandsworth.

13 December

The monthly lockdown for staff training is swiftly approaching. We always find a way to swerve the bang-up, usually by attending a focus group or library talk. This month the only option is to join the Liberty Choir, who performed with such gusto at the Trinity fair. Affectionately known as Spinsters and Spiceheads, the choir consists of a dozen women of a certain age who visit Trinity every week to sing with some of our more troubled drug addicts. In a few days they will be performing at the Prison Employee Awards.

Today I go to a practice in the K Wing chapel. On arrival, I'm immediately given a crushing bear hug by MJ, the charming Texan woman who runs the choir. The other women smile at me like psychiatric nurses. More inmates drift in; I count four spice dealers, six spice addicts, and a couple who sit in both camps. Dean unexpectedly appears, and I'm slightly concerned that he's turned up by mistake.

MJ has an infectious energy, and gets everyone hooting gibberish to warm up our vocal cords. We then belt through various eclectic classics, and there's no denying that the singing is very therapeutic. Hardboiled prisoners who normally strut about the wings like peacocks quickly lose their inhibitions and let rip. It's a joy to watch if not to hear.

At the end, MJ makes an announcement about our upcoming gig.

'Don't forget that we're performing at the awards ceremony tomorrow.' There is some concern over whether we'll get near the buffet, but she warns that she's facing an uphill battle just getting everyone unlocked.

14 December

It takes ages to get everyone opened up for choral duties. Word has got round that it's the only way to dodge today's lockdown, and the choir has expanded considerably. Officer Abioye is managing the register, which is a brave choice as he has a limited grasp of English. Everyone stands around impatiently while he makes a total hash of ticking off the names. One of his colleagues panics that they'll miss the canapés, and just lets everyone pile out of Trinity. Anyone who escapes now could easily make it to France before the alarm is raised.

We enter the main chapel right next to the buffet. After all the anticipation, the spread is pretty unimpressive. We process down the aisle and onto a raised platform. Bickers sits at the front of the congregation, still wearing the same Dickensian outfit from Truss's visit. Behind him are about 80 stony-faced officers, looking as if they're cleaning up a dirty protest. The civilian staff are right at the back. Linda gives me a big thumbs-up. There's a live mic on the stage, and the audience briefly hears two prisoners discussing which of the female screws they'd rather fuck, before someone kills the feed.

MJ takes the floor in a black trouser suit and optimistically introduces us as 'the best singing voices I've ever heard'. We kick off with a stirring rendition of 'Price Tag'. It's a bloody tricky number, and I lose the thread completely during the middle rap. In retrospect, it was probably a mistake to then segue directly into Vivaldi's Gloria. This only just worked in rehearsal as we had a phalanx of women singing soprano. Unfortunately, most of the female volunteers haven't turned up for today's performance, so the ratio of spiceheads to spinsters is about 4:1. Our performance is a complete washout, and we all mutter 'in excelsis deo' before grinding to an embarrassing halt.

MJ introduces our final number: 'Christmas' by Phil Spector, an ironic choice given that Spector himself is currently serving 19 years for murder.[9] It's a mercifully easy ditty, essentially chanting 'CHRISTMAS!' over a standard fifties chord progression. We hit the ground running, and pass a tipping point where more of us are singing in tune than out. MJ encourages the audience to clap along, and, possibly out of a desire to hasten the end, the screws reluctantly do so. I can't stop myself doing a cheeky shuffle dance at the front, and spot Linda doubled up in hysterics. During the applause, Bickers leaps up to thank MJ, thereby preventing her from calling an encore.

We are funnelled back down the aisle. A ginormous screw guards the buffet, his eyes daring us to snaffle so much as a vol-au-vent. We emerge from the chapel on a high, laughing in the brisk winter sunshine. I even catch Dean flashing a smile.

In the evening, a slip comes under our door informing Scott that he's being shipped to HMP Highpoint tomorrow. We hold an emergency backgammon tournament and deliberate his options. SO Romley has threatened to bend Scott up if he refuses another transfer, which would be a sad end to his Wandsworth career. He has spent the last week rinsing legal advice out of Fenton, so he's now more relaxed about moving on. Highpoint has pretty positive reviews, and he concludes that it's time to cash in his chips.

I reflect on how my fortunes have changed since I moved into this cell. Two months ago I was still a complete wreck, and had barely recovered from the trauma of the trial. I've now absorbed much of Scott's bullish self-assurance; as he puts it, 'You've really grown a pair since you came in here.'

Word of Scott's departure soon spreads, and in the morning prisoners queue up outside the cell to say goodbye. I call his wife to tip her off about his transfer, and then give him one last wave through the observation panel. He flashes his irrepressible cheesy grin, and that's the last I see of him.

Friends in low places

It's worth reflecting on how I feel about Scott. I later looked up his crime, and it was very uncomfortable reading. It was an unfathomably complicated fraud, which involved lots of investors losing money. I found it very difficult to reconcile what I read with the person I had got to know so well. I refuse to condone what he did, but even after seeing the extent of his crime, I still maintain that he is a stand-up guy.

If my time in Wandsworth taught me anything, it's that good people can do bad things. When I first met Scott, I had no way of researching his financial machinations. I had to judge him on how I found him, which was extremely friendly, decent and charitable. He was also eccentric and childish, and he regularly cheated at backgammon. He spent many hours counselling some deeply unpleasant and dangerous prisoners, and he'd often help contacts the other Listeners had refused to see. By the time I met him, he'd already spent two years in Wandsworth, which may have made him nicer. What I do know is that he took his bird on the chin and carried on smiling, which counts for a lot in my book.

I end up taking Scott's place in many ways. Disgruntled cons just assume that I'm equally qualified to provide admin support services. His departure also means that there are only four Listeners covering the whole of Trinity. Scott was the go-to Listener for the most troublesome contacts, so officers start bringing them to me instead.

8

Murder and Mutiny

In which Listener requests skyrocket and I start to buckle under the strain. I help someone with a deadly secret, which leads to a dangerous dispute with the local barber.

Things I learn:

1) How to start a riot

2) Why some people come to prison by choice

3) The fluctuating price of fish

I finally become eligible for Cat D, and foolishly think there is light at the end of the tunnel.

15 December

I urgently need to find another cellmate. My sights narrow on Gary, the young Scouser who shared my old cell with Ted, and it takes him about three seconds to agree to move in. Gary isn't a Listener so shouldn't really be in the Executive Suite, but there is such chaos in Trinity right now that no one notices. I soon hear the full story of how he ended up inside.

'I was basically a degenerate cokehead,' he happily admits. 'I started importing drugs to fund my habit. I was so twisted on gack that I actually thought it was a top idea to carry a suitcase full of weed through Dublin airport.'

He was almost through the gate when a customs officer asked to have a look in his luggage. 'At that moment, I knew I was fucked. There was twelve kilos of the finest Ambrosia Haze in there, which I'd vacuum-wrapped into half-kilo blocks. I'd had a nightmare shutting the case. There wasn't even room for me kecks.' He acts out what happened next. 'I put the bag on the customs desk and started to unzip it. The blocks of weed were so tightly packed in that one of them popped out and landed by the officer's feet. He said, "What's all this then?" I just stood there and said, "What do you think it is? It's a suitcase full of drugs, and you've caught me red-handed." They don't fuck about in Ireland. At one point I was looking at eight years. I pleaded guilty and got away with four.'

Gary accepts full responsibility for his lot. He's now completely clean, and is convinced that prison has saved his life. 'Before I came inside, I was hoovering ten grams of bugle a day. If I'd carried on, I wouldn't have seen thirty.'

16 December

Les quits Listening, claiming that the work is tipping him over the edge. The lack of Listeners means that the rota has gone out the window, and I'm now seeing around three contacts a day. The call-outs range from 10 minutes to over an hour. Often it's just prisoners letting off steam, and I hear the same complaints over and over again: too much debt, facing new charges, baby mama has stopped bringing child to visit, taking too much spice, fallen out with cellmate, can't handle the sentence. Some prisoners are effusive in their gratitude; others less so. I'm queuing for lunch when an officer asks me to speak to a 'raving nutbag on the Fours'. The cell door is locked and I peer in through the observation panel to see that the prisoner is openly taking a shit. The sod hasn't even pulled the privacy curtain, and just sits there toking on a massive spliff. I tap politely on the glass, and he looks at me with withering disdain. 'Fuck off and come back in five minutes.' I shut the flap and never return.

I head over to see Dean, the underfed teenager on K Wing, who has now come off the monitoring programme. He's been allowed to leave the observation cell, and we move his things into a normal pad. His new room has the luxury of a door and a proper bed. He's a bit more communicative, and we chat about his background. He was abandoned by his parents and has been in and out of care homes since he was 11. He was initially at Pentonville, but was transferred following the recent murder. An officer told him that he was being shipped to Wandsworth as 'we don't want anyone else dying here'. For the first time it strikes me that this lad is closer to Kit's age than to mine. I swear to myself that when I get out, I'll try to stop the system brutalising children this way.

After 7 p.m. we're supposed to see contacts in pairs, and my new wingman is Lunn. Tonight we're introduced to a young Mexican called Rudi, who bursts into tears even before we've sat down. Rudi was convicted of possessing a false passport, and was given a short sentence. He was supposed to get out just before Christmas, but his release has been blocked by the Immigration Department. The authorities didn't trust him to make his own way home, and want to repatriate him directly to Mexico. He is desperate to get out of the UK, but Immigration can't arrange a flight for a few more weeks. The authorities are therefore trying to expedite his departure by keeping him in Britain for longer.

Rudi's girlfriend is in a really bad way. They have a young son who is quite ill and is being looked after by relatives in Mexico. However, his girlfriend is refusing to go home until Rudi is released. When she heard that his departure had been delayed, she self-harmed quite badly and ended up in A&E. She has since come to visit, but was heavily medicated and barely spoke. Rudi has a meeting with an immigration officer tomorrow, and begs one of us to accompany him. I am completely stretched, so Lunn agrees to take the reins.

17 December

The BBC reports a riot at HMP Birmingham. Inmates have taken over an entire wing and are chanting 'We want burn!' It later emerges that the riot's ringleader was actually the wing's violence reduction representative.[1] The MoJ insists that it's completely in control of the situation, while the news coverage indicates the exact opposite. Prisoners start tweeting photos of themselves wearing officers' helmets and smashing up the wings.[2] The BBC shows a Tornado squad tooling up, all dressed in black and wearing balaclavas, looking as if they've failed to get into the SAS on fitness grounds.

The reporter interviews a former resident of HMP Birmingham, who doesn't want to be identified. He's zipped a parka hood around his face and strongly resembles Kenny from *South Park*. I can understand his shyness, but he doesn't project a particularly appealing image. This could be one of the reasons why the public are so apathetic about the plight of prisoners, as the media rarely features coherent offenders. Six of the Birmingham rioters are later convicted of 'mutiny'.[3] This archaic charge is in keeping with the Victorian culture that permeates the penal system. I wouldn't be surprised if they were forced to walk the plank.

Twenty refugees from HMP Birmingham arrive in Wandsworth a few days later, and I hear some colourful accounts of the recent carnage. Apparently trouble initially flared because they'd had cold showers for three days.

Connor is unsympathetic. 'Fucking lightweights. Our showers have been freezing for two weeks.'

The butterfly effect

Events in one prison often had consequences elsewhere in the system. The Birmingham riot had a surreal impact on Wandsworth, and I was soon awoken at 3 a.m. by a screw shining a torch in my face.

'Morning, Chris. There's a right fruit loop on G Wing; he tried to stab an officer earlier. Do you want to talk to him?'

I told myself that on the outside I'd have killed for an invitation like this, and hunted around for my flip-flops and dressing gown. I stumbled onto the landing and was escorted by five screws in Tornado gear, who fanned out around me as though they were guarding Hannibal Lecter. These excessive minders were due to the Birmingham riot being started by a convict stealing an officer's keys. I had a mild out-of-body experience from my ludicrous predicament – being accompanied by a small riot squad through the darkened wings of a high-security prison dressed in little more than my pants.

I tapped on the contact's locked door. 'How can I help?'

'Got any burn, bruv?'

I turned back to my personal Tornado team. 'Reckon we can pick up some flapjacks on the way home?'

19 December

Signs go up around Trinity announcing a festive board game competition. Chess, backgammon and draughts are all extremely popular, and the event promises to be a powerful moment of community cohesion. I sign up for the backgammon league, but realise that I'll need to up my game to beat Howard, Scott's former biohazard partner and the backgammon king of Wandsworth. This is going to be tricky, as I'm currently unable to practise. Scott bequeathed me his spare backgammon set, but he then lent it to some Romanians on the Fours. I head up to the top landing to claim my inheritance, but the Romanians refuse to understand a word I'm saying.

Later on, I'm moaning about the situation when I'm overheard by Tommy, the weasel-faced Geordie drug dealer. 'Leave those Romanian cunts to me,' he winks, and heads purposefully upstairs. I sit wondering how best to arrange an alibi. Tommy's Romanian is obviously better than mine, and he swiftly returns with my backgammon set. I peer inside, delighted to see that none of the pieces have been extracted as payment. It does now mean that I'm indebted to the hardest dealer on Trinity.

20 December

Martyn and I are delivering canteen on G Wing. We've now perfected our 'bang and run' technique, in which an officer opens the door, Martyn tosses in the bags, and I mark the name off the list. Like an Italian sports car, this process maximises speed at the expense of reliability. I realise, too late, that the guy in G4-24 has now moved to another pad, so we go back to retrieve his groceries. The cell is now occupied by one of the many tramps who've been admitted over the festive period. They've usually deliberately committed a minor offence just to get a roof over their heads and some food. This lucky vagrant clearly thought Christmas had come early when we accidentally lobbed someone else's canteen order at his feet. It's only taken us two minutes to return for the groceries, but he hasn't let a second go to waste. The canteen bags have now completely vanished. On the table are three suspiciously open tins of chicken curry, the contents of which are spread over the tramp's beard.

The officer, Mr Hart, is normally pretty cheerful. He is not cheerful right now. 'Did you get any canteen in here?' he demands.

'No.' This is a bold answer, as we all saw the bags go in.

Hart becomes more irate. 'Where did you get all this food?'

'I traded it.'

'What with?'

The cover story obviously hasn't been bottomed out this far. The tramp just licks curry from around his mouth in a desperate attempt to destroy the evidence. Hart orders the poor bastard to stand against the wall and pulls back the mattress to reveal packs of noodles, Haribo and cereal. I'm seriously impressed at how quickly the food has been sequestered away.

The rightful owner of this produce is less impressed. It was ordered by a lad called Foley, who's moved to the pad directly opposite and has been watching events unfold through his observation panel. Now he starts screaming blood-curdling threats. Mr Hart locks up the tramp for his own safety, and the situation immediately deteriorates. Foley owes much of this canteen to his new cellmate, who is in turn heavily indebted around the wing. News of their insolvency quickly spreads, and a complex network of prison debt begins to unravel. It reminds me of the collapse of Lehman Brothers, where the contagion from toxic loans swiftly infected the entire economy. The landings descend into uproar, and Martyn and I retreat from the field of battle.

Hours later, I gingerly return to deliver the visit slips. G Wing is still reeling from the recent economic crash, and dozens of inmates have been trying to exact retribution on the occupant of G4-24. I can't resist peeping in through the observation panel. The tramp has come up with a canny strategy to prevent anybody demolishing his cell, and has smashed everything up first. The bed, desk, sink and loo are in pieces, and water gushes from a broken pipe. He sits in the middle of this devastation grinning like Satan himself. A team of screws wearing blue plastic gloves march up from the centre and drag the deranged wretch to the punishment block. This was probably his intention in the first place, as he's now been spirited away from mortal danger.

Water continues to flow into the cell. The bottom of the door is 10 inches off the ground, so it will soon start flooding onto the landing outside. I feel that my cavalier approach to canteen delivery is partially responsible for this disaster, so I wade inside. The water is full of broken furniture and Foley's canteen. I discover that the tramp helpfully snapped the pipe just above a valve, so the leak can easily be stemmed with a screwdriver.

Troublemakers always end up on the Fours, which means that when they flood their cells it causes the maximum damage. Water has begun to cascade down onto the three lower landings and starts flowing into the locked cells. One guy is in the middle of an appeal, and his paperwork is piled on the floor. Another prisoner is making Christmas cards for his children, which get completely soaked. I run round the affected cells telling the occupants to get their stuff off the ground. Two officers finally appear to deliver the evening meal.

'Guv, water is going into a dozen cells,' I shout down. 'It'd be really easy to stop the leak; we just need a flathead screwdriver.'

One of them looks up with an indifference bordering on paralysis. 'Carillion have been called. Nothing we can do.' Maintenance response times are currently between three and six hours. The officers start delivering mangy sandwiches and I make a sharp exit.

21 December

At the end of today's inductions, Danielle discreetly gives me a dozen M&S mince pies. I feel like a soldier at the front, receiving parcels from home. She has been nothing but kind and supportive since I started working with her, undermining the stereotype of prison staff being uncaring automatons. I thank her profusely.

'It's more than deserved,' she smiles. 'I think of you as a colleague, not a prisoner.'

Later on, an empty brown envelope is shoved under my door. A friend posted in some Christmas decorations, and an angry note on the envelope informs me that the contents have been confiscated. I now add 'paper stars' and 'snowflakes' to the burgeoning list of unauthorised items, which doesn't seem to extend to illegal drugs. Someone on H Wing has received a bumper Christmas delivery of skunk, which can be smelt on every landing. Gary sniffs the air and confidently asserts that the strain is Mango Kush. Even the screws admit that the smell is more pleasant than the usual stench of rotting rubbish.

I'm increasingly nervous about Tommy. Ever since he retrieved my backgammon set, he's been making dark hints that I now owe him. I'm therefore delighted when I run into him dragging his stuff in clear bin bags.

'Got busted with a phone,' he snarls. 'Cunts put me on Basic.'

Basic is the lowest possible IEP level. Naughty prisoners are locked in a cell all day without a TV, and only allowed two showers and exercise sessions a week. They can't even go to the servery; instead, other prisoners deliver food to their door. I suppress my delight at Tommy's misfortune, and offer my condolences. He just gives me a mad-eyed stare. 'I'll only be there a couple of days before I shank a screw and go to the block.' I promise to drop round some newspapers.

22 December

Martyn walks in with a colossal smile. 'I'm going to Ford tomorrow!' He's got a good line in restricted information, which is ironic given his offence of insider trading, and he's had advance notice from a friendly officer. I'm extremely happy for him that he's escaping, but also gutted to be losing my best friend. I hug him goodbye, and say that I'll be following him to Ford imminently.

Trading places

I later look Martyn up online and read of his spectacular downfall. He'd made it to the top of the financial world, advising the government on the banking bailout in 2008. He then took over Deutsche Bank's merchant banking division for the whole of the UK. In 2010, he was arrested for using his knowledge of blue-chip clients to trade personal shares. It took six years for the case to get to court, and Martyn was convicted and given four and a half years.[4] His actions appear less harmful than Scott's crime, as there weren't any direct victims, but it's not for me to cast judgement.

What I can say is that I have never met a more cheery, upbeat and kind-hearted soul than Martyn Dodgson. He helped me through the worst period of my life, and never once asked for anything in return. It's very easy to be generous when you're subbing your mate in Starbucks. It's a lot harder being altruistic when the shit's against the wall, and you won't find any shittier walls than in Wandsworth. I'd pick Martyn for my team any day of the week.

23 December

The news reports another riot, this time at HMP Swaleside, where 60 prisoners have taken over an entire wing. Mobile phone footage shows inmates letting off fire extinguishers, waving around pool cues and shouting 'Swaleside is burning!'[5] It's self-evidently a full-blown riot, but the MoJ keeps calling it a 'disturbance',[6] in their latest attempt to rebrand their way out of the prison crisis.

I stop by Tommy's new cell on G Wing. He's been stuck inside for several days, and looks completely frazzled.

'You seen what's going down at Swaleside?' he asks.

'That's some disturbance.' I make a misguided attempt at humour. 'Everyone else is kicking off; why isn't Wandsworth pulling its weight?'

He flashes me a terrifying grin. 'We're planning it now. Gonna tear up on Christmas Day, spread the word.'

I nod conspiratorially. The last thing I need is a riot just as I'm due to be recategorised. Hopefully the Christmas regime will prevent anyone getting out long enough to start a disturbance. I pretend that I'm being called by an officer and scamper off.

We have all been looking forward to the Christmas board game tournament. I've been practising my backgammon for hours, in preparation for my battle with Howard. I have envisaged our showdown as the Wandsworth equivalent of Kasparov versus Karpov, watched by dozens of prisoners hanging on our every move. The reality is a bit different. I'm walking through G Wing, which is completely deserted apart from two lads seated opposite one another on the Twos. As I get closer, I realise that they're playing draughts, and I've just increased their audience to a total of one. This, it seems, is the Trinity board game championship – two Polish drug dealers sitting on a deserted landing. The tournament was supposed to build community spirit, but the community is all banged up in their cells due to staff shortages. The chess league dies completely. Nobody can be persuaded to lend their chess set out, as they aren't able to watch the game and keep an eye on it.

24 December

Christmas Eve. The meanest possible selection of screws are on duty, including Moss and Romley. They enforce complete bang-up across Trinity. We're eventually unlocked for lunch, and a couple of prisoners dash across the landing to call home. Officer Moss is lying in wait and bellows, 'OFF THE PHONES!' into their faces. I stand in line for the servery and spot two elderly Samaritans arguing with SO Romley. The

Samaritans are supposed to visit the Listeners every week to check on our well-being, but they are being blocked from entering H Wing. I can't hear what's being said, but I'm guessing Romley has decided that these old ladies pose a security risk. One of the Samaritans recognises me and darts over, and asks me to tell the other Listeners what has happened. Romley follows and escorts the brave old dear away.

I could really do with the Samaritans' support, as the Listening has become extremely gruelling. I'm now seeing up to five contacts a day. At one point I say goodbye to a prisoner only to see that a small queue has formed outside the Listener Suite. The demand is fuelled by people missing their families over Christmas, a sharp rise in bang-up, and the level of psychiatric care going off a cliff. Most of my contacts have at least one mental illness, and many wait weeks to see the mental health team. I witness constant despair and trauma during the Christmas period and get increasingly upset at my inability to provide significant help. I often feel like I'm hanging round the executioner's steps, simply giving people a friendly smile as they're led off to their fate.

25 December

Christmas Day. Thankfully one of our favourite screws, the BFG, is on duty. He's about six foot four, well into his sixties, and is always extremely courteous. He opens us up at 9 a.m. and politely asks if we want a phone call and a shower. I speak to Kit and it makes me unbearably sad not to be with him. I spend the morning seeing contacts, and at lunch, a smirking officer pops by. 'Do you want to have a word with Spice Attack?' I deduce that he's referring to Samuels, the Jamaican spice addict upstairs. This new nickname is both unprofessional and painfully accurate – Samuels has keeled over three times in the last week. The officer won't unlock him as he's 'having a mental', but the Jamaican refuses to talk to me through his door. I tell the officer that I'm happy to have him in my cell, but the screw just walks off. I inform Samuels that nobody will let him out, and he goes absolutely tonto.

For the rest of the day we sit in our beds watching TV and munching chocolate. 'This is just like spending Christmas day in Hull', remarks Gary. Every film I watch over the festive period manages to accentuate the bleakness of my situation. It's either courtroom dramas (*The Runaway Jury, Kramer vs Kramer*) or stories about lost kids (*Finding Nemo, Home Alone*). I even well up during the slapstick comedy *Liar Liar*, as it's a double whammy – a courtroom drama about parental abandonment. Despite these pitfalls, watching movies remains a great way to kill time. I now rate films by their duration rather than their artistic merit. Linda has recently ordered me in a DVD player from Argos, which is a total godsend. The main library has a decent collection of DVDs, though it's devoid of 18-certificate films.

No sex, please, we're prisoners

Violent and sexually explicit films were outlawed in prisons by Chris Grayling in 2013. According to ITV News, inmates would be banned from watching films like '*Hostel* and *Reservoir Dogs*'. Grayling said that privileges that allowed prisoners to boast about their 'easy life' were 'not right and cannot continue'.[7] This puritanical rule had no effect whatsoever: 18-certificate films were often shown uncut on BBC, ITV and Channel 4 and broadcast into every cell in Wandsworth. This meant that impressionable prisoners could easily view adult-themed films every night. During my sentence I watched both *Hostel* and *Reservoir Dogs* on the prison's own TV system.

Film4 keeps showing *The Shawshank Redemption*. Gary and I watch it every time it's on, and play our favourite game of comparing the on-screen facilities to those in Wandsworth.

'They've got *four* washing machines in their laundry,' says Gary. 'Lucky fuckers.'

'I know Tim Robbins just got raped in the shower,' I note, 'but they do at least have decent water pressure.'

26 December

The wings are filling up with homeless people who have come to prison on purpose. I'm called to see an emaciated guy called Greg, who looks 45 but turns out to be 27. He stole a bunch of designer clothing from John Lewis and walked out of the store expecting to be collared. The alarm didn't sound, and the security guard refused to take any notice of him. Greg then trekked up and down Oxford Street with an armful of women's clothes – which he couldn't even wear to keep him warm. He eventually succeeded in getting arrested, and has been on G Wing for a fortnight.

His face is covered in cuts and scars. I assume this is due to fighting, but the injuries are actually a result of his epilepsy. 'I have loads of fits and bash my face up rotten.' Prison beds are surrounded by hard wooden boards, so Greg's seizures knock him black and blue. I write out a general application asking for him to get a padded bed, knowing full well it won't receive a response. This is the most depressing part of the job: trying to offer hope to the hopeless.

Another self-incarcerating vagrant has taken over the H Wing laundry, and he has a surprisingly fickle taste in tinned fish. The 75p tuna in brine has long been the basic unit of prison currency, but the new laundryman doesn't consider this legal tender. Henceforth he will only accept the 95p tuna in sunflower oil.

Gary is fuming. 'That tramp eats all his food out of a bin anyway.'

I can't resist it. 'Looks like beggars can be choosers.'

27 December

I'm called to the Listener Suite and sit down with a scrawny 19-year-old called Evan. He tells me that he's recently tried to kill himself, and shows me where he's been self-harming. I've started to gauge a contact's problems by the number and severity of the cuts on their arms, and I'd put this lad halfway between a cry for help and the real deal.

He was arrested a few days ago for a driving offence, and is going to be inside for a couple of months. I still find it incredible that teenagers are imprisoned for minor motoring violations. He explains that his mother recently died and he doesn't feel that he has much to live for. I can't help feeling that he is holding something back, so I probe a bit more and discover that he hasn't spoken to his younger brother over Christmas as he hasn't got any phone credit.

At the end of the session, I track down Miss Black. When I first moved onto Trinity, I went with the general consensus that she was a sex-starved curmudgeonly old bat. Having done a couple of months' Listening, I now realise that she is quietly very professional and diligent. I explain Evan's predicament to her, and she allows him to call his brother from the office phone. I later swing by his cell with chocolate, mince pies and tangerines, in a desperate attempt to feed him away from suicide.

Babes in arms

I was constantly shocked by the number of teenage boys in Wandsworth. Previously 18–21-year-olds had always been detained in special young offender institutions. By the time I was imprisoned, the system had changed, presumably for cost reasons, so that anyone aged 18 or over could end up in a place like Wandsworth.[8] This despite the fact that a House of Commons Justice Select Committee concluded that anyone under 25 should not go to adult prison. It argued that those in this age group 'offend the most but have the most potential to stop offending … While the brain is continuing to develop there is a risk that problems will be compounded by involvement in the criminal justice system itself and that opportunities will be missed to repair the developmental harm.'[9]

28 December

I have another session with Evan. The good news is that he's finally spoken to his brother. The bad news is that the police have just raided Evan's flat. I ask what they were searching for, and he starts looking terrified again. He prevaricates for a while, and then admits that he's suspected of attempted murder. I take a deep breath and ask him to start from the beginning.

He lights a roll-up with trembling hands. 'Six months back I was walking home with me girlfriend. We were jumped by three boys.' Somewhat fortuitously, Evan was carrying a blade. He stabbed one of the assailants, who promptly went into a coma. I'm quite dubious about his version of events, and suspect that it wasn't entirely self-defence. The hospital are now considering switching off life support, which means that he could be facing a murder charge.

My moral compass is all over the shop, as my view of Evan oscillates between 'pitiful victim' and 'evil scumbag'. Throughout my life I've envisioned a stereotypical murderer, loosely based on Jack Nicholson in *The Shining*, menacingly waving an axe at helpless victims. This image couldn't be further from the terrified twitching child in front of me right now. I feel duty bound to support him, even though I risk helping him evade detection.

'Is there anything linking you to the crime?' I ask.

'The feds were looking for jeans and a coat I was wearing that night.'

'What about the weapon?'

'They won't find it.' He is pretty confident about this.

'Where are the jeans?'

He looks down at his legs. 'I'm wearing them.'

I nearly burst out laughing at his monumental stupidity. 'Are you sure it's a good idea to hang onto potentially incriminating evidence?'

'They've been washed.'

Give me strength. 'Look, Evan, the Trinity laundry is not renowned for its thoroughness. I'm no expert on forensics, but those washing machines are unlikely to remove all trace of your victim's DNA.' Before I can consider the consequences, I suggest that he cuts up the jeans and flushes them down the loo. He mulls this over, weighing the loss of a nice pair of jeans against getting life for murder.

'What about the coat?' I ask.

'I had it on when they nicked me last week. It's in my prop box.'

I give up. Evan has put damning evidence of his own guilt right into the hands of the authorities. That said, Wandsworth's property department is in total meltdown. Even Scotland Yard's finest might struggle to fill in the paperwork necessary to access the clothing.

29 December

I bump into Evan in the Trinity centre. He's carrying all his stuff in clear plastic bin liners and is being escorted by a female officer.

'Where are you going?'

'E Wing,' he replies. 'Guv said so.'

E Wing is easily the most dangerous wing in the prison. It's become particularly demented over Christmas, and will clearly exacerbate Evan's suicidal tendencies. He's being accompanied by Miss Harley, an officer with a notoriously high opinion of herself.

'Sorry, miss, can I ask why you're taking him there?'

'We're clearing all remand prisoners off Trinity,' she snaps.

I struggle to keep my temper. 'Trinity is full of remand prisoners that you're not moving. This kid is going to get eaten alive on E Wing.'

'I'm just following orders.'

My mind is immediately drawn to the Milgram obedience experiment, and for a split second I forget that I'm a prisoner. 'If your orders are to get Wandsworth's suicide rate up, then this is the best way to go about it.'

Les overhears our confrontation and swoops in. He still sees himself as the King of Listening, and has a long-standing crush on Miss Harley. He places a condescending hand on my shoulder. 'Sorry he's speaking out of line, Miss H. He's a bit wet behind the ears and we're still showing him the ropes.'

This really gets my back up, as Les has recently stood down from working as a Listener. Evan shuffles off, and I call out, 'I'll come and find you on E Wing!'

Les shakes his head at me. 'When I started Listening, I wanted to save the world as well.' I bite my tongue and flounce off.

30 December

Gary reports that Les invited him into his cell, offering him some cereal in a 'pretty pathetic attempt' to win his confidence. Apparently he then launched into a tirade about me not giving him due respect as the 'number one Listener'. He warned Gary that he is tempted to go 'all street' on me unless I apologise.

Gary struggles to take this threat seriously, pointing out that Les is 'just a fifty-year-old hairdresser'. He told Les that his loyalty lay with me, but still took the cereal before he left.

I run into Les in the middle of S&Ds. I try to build bridges, but he tells me to get fucked. 'I've been hearing that you've been taking Listening calls while you're not on duty!'

'That's exactly right. Ever since you jumped ship we've been really up against it.'

Our bickering causes quite a scene, and we're soon surrounded by a gaggle of bemused cons. Lunn intervenes and takes us aside to mediate. He insists that he has nothing but praise for my Listening work, which takes the wind out of Les's sails. I grudgingly admit that I was rude to Miss Harley, and accept the need to keep the officers onside. We all start agreeing with each other and apologising, and the air is quickly cleared. Les holds out his hand just as I move in for a hug, and he takes a step back. 'We're in prison, Chris. We don't hug.'

31 December

The last hours of 2016 draw to a close, and Gary insists that we watch *Match of the Day*. H Wing is full of Chelsea fans, and whenever their team score there is an explosion of door-kicking. The night screw, already spitting feathers from doing the worst shift of the year, furiously tries to curtail the noise. 'Stop that fucking racket or I'll give everyone an IEP!' His ranting just provokes even more door-thumping, reminding me of schoolkids humming to wind up their teacher.

The clock chimes midnight; I have now spent exactly six months in prison. I'm amazed at how quickly the time has flown. The longer I'm here, the faster reality slips past. Maybe my brain is slowing down, like a hibernating mouse, reducing all higher cognitive processes for survival. I've stopped missing most of my middle-class trappings. I no longer crave alcohol or nicotine, I actually like the taste of instant coffee, and I don't find the hard bed uncomfortable. I am now an integral part of the Wandsworth ecosystem, and have seamlessly replaced Scott as the admin sage of Trinity.

1 January 2017

We've run out of loo roll. It's usually dispensed at the servery once a week, but nothing was handed out over Christmas. I ransack the cell, hoping that Scott squirrelled a stash, but with no success. On

S&Ds I head down to the screws' office, where a dozen other inmates are queuing for the same reason. We wait patiently for 15 minutes, until Officer Moss merrily announces that there isn't any bog roll on Trinity. 'You'll just have to make do.'

Happy New Year.

2 January

The new year has brought some new officers. We have a fresh-faced SO in his twenties, who's tall and blonde and is immediately christened 'Hitler Youth'. He's soon spotted writing the date into the dust on a stairway so he can later check if it's been cleaned. The cleaners are up in arms; Howard is so worried that he's actually considering doing some cleaning.

I suggest a 'fake news' strategy, and demonstrate by writing a date from the nineteenth century in the dust on a nearby wall. Hitler Youth's enthusiasm does not last, and he quits after just three months.

Our favourite new officer is the Hipster Screw. He's about five foot two and sports an immaculate Shoreditch beard. On his first day he gets accosted by a burly inmate, who demands, 'Does your mum know you're in prison?' One afternoon I spot the Hipster Screw striding purposefully down a landing. He hasn't properly secured his belt, which holds his keys, handcuffs and radio, and it all slides down to the floor. 'Oh crap!' he sighs as he tries to reattach the belt unnoticed, before realising that he's being watched by a dozen grinning prisoners.

There's also a new night officer who is causing much mirth. It's difficult to describe him without referring to the Hunchback of Notre Dame, as he has a mild hunch and clanks around muttering to himself. One of his few jobs is counting everyone at night, which he undertakes in a highly unconventional manner. He simply goes up to each door and asks, 'How many in here?' This trusting approach could easily enable a prisoner to escape, as long as their padmate stayed behind to vouch for their presence. His naïve questioning provokes frequent unhelpful answers, including 'none', 'three and a half' and 'four hundred and thirty-five'. These wisecracks usually bugger up the hunchback's count, and he has to start again from the beginning.

3 January

Freeflow is finally back on, and I head to the mains to do the inductions. I spot a screw handing out loo rolls, and join the queue. The officer recognises me, and grunts, 'You don't live on E Wing.'

'There isn't any toilet roll on Trinity, guv.'

'This is all for E Wing.'

'I'm sure the shit is pretty consistent across the wings, guv.'

He gives me just one roll. I later bump into Evan. He seems to have settled in well on E Wing, and I detect a wisp of spice in his eyes.

Ongoing storylines

I rarely knew what became of my Listener contacts after I talked to them. The chaotic nature of the prison meant that it was difficult keeping tabs on my friends, let alone the inmates I'd seen in Listener sessions. Wandsworth had a high turnover of residents, so people would simply vanish from the wings and there was no way of tracing their whereabouts. Some contacts wouldn't want it publicised that they had seen a Listener, as it could be perceived as weakness, so it might be dangerous if I went round asking questions. Since getting out, I'm often asked, 'Has anyone you sat with ever killed themselves?' to which the painful answer is 'I don't know. Probably.' A lot of my Listener contacts had strong suicidal tendencies, and they were in a place almost structurally designed to make them take their own lives, so I think it's more than likely.

---

4 January

Tommy has finally come off Basic. He saunters into my cell flashing his mad eyes.

'You didn't come and see me on G Wing, you cunt. What food have you got? I'm going to rob you.'

He swipes a tin of mackerel, a bag of rice and an onion, and walks back out. This presents a bit of a quandary, as he is the go-to gangster for protection services. I'm unsure of protocol if the person giving me grief is actually him.

At night we receive another unwelcome guest. Just as I'm nodding off, I hear a scratching from under the desk. I gently poke the bin with a broomstick, and a rat flies out and scampers under Gary's bed. He shrieks and jumps on a chair, as if he's in a *Tom and Jerry* cartoon.

I enjoy this situation hugely. 'You've survived the toughest jails in Ireland, but you're now being bullied by a four-inch rodent.'

Gary refuses to get down until I chase the rat out of the cell. Wandsworth is infested with vermin, thanks to the piles of rotting rubbish. I'm surprised there hasn't been an outbreak of bubonic plague.

6 January

I receive some paperwork about my upcoming proceeds-of-crime hearing. HMRC has hired a new forensic accountant to calculate my financial benefit. They accept that I wasn't paid personally, but I am on the block for the money retained by the production company to fund *Starsuckers*. The accountant has actually estimated down what was alleged in court, and the financial benefit attributed to me is just over £100,000. The silver lining is that the CPS can only demand payment of this lower figure. I had assumed that I would probably have to sell my house to settle the confiscation, but it's looking now as though I might get to keep it.

None of my neighbours can believe that I've been given a five-year sentence for such a comparatively small amount of money. Someone a few doors down stole a million quid from the Department of Education and blew it all on a luxury flat. He only got three and a half years.

8 January

Gary is counting the hours until his imminent departure. On 21 January he'll have served exactly two years, which is half his sentence. His girlfriend has stood by him, and they're planning to start a family as soon as he's released.

'We're heading for some *serious* headboard techno,' he informs me. Sex remains at the forefront of his mind. This morning he announces that he has a 'right diamond cutter' under the covers. While I brush my teeth, he describes the explicit dream he's just had about his missus. 'She had a face like a plasterer's radio.'

10 January

Tomorrow is officially the day of my recategorisation. Tracey reveals that recats are running about a fortnight behind, but I'm strangely relaxed about the delay. Two weeks isn't much given that I've got two more years to serve; it's all time off the total anyway. Everything points towards me being made Cat D, meaning that I'll be at Ford by the end of the month. Gary finishes his sentence in a week and a half, and we toast our good fortune, both believing that our darkest days will soon be over. I feel as if I've been cut free from a sunken wreck and am starting the long swim back to the surface.

9

Courtrooms and Cheeseburgers

In which Gary and I both get stuck in Wandsworth. We refuse to ride the bang-up, and wage admin warfare with the authorities.

Things I learn:

1) The Offender Management Unit can't count

2) How to conceive in prison

3) A novel way to solve the housing crisis

We score a partial victory for Gary, but my prospects take a turn for the worse.

11 January

I'm shortly due back in court for my confiscation hearing. I am desperate to know what's going on, but can't raise my lawyer on the phone. Danielle lets me nip out of the inductions to call, and I eventually speak to my lawyer's assistant, who clearly learnt her bedside manner from Dr Harold Shipman.

'So you're going to have to sell your house,' she sniffs.

This is a bolt from the blue. 'Surely the lower benefit figure means I can borrow the money instead?'

'Yeah, but you're getting hit with a prosecution bill as well.' Guilty offenders are now charged for the costs of their own prosecution. It's akin to being castrated and then getting invoiced for the shears. My panic attack is made worse by my legal adviser's brutal tone.

'You'll probably end up owing over two hundred thousand. There'll be a hearing in a couple of weeks. I've got to go.' And she hangs up.

I stagger back to the classroom, and pour my heart out to Danielle. That house was my rock, where I intended to rebuild things with Kit on my release. Danielle is sympathetic and understanding, and tries to cheer me up. She jokes that she'll pay me for both Christmas *and* New Year's Day. 'That's two pounds forty in the kitty for a start.'

12 January

Gary's due to go home next week, and he's bouncing off the walls in anticipation. This afternoon a young probation officer asks him for a quiet word. Twenty minutes later, Gary reappears, pale and hyperventilating. It's obvious that something is terribly wrong.

'They've just given me another six months!' he gasps.

The probation officer told him that there had been a 'bit of an error' with his sentence calculation; his release date has now been pushed back to 31 July. The mix-up stems from the fact that he was originally sentenced in Ireland, where offenders serve three quarters of their total sentence.

We dig through all Gary's paperwork. He previously submitted several general apps asking to see OMU to clarify his release date. A month ago, Tracey sent back a clear written response: *Your release date is confirmed as 21 January 2017.*

We take this document to Tracey's office, and she looks Gary up on NOMIS. The screen now shows his release date as 31 July. Tracey hits peak flailing and offers him some additional visits, as though this compensates for six more months in prison.

Gary stumbles off to call his family. His mother hasn't visited him in Wandsworth, as she's been too upset to see him in these conditions. He breaks the news that she now won't see him until July, and she's completely devastated. The most upsetting call is to his girlfriend, Emma. She's stood by him throughout, and is distraught that her life is being put on hold yet again. Tragically, everyone assumes that the delay is Gary's fault.

Now it's very easy for me to accept that Wandsworth has miscalculated someone's sentence by half a year. I've observed OMU's failings for some time, and such disasters are commonplace. But Gary's family simply cannot accept that public officials could be this inept. His brother suggests that the increased sentence is a result of Gary misbehaving in prison. Like the boy who cried wolf, he is now being judged as the unreliable cokehead who was jailed two years ago.

Prisons make hundreds of brutally unjust mistakes every day. Fighting the system is rarely successful, and just grinds you down. It's usually best to simply 'ride the bang-up' – laugh at the problem and cross off the days. But increasing Gary's sentence crosses a line, and we resolve to fight it tooth and nail.

13 January

I go back through all of Gary's key dates. He was initially arrested in the Republic of Ireland in January 2015, and has been in custody ever since. He did 19 months in a Dublin prison before being repatriated to the UK last August. Ireland and Britain make prisoners serve different proportions of their sentences, so there are two ways to calculate Gary's actual jail time. OMU have belatedly opted for the method that produces the longest duration, and I suspect there's little chance of him being released before July. His best bet is to shame

OMU into giving him a Cat D immediately, so he can at least spend his remaining time in open prison.

Gary starts to fill out a COMP1 complaint form, but I insist that we unleash a COMP2. This is the highest level of complaint, and goes straight to the governor. I type up a letter that mixes forensic analysis with belligerent sarcasm: 'OMU is failing in its most basic function of knowing how long prisoners are meant to serve, and making up release dates as they go along. This is tantamount to arbitrary detention, which was supposedly prohibited in the Magna Carta in 1215. Wandsworth is famous for its archaic approach to criminal justice, but I didn't realise that you hadn't left the Dark Ages.'

Gary has another bad call with his girlfriend. He's worried that their relationship won't survive this latest catastrophe. I'm worried that he might start using drugs again.

14 January

We try to recruit official advocates to the 'Free Gary' campaign. Gary tells the education staff what's happened, and Linda immediately picks up the phone and starts berating OMU. I'm deeply touched that she's willing to take up the case of a prisoner, even though she has no obligation to help whatsoever.

Meanwhile Gary's gran is in a bad way. He was going to stay with her when he was released, and she's spent all week getting the house ready: new sheets for the spare room, a flat-screen TV on the wall, and all his favourite food in the fridge. The news that her grandson won't be coming home has hit her hard. To add insult to injury, she's just received a letter from the local probation office informing her that he will be arriving on 21 January. Cheshire Probation were obviously working off the same wrong release date, and wrote to her before the sentence was changed.

The letter might have caused Gary's gran considerable distress, but it also restores Gary's credibility among his family. It shows that the whole system is up shit creek, and quashes any suspicions that the situation is his fault. Gary's mother is apoplectic, and pens an extremely angry complaint to the Wandsworth authorities.

Gary and I continue our angry correspondence, and send a scathing letter to the Independent Monitoring Board. This is a group of volunteer observers who claim to 'monitor the day-to-day life [in prison] and ensure that proper standards of care and decency are maintained'.[1] Given the appalling standards of care and decency in Wandsworth, I've always been somewhat dubious about their effectiveness. We're soon visited by an elderly woman with an IMB badge, who looks as though she's about to play the piano in her local church.

'I spoke to Governor Daniels at OMU,' she trills. 'He's *very* upset about the situation.' Evidently Daniels is the real victim in all this.

'Not upset enough to apologise,' Gary shoots back.

'He said that there was a computer glitch, and someone at the MoJ entered the wrong release date. He's *really* sorry.' She is doing little to contradict the general view that the IMB is just a shill for Wandsworth's management.

Gary's blood is beginning to boil. 'They should give me a Cat D now and get me to open prison!'

The IMB woman starts to retreat from our locked door. 'If you want to be recategorised, you'll have to fill in a general app.'

I start explaining that it was filling in a general app that got Gary into this mess, but she just walks away.

16 January

Gary's girlfriend Emma is still furious, as she's waited patiently for Gary for two years and is keen to start a family. Given that she's in her early thirties, she is loath to stomach any further delays. Gary and I brainstorm ways that they might get the conception party started before July. If he's sent to open prison then he'll be allowed out on day release, and they could just decamp to a nearby hotel.

17 January

Teasnitch, the smarmy Greek who makes the officers' tea, sticks his head round the door.

'Hi, guys, we need a hand in the wing rep meeting. Couple of the reps have been put on Basic and can't attend. Reckon you could step in?'

Gary and I readily agree, and we go into the K Wing chapel room. We're soon joined by two custody managers, the most senior officers in the prison; Governor Yeti, who professes to be in charge of Trinity; and the kitchen manager, Pete. These meetings are supposed to be a platform for the wing reps to air problems concerning the prison community. However, it becomes quickly obvious that the reps are only here to brown-nose for their own purposes.

'Can I just say to Pete that last week's cheeseburgers were *delicious*,' pronounces Teasnitch. Pete is wearing disgusting chef's whites that don't quite cover his pot belly, and gives Teasnitch a bashful wave. I actually saw these burgers. If Pete served them to paying customers, he'd receive a public health prosecution.

Les gives a maniacal double thumbs-up. 'Pukka, Pete! Those cheeseburgers were pukka!' Les is due to be sentenced for further charges soon, and clearly thinks that praising the catering will somehow get him a more lenient punishment.

Yeti has helpfully prepared the agenda, which is quite odd given that it's purportedly a prisoner-led forum. He starts by acknowledging that Trinity has recently become 'a bit messy'. This is something of an understatement: rubbish has gone uncollected for weeks, there are rats everywhere and the laundry stinks of sewage.

'My vision is to appoint officers as Cleaning Champions, who will own the hygiene journey.' Yeti uses the word 'vision' a lot. He proposes that the Champions' photos will be displayed on a board so they can be alerted quickly whenever someone disgraces themselves in the shower room. There's no additional pay for this role, and unsurprisingly there hasn't been a stampede of volunteers.

Two people tried to kill themselves on Trinity last week, but this has not made the agenda. Instead we deliberate Yeti's vision for a ramp into the shed in the yard. It transpires that Carillion still haven't constructed the ramp, as the shed light is broken. We spend the next 10 minutes discussing how best to change a light bulb. Next we debate why powdered custard has disappeared from the canteen.

The meeting draws to a close and Yeti finally opens up the floor to the assembled reps. 'So do the men have any issues?'

First to speak is Dobby, a weaselly inmate who looks much like his Harry Potter namesake. 'I just want to say how safe I've felt on Trinity these last few weeks. We should congratulate the officers on how easy it is to walk down the landings.' Dobby has been lobbying hard for a single cell, and this toadying is obviously intended to seal the deal.

Finally it's my turn. 'Lots of prisoners are struggling to talk to OMU.'

CM Walden replies in a dull monotone. 'Men need to submit their enquiry on a general app. Tracey will deal with simple queries; everyone else goes to the OMU surgery.'

'But Tracey has been issuing dud information. A prisoner – sorry, *man* – was given the wrong release date on a general app. He was about to go home when he was told he had to serve an extra six months.'

Walden is unmoved. '*If* that's true, he should raise it through the proper channels. He should send in a general app.' I sit dumbstruck at this circular insanity, and Teasnitch seizes the opportunity to rhapsodise about the bloody cheeseburgers again. This whole rigmarole is observed by an elderly member of the Independent Monitoring Board. I say observed, but he actually nods off after 10 minutes and spends the rest of the hour snoring quietly.

18 January

Connor, my friend on the inductions, is finally sentenced at the Old Bailey. He's been on remand for a year, along with several associates, accused of running his high-end cocaine delivery service. He gets 15 years, which seems utterly preposterous, especially as there were no allegations of violence.

Connor returns from the Bailey looking only mildly put out. I ask him how he's feeling, and he just shrugs. 'Fuck all I can do about it, is there.' He is a big fan of mindfulness, and regularly meditates to keep a level head. It also helps that he's been to prison before, so he knows that it will definitely end one day.

> ### Different strokes for different folks
>
> Sentencing disparity was a regular cause of heartache. There was nothing worse than seeing someone else get a much lighter punishment for a far worse crime. Connor's 15-year sentence seemed even more ridiculous when I later looked up some other convictions in the same month. 'Career paedophile' Roy Reynolds was convicted for 20 historic offences committed against eight boys, some as young as nine. He got 16 months.[5] A caretaker who superimposed pictures of children onto youngsters being sexually abused received three years.[6] A previously convicted paedophile was spared jail after admitting possession of hundreds of Category A child abuse images.[7] This disparity basically implies that it's more acceptable to abuse children than to sell a drug consumed by half the Tory party.

19 January

A bunch of sentenced Cat C prisoners arrive on Trinity from the mains. Our new neighbours also include several qualified Listeners, which means I can go back to doing normal shifts. One of them, Carney, has something of the Artful Dodger about him. He's completely bald, talks in a camp cockney accent, and got three years for some fairly unusual housebreaking.

'I'd only jemmy empty flats. I'd change the locks quick-smart and then put the address on Gumtree.' He would only accept offers from foreigners, and insist they pay the first three months' rent upfront in cash. He would hand over the keys, ditch his phone and then leave them to it. It's a very twenty-first-century crime, and Carney is adamant that he was simply helping to solve London's housing crisis.

20 January

It's finally time for my confiscation hearing at Southwark. I'm woken at 6 a.m. by an officer tapping on the door. I assume that it's a Listener call-out, and stumble out of bed asking who the contact is. The screw tells me that I'm due in court, and I get ready in the dark to avoid waking Gary. I eat a bowl of muesli and chuck the remainder in the loo, realising too late that I've thrown my spoon in as well. This sets the tone for the rest of the day.

The wings are completely deserted as I'm led to reception, and my heart starts thumping as I retrace my first steps in prison. I'm presented with my creased court clothes. The curry stains from July now look like an experiment to recreate primordial life.

Six of us are bound for Southwark, and we're herded into a filthy holding cell. I natter with the Chinese computer hacker who previously drew Ted's unwarranted ire. Another prisoner does some yoga in the corner, which is pretty brave given the revolting state of the floor. We're called out to a big white Serco van, and locked in a tiny cubicle in the back.

The van pulls out of the main gate, and my head starts to spin. I haven't left Wandsworth in seven months and I feel as if I'm being wrenched from a womb. We crawl through the morning rush hour and turn onto Albert Embankment. The traffic is practically gridlocked up to Waterloo. I peer out of the window at Big Ben. It's already past 9 a.m. My hearing starts in less than half an hour and we're still nowhere near Southwark. I resist the urge to shout a quicker route at the driver.

We arrive with minutes to spare. I'm cuffed and taken up to the tatty reception desk.

'Welcome back, Mr Atkins. Would you like a tea or coffee?' The guard is the same Eric Idle lookalike who escorted me when I was sentenced. I'm thrown by both his politeness and his extraordinary powers of recall. I'm taken to meet my barrister and it's just as well that everything's been agreed in advance, as we only have 30 seconds to confer. Eric Idle briskly shepherds me up to Court 5.

The prospect of returning to this place has been filling me with dread. The trial was the worst trauma of my life, and I've been replaying it in my head ever since. I nervously enter the dock from the back and quickly realise that it's just a dull, functional room. I'm suddenly not scared of it any more, and I'm overwhelmed by a huge sense of relief. I almost want to get up and dance.

We are surrounded by mountains of paperwork for another case. Eric Idle tells me that they're halfway through the HBOS trial, which has been getting loads of press. Some bankers allegedly fleeced £230 million and blew it on luxury boats and sex parties. My hearing is in the same courtroom with the same judge, and is scheduled just before their day starts.

After a few minutes, the CPS barristers float in. I actually got on reasonably well with my prosecutor, and he gives me a smile. I return a friendly wave. Judge Beddoe sweeps in and says that he wants to wrap everything up immediately. One of the other lawyers has some last-minute questions about the figures. There isn't time to deal with it now, so the judge tells everyone to come back in four weeks. This is deeply annoying. I've agreed to all the CPS's demands, so there should be no need for me to return again. I hurriedly scrawl this on a tissue and bang on the glass window of the dock. A paralegal runs up, and several people pass the note to my barrister, who stands up and asks if I can appear by video link at the next hearing. Judge Beddoe, a renowned stickler for protecting the public purse, readily agrees. 'I can't see why Mr Atkins was even brought here today. Is he trying to move to a less uncomfortable prison?'

I give an enthusiastic thumbs-up. My barrister, who's unable to see me, stands up and says no.

The judge frowns. 'There appears to be some confusion about this.'

My barrister turns round to see my idiotic waving. 'It would seem that my client does indeed want to move establishment.'

Beddoe stands up. 'Well, I have no problem with that.' He sweeps back out in a way that only judges can. I'm convinced they give them sweeping lessons at judging school.

I'm led back downstairs, mildly pleased that this will be my last visit to Southwark. The van doesn't leave for another seven hours, and at lunchtime Eric Idle gives me another microwaved curry. Much of it gets spilled over my court clothes again, adding an extra layer to the original festering stains. I find myself longing to return to Wandsworth.

We're finally herded back into the van. The Chinese hacker got 18 months, which was a lot less than he was expecting, so he's definitely won at court today. The driver takes a more sensible route home, and we pull up outside Wandsworth at six o'clock. I wait patiently to be let out, but we just sit in the car park. The driver explains that there are several vans in front of us, then disappears for a smoke.

The temperature quickly plummets. It's supposed to go below zero tonight, and none of us have coats. My fellow travellers soon start screaming and kicking, and the van begins to rock. The driver ignores us, so I give the cubicle a few kicks just to keep my feet warm. It occurs to me that people being prosecuted while on remand would have to endure this experience every single day. I can see now why prosecutors are always keen to oppose bail, as people attending trial while in Wandsworth are going to be massively disadvantaged compared to those living at home.

After 90 minutes of this freezing misery, we're eventually led back into the prison. Mercifully, one of the Annexe posse is working on reception. He deftly produces a steaming plate of pasta, which I practically inhale. I return to H Wing at 8.30, over 14 hours after I left. The taxpayer has just spunked several hundred quid transporting me 15 miles for an utterly pointless hearing. It would have been easier and cheaper to go on a day trip to Greece.

22 January

Today there's a graduation ceremony for newly qualified Listeners. I've been looking forward to this quite a lot, as we've been allowed to invite two visitors each. I head to the centre to join the other Listeners, a group that unfortunately includes Montague. I find this prisoner mildly irritating, as he's always babbling in a bizarre mid-European accent. He is currently rambling about seeing his daughter, who's flying in for the ceremony. Montague is clutching a large clear evidence bag of trinkets that he intends to give her.

We are finally led to the main chapel, where our visitors are waiting for us. I've invited Lottie and my friend Nazia, who has been looking after my affairs on the outside. Hanging out in a cold church would normally be pretty awkward, but it's far more relaxed than the visits hall. There are only two officers present; they sit at the back keeping a low profile.

Today's ceremony is run by the governor who manages the prison day to day. She gives a brief speech about the importance of the Listener scheme, and thanks us for doing such difficult work. We're called up to collect our certificates and shake her hand. Leroy, a ripped south London hood, doesn't leave the stage.

'Becoming a Listener has been deep, you get me?' he announces to the congregation. 'At first I thought it was just grasses chattin' shit, yeah, but since I been out on the wings I've *changed*. I seen brothers on the floor, swear down, and pickin' 'em up needs big *heart*.'

I'm unsure if Leroy's impromptu speech is genuine, or if he's trying to influence his upcoming recategorisation. The governor wisely lets him finish, and we all give him a nice round of applause. Montague claps with particularly manic enthusiasm. I notice that he's sitting all alone, while everyone else is surrounded by their guests. His daughter obviously hasn't turned up, but he's still beaming inanely, clutching his bag of tatty keepsakes. I realise that he's probably having a breakdown, and suddenly feel sorry for him.

Days later, it emerges that another fellow Listener had a secret graduation party in the chapel loos. Cally is part of the Annexe posse, and his wife came in to watch the ceremony. While Leroy was causing a distraction, she quietly nipped to the toilet, and Cally followed her in. They didn't let a second go to waste, which is just about how long it lasted, given that Cally's been inside for 12 months. They emerged separately, flushed with the Holy Spirit, and the screws didn't notice a thing. Cally is now treated like a rock star around the prison, and there's been a spike in applications for the next Listener training.

23 January

Our cell door unexpectedly flies open, and a large security officer marches in. Screws rarely enter cells, as they're terrified of being held hostage. The officer completely ignores us and starts poking around under our beds.

'Can we be of assistance, Officer?' I ask.

The screw shows us a printed mug shot. 'You seen this prisoner? He's gone AWOL.'

Gary peers at the picture. 'Good-looking guy. If he turns up, we'll drop you a text.'

The screw stomps back out, and the lockdown continues all day. We watch the evening news, but there's no mention of a Wandsworth breakout. Days later, I ask Officer O'Reilly where they found the missing prisoner. He checks that he won't be overheard, and whispers, 'In his own fucking cell.'

Offender Anarchy Unit

Every time I thought that OMU had reached the pinnacle of utter fuckwittery, it immediately exceeded itself. A former security consultant called Nichols had got three years for stealing dozens of Burberry handbags from his former employer. With only 18 months to serve, he should have got his Cat D straight away. But OMU kept knocking him back, citing 53 previous convictions and 10 fake identities. This was news to Nichols, who was definitely inside on his first offence. OMU replied that this was exactly what someone with 10 fake identities *would* say.

Another time I was doing the inductions when I bumped into Brendan, someone I knew from Trinity. I was surprised to see him on E Wing, or indeed anywhere in the prison, as he'd been released the previous week.

'What are you doing back here?' I asked.

'Fucking OMU. They brought me back to serve an old nicking.' He had been caught with a mobile phone earlier in his sentence and given an extra 28 days. 'I kept asking if I'd served the extra days, and OMU said it'd definitely been added to my sentence. I got out Friday, went for tea at the Ritz with my mum on Saturday, then on

Sunday I was arrested for being unlawfully at large.' OMU admitted that they hadn't factored in the 28 days, and had let Brendan out a month early.

Wandsworth sometimes accidentally released extremely dangerous prisoners. An armed robber was turfed out just weeks into a nine-year sentence. He then taunted the authorities by Instagramming selfies in pubs and in front of a police van.[11] Nationally, over 300 offenders were wrongly released between 2011 and 2017.[12] This was usually due to people sharing the same surname, or court officials writing down the wrong sentence.

24 January

Gary finally gets a response to our numerous written complaints. He opens a letter from Governor Daniels, the head of OMU, which unsurprisingly blames everyone except OMU. Daniels claims that a computer error at prison HQ caused Gary's release date to 'drop off' the system. He then criticises Tracey for sending Gary a note with the wrong date. The tone is like a bland corporate apology, and manages to sound contrite without ever saying sorry. In recompense, he offers to bring Gary's recategorisation forward to 21 February. Given the delays at OMU, he is unlikely to actually leave Wandsworth until March. Gary accepts that this is the best result he can expect, and focuses on ensuring that they definitely issue his Cat D.

OMU give a lot of weight to rehabilitation courses, so Gary starts signing up to every programme on offer. I soon hear of a new horticulture class, and put his name on the list. When I tell him about it, he is not enthused.

'That's a fucking terrible idea.'

'Why not? Bit of fresh air will do you good.'

'I got four years for importing home-grown marijuana. They might think that gardening lessons are a bit inappropriate.'

'I'll take your name off the list.'

25 January

Newspapers are usually delivered by Fenton, the former lawyer. He's pretty efficient, and even on days without showers, phone calls and heating, I still get a *Guardian* shoved under my door. Last week, several TV guides went missing and the paper round was reassigned to the officers. Subsequently the papers start arriving four days late, making their contents fairly redundant.

Today I nip into the centre office. 'Guv, can I have my paper?'

'We haven't sorted them out yet.'

'Mine's the *Guardian*. The only *Guardian* in Wandsworth actually.'

The officer throws the paper at me in disgust. 'Get that commie filth out my office.'

All the news that's unfit to print

Most prisoners preferred to read the *Sun*, the *Daily Star* or the *Daily Mirror*. The popularity of these tabloids was quite surprising, given that they all printed nonsense about prisons being too cushy: *JAILS TO GET EVEN SOFTER;*[13] *PAMPERED PORRIDGE! INSIDE HMP BERWYN;*[14] *EXPOSED: PRISONERS PARTYING ON DRUGS, VODKA & FAST FOOD.*[15] This false narrative fostered a public perception that prisoners were all living the life of Riley, and enabled politicians to make prison conditions even worse. In 2012, Chris Grayling thundered that he would 'stop our jails being like holiday camps'. He promised to make life harder for criminals in order 'to rebuild shattered public confidence in the justice system'.[16]

By 2017, violence, suicides and self-harm were at record levels, but the tabloids still perpetuated the myth that prison was an easy ride. Politicians have started to shy away from supporting such stories, and in fairness Liz Truss said on LBC, 'I visit prisons all the time. I can assure you that they're not holiday camps.'[17]

26 January

We keep a stack of newspapers by the door, so I can always grab reading material whenever I leave the cell. This is invaluable whenever I'm waiting for a gate to be unlocked, but there is precious little respect in prison for reading. Today I'm standing in a corridor engrossed in an article, and a random inmate bumbles up to me.

'These screws are fucking useless. I didn't get any burn on the canteen last week, as they hadn't put my money on from the week before ...'

Far from indicating that I want be left alone, reading is akin to announcing 'I'M BORED! PLEASE COME AND TALK TO ME!' I try holding up my *Guardian* so it covers my entire upper body, but the prisoner just looms over the top, tossing on about his bloody tobacco. I usually grudgingly engage in these conversations, just in case the inmate is a complete psychopath, though I'll try to start reading again at the first available pause, which occasionally ruffles some feathers.

Burn before reading

Contempt for the written word is a consequence of the appalling literacy levels in prison. Half the inmates in British jails are functionally illiterate,[18] and up to 30% have learning difficulties.[19] Given the captive audience, prison should be an ideal place to address the problem. The Shannon Trust, an excellent charity that teaches literacy behind bars, launched its 'Toe by Toe' scheme in

Wandsworth 25 years ago. This works by encouraging educated prisoners to teach their fellow inmates. It has since taught over 50,000 prisoners to read across the country,[20] but receives no government funding despite the obvious benefit to society.[21] Alongside the Listeners, it's arguably the most effective scheme running in prisons, but it is massively hamstrung by most inmates being locked in their cells all day.

27 January

Coordinating the 'Free Gary' campaign has helped distract me from my own problems. I was due to be recategorised on 11 January, but have heard nothing from OMU. Every day I ask an officer to pull up my NOMIS page to look at my status, and it's like constantly checking Tinder to see if a girl has messaged me back. As with Tinder, the feedback from NOMIS has been bitterly disappointing, and there hasn't been any activity for two weeks. On today's check I see a new entry: *Initial assessment – Cat C*. Underneath is an empty box marked *Final result*. The officer has no idea what this means, but it doesn't sound positive.

Prisoners are eligible for Cat D when they have less than 24 months to serve. I now have 23 months to go, so there must be another reason why I'm being pushed back. The security categorisation is a measure of our risk. I've toadied non-stop for seven months, so they can't believe that I'm too risky for open conditions. The prospect of being kept at Cat C – and stuck in Wandsworth – is too bleak to contemplate.

I track down Miss Black, who used to work at OMU, and ask her to pull up my NOMIS page. She sucks her teeth as she looks at it, like a builder viewing some dodgy plasterwork.

'That's a bloody confusing entry. It looks like you're getting a Cat C, but you won't know for sure until they fill in that final box.'

'Why am I being rejected? I've got less than twenty-four months to go.'

'Have you got any court appearances coming up?'

'Just my final confiscation hearing.'

'They'll probably make you Cat C so you stay in Wandsworth to attend court.'

My blood turns to ice. 'But my confiscation has all been agreed. The judge said I didn't even need to attend the final hearing.'

'The system doesn't know that. Get something in writing saying you don't need to turn up, or you'll probably get stuck in this craphole.'

I call my solicitor, but he's too busy to talk to me. I leave a message with a paralegal, asking for a letter confirming that the judge was happy with me moving prison. My solicitor then sends a curt response, refusing to write the required letter. After several calls, I finally get through to him.

'I just need a simple letter explaining what happened at the last hearing.'

'No.'

'Why not?'

'I won't lie to the prison on your behalf.'

'I don't want you to lie. Just confirm that the judge had no problem with me moving prison.'

'That's not what he said.'

This really throws me, as my solicitor wasn't even at the hearing. 'I promise you, he did.'

'It's not the kind of thing a judge would say. I won't be part of you tricking Wandsworth to get to open prison. You'll have to stay there until you've paid your confiscation.'

This is complete bollocks, as Wandsworth OMU regularly give Cat Ds to prisoners with outstanding confiscations.

'I just need an accurate record of what was said in court,' I say through gritted teeth. 'Can you get a transcript?'

'It's not worth it. This is really grating on me, Chris.' He eventually agrees to write a note about the hearing, but refuses to mention what Beddoe had indicated about moving prisons. It doesn't arrive for a fortnight, thereby rendering it completely useless.

This lawyer used to be all smiles, presumably salivating over the fees he'd earn from my case. In fairness, he worked extremely hard before and during my trial. Now that it's all over and I'm stuck in prison, however, it seems he's content to leave me hanging. Discussing it with other inmates, I'm told this is par for the course.

29 January

My outlook isn't helped by seeing wholly unsuitable prisoners getting handed Cat Ds like sweets on Halloween. Marsh, an amiable young rascal, bounces into the cell grinning inanely.

'Just got my Cat D, innit!'

'How the fuck did that happen?'

'OMU just sent me a slip. Gonna have *bare* party at Ford.'

Marsh has recently had a fight in the showers, got into a slanging match with the SO, and was caught stealing a screw's Thermos mug. OMU have overlooked these trifling issues and decided that he is the right material for open prison. He lasts just three weeks at Ford, before he's kicked right back to Wandsworth.

Later on, we are paid a visit by Deputy Governor Gallagher, who has got involved in Gary's case. This is good news, as she is known to be efficient and compassionate. She's received a letter from Gary's mum castigating Wandsworth for misleading her family about his release. Gallagher has drafted a response, and I'm pleasantly surprised by the tone. Most prison communications are written in bad eighties management-speak, but her letter is breathtakingly frank and firmly blames her colleagues in OMU. She makes it clear that none of this debacle is Gary's fault, and that he's behaved extremely responsibly throughout. She promises to do his 21 February recategorisation personally, so that it definitely happens on time. Given that most recats are running a month behind, this is an extremely welcome bonus.

At the start of January, both Gary and I were expecting to leave Wandsworth within a couple of weeks. We both underestimated OMU's capacity to demolish our plans, though I'm impressed at how we've rallied in response. Gary has at least won a partial victory, but my own future remains mired in uncertainty.

10

Despair and Dancing Queen

In which my psychology studies open a chilling window into the prison's mental health crisis. I witness relentless self-harm, and become completely desensitised to the bloodletting.

Things I learn:

1) How spice is getting into the prison

2) Rehabilitation programmes can actually increase crime

3) The downsides of prostitutes keeping diaries

Gary flies the nest, but my wings are painfully clipped by OMU.

30 January

At 1 a.m. I'm asked to see a prisoner who I've heard is pretty excitable. I first call on another Listener up the landing. 'Jake. Jake! Can you do this Listen with me?' Jake is a former professional boxer, with a lethal right hook, and he eventually agrees to be my wingman. Inside the Listener Suite is a large, agitated prisoner who announces that he hasn't taken his antipsychotic medication. Before I can ask why, he starts demolishing what's left of the furniture. Moments like this are really something. The adrenaline goes into overdrive, and a voice in my head says, 'Well, we're really living now aren't we?' Thanks to Jake's presence, I don't come to any harm, and I swiftly call the night screw.

'What was his problem?' he asks.

'This guy doesn't require a Listener, he needs a fucking exorcist.'

That way madness lies

The MoJ won't publish how much of the prison population has mental health problems, but it's estimated at around 50%.[1] Bickers once asserted that the figure in Wandsworth was 90%.[2] The Listeners were often the last line of defence, and we were constantly dealing with people who should blatantly have been in psychiatric care. One evening I sat with a rotund Ghanaian called Charlie, who was in the middle of a psychotic episode, ranting and screaming as though he was speaking in tongues, until his mania finally dropped.

'I'm so sorry, I'm so sorry,' he kept saying.

'It's all right, mate,' I reassured him. 'All in a night's work.' By this stage I had got used to behaviour that would have completely freaked me out just a few months before. I promised to write a medical application for Charlie demanding he see the mental health team, and pressed the cell bell. Several night screws soon rocked up. They took one look at Charlie and pinned him against the wall.

'What have you taken?' one officer screamed. 'What drugs have you got on you?'

'I done nothing, swear down!' Charlie stammered.

'What's that then?' the officer shouted, pointing to the foam around Charlie's lips.

I gently raised a hand. 'Um, he's got paranoid schizophrenia and has, quite literally, been foaming at the mouth. I can promise you he hasn't taken any drugs.'

The mental health crisis was most starkly illustrated by the spiralling suicide rate. MoJ statistics revealed that self-inflicted deaths had reached a record high in 2016: 119 inmates killed themselves, one every three days.[3] In 2015, Wandsworth had the highest suicide rate in the country.[4] The Royal College of Psychiatrists blamed the figures on the swingeing cuts to mental health services. Professor Pamela Taylor said: 'Mental health teams are struggling to help prisoners in desperate need. In many cases there is no one available to escort prisoners to in-prison clinics from time to time, even when a psychiatrist goes to a prisoner's cell, as there are not enough prison officers present and the cell door can't be unlocked for safety reasons.'

Increasing staff shortages, coupled with incessant bang-up, means that prisons are morphing into warehouses for the mentally ill, steering them towards suicide out of public view.

1 February

The verdicts are finally in on the big HBOS trial that has been going on in my Southwark courtroom. The BBC reports that six defendants have been found guilty of a £230 million fraud. Over the course of several years, a corrupt HBOS banker, Lynden Scourfield, forced small businesses to use a preferred restructuring firm. This outfit was run by a shark called David Mills, who asset-stripped the businesses, forcing many into bankruptcy. All the while Mills was paying huge bribes back to Scourfield, which were spunked, quite literally, on sex parties with hookers.

A few hours later, I'm doing the inductions, and in stumble the HBOS bankers I've just seen on the news. I'm surprised they're here so quickly, as they won't be sentenced for a few more days. Apparently their lawyers begged for them to spend the intervening days with their families. Judge Beddoe just peered down his Dickensian nose and sniffed, 'The party's over' before sending them straight to Wandsworth. This makes me quietly thankful I was bailed between my conviction and sentencing. According to prison rumours, they had a farcical arrival at reception. I thought my bang-up bag was excessive, but one of the HBOS bankers turned up with a massive Louis Vuitton trunk. It needed two screws just to pick it up.

When I first arrived, I naturally gravitated to other white-collar criminals, and fell into the trap of thinking that our crimes were somehow less harmful than those committed by other inmates. Reading how lives were shattered by the HBOS gang, I now feel pretty disgusted at being part of the same criminal fraternity. Mills, the ringleader, had a fleet of luxury cars, one with the personalised number plate MIILSEY.[5] He also owned a £2 million yacht, which he'd actually called *The Powder Monkey*.[6] His wife was also prosecuted, and she struggled during cross-examination. The prosecutor asked about their palatial country home, Toddenham Hall. Mrs Mills sniffily corrected him: 'Actually, it's Toddenham House,' which apparently didn't go down well with the jury. I ask Mills what length of sentence he thinks he's facing.

'I reckon I'm looking at around eight,' he replies bullishly.

I nearly laugh out loud. My squalid crime was a fraction the size of their scheme, and we didn't bankrupt family businesses and blow the proceeds on call girls. Beddoe gave me five years, so Mills isn't walking away with anything in single figures.

A few days later, they return to Southwark. Mills is given 15 years, one of the longest ever sentences for fraud. Judge Beddoe then turns his ire on Scourfield. 'I do not know when or how David Mills got his hold on you, but that he did. He is the devil to whom you sold your soul, for sex, for luxury trips – for bling and for swag.'[7]

Scourfield only receives 11 years. He earlier sensibly pleaded guilty, as the evidence was pretty overwhelming. One of the prostitutes had kept a diary of their sex parties, which was read out during the trial. She noted that Scourfield had 'movie star looks', though sadly for him, she was referring to Danny de Vito.[8] Michael Bancroft, a doddery banker in his seventies, gets 10 years. He'll have to serve five, but given his frail health, this may turn into a life sentence.

2 February

An emergency whistle goes off on G Wing. I stand on the balcony to watch the mayhem, as all the nearby officers race to the scene. It's a remarkably inefficient system, as nobody initially knows where the problem is. A dozen overweight officers hurtle around the Twos like sugar-crazed toddlers, screaming, 'WHERE IS IT?'

Eventually a screw pops up from the Ones. 'Panic over! It's only a self-harmer.' The alarm was sounded by a new civilian worker who'd seen a prisoner cutting up for the first time and hit the alarm. As soon as they hear this, the officers all relax and stroll away gossiping.

I end up witnessing so much self-harm that I become completely desensitised to it. One afternoon I'm called to a prisoner's cell, and I can guess what his problem is from the stench, even before I open the flap. There's blood and faeces up the walls, and all the furniture's been trashed. The gaunt, bearded inmate is stripped to the waist and has got deep welts all over his arms and torso.

'Got any burn, bruv?' he says through a large number of missing teeth.

'I don't smoke.'

'Go to next cell, I beg you. My brethren will tick me some burn, innit.'

I put on a cod New York accent. 'No can do, the captain will have my badge.'

He doesn't get the joke. 'Get me burn or I'll cut up.'

The first time someone said this, I really lost the plot. Now I'm completely impervious to such threats, and deal with the trauma by cracking increasingly tasteless jokes. It's a necessary defence mechanism to stop myself breaking down over the relentless pain and suffering.

Do no self-harm

At an official level, there was a complete indifference towards self-harm in Wandsworth. The prison even stopped counting the number of incidents. The Bishop of Southwark asked the MoJ how many instances of self-harm there were in Wandsworth in 2016. The government gave the number as 118.[9] For the whole year. This figure was patently rubbish. I personally saw a dozen inmates cutting up each week, and I only did Listening in a small part of the prison.

I strongly suspect that the authorities downplayed the extent of self-harm to avoid the obvious conclusion that it was caused by the crippling bang-up. I came across some compelling evidence for this link in my psychology studies. In the 1950s and 60s, Harry Harlow conducted experiments into parent–child attachment in an effort to understand whether the parental bond in humans was innate or learned. In some of these experiments he took infant monkeys from their mothers and locked them in solitary confinement for two years. The primates performed endless rocking and pacing actions, became incapable of socialising with others, and violently attacked and bit their own bodies. This could just as easily describe half the residents of G Wing after a long lockdown, and shows how prolonged isolation can cause self-harm. Modern laws would prohibit Harlow from repeating his experiment today, but it's still acceptable to inflict this terrible treatment on human beings.

3 February

I have a visit with Lottie and Kit. While Lottie queues up for coffee, Kit sits on my lap, clasping my hand.

'When I'm at Mummy's house, I miss you,' he says. 'A lot.'

I kiss him on the head so he can't see me crying. I have to get out of this place, but the inaction of my lawyer combined with the incompetence of OMU threatens to trap me here.

As I return to the wing, an officer hands me a slip: *RECATEGORISATION NOTIFICATION: OFFENDER TO REMAIN AT C CAT.* There's no reason given whatsoever.

'Fuck me,' he exclaims, peering over my shoulder. 'If a sniffer like you can't get a Cat D, then no one can.'

My panic quickly turns into relief, as the bad news at least hands me a sliver of control. I type a caustic letter to OMU, demanding to know why I've been kept at Cat C. I also reflect that writing endless recat appeals for other prisoners has provided me with excellent training for my own battle. I attach the letter to two general apps, a COMP1 and a COMP2, and copy in the IMB, the highly ineffectual monitoring board. I also muster the support of Danielle, Linda, Miss Black and Officer O'Reilly, and ask them all to find out why I've been knocked back.

4 February

Governor Bickers has recently appeared before the House of Commons Justice Committee, along with the governors of the other 'trailblazer' reform prisons, to give evidence about progress in Wandsworth. A friend has posted me the transcript, which makes for highly entertaining reading. What Bickers' testimony lacks in accuracy, it more than makes up for in enthusiasm.

'The other thing we did early in the summer was to change our regime to make it consistent and deliverable ... In reality it meant that more of our men got more time out of cell than they were getting previously ... We were able to get men engaged with education and work consistently for the first time in a very long time.'[10] This is complete codswallop. The regime has been continually scaled back since July, resulting in much less time out of the cells. The five main wings have been on emergency lockdown for months.

Bickers goes on: 'My sense of success for us will be when I see prison officers sitting on the ends of beds helping men read and write letters.' The thought of Officer Moss sitting at the end of my bed still gives me nightmares.

'If you are a member of staff walking along A Wing today, would you feel significantly different? The staff would say it has improved a bit.' I recently spoke to the SO on A Wing, which he describes as a 'fucking war zone'. The *Mirror* later publishes a secret recording of a Wandsworth officer warning that the prison is about to 'go up like dynamite.'[11] This is not mentioned in Bickers' testimony.

'We might have this wonderful cascade of positivity, but, specifically for Wandsworth, staff can see it coming, they can probably feel the change in some ways.' The only thing that's cascading in Wandsworth is the water from the flooded cells on G Wing.

Bickers can't resist flying the flag for the Purple Army: 'Currently we have 27 men going through a training programme to be peer advisers working entirely within the prison.' In reality we are down to just three of us in peer advice training on Trinity, and we've yet to advise any peers. There still hasn't been a single lesson on the mains, as the officers refuse to unlock the trainees.

All of Bickers' questionable claims are accepted by the politicians without a murmur. One of the MPs calls him the 'crème de la crème of prison governorship', and his evidence quickly becomes the official line. The fiction about the Purple Army is later regurgitated in the Commons by a former prisons minister, Andrew Selous: 'I commend what is happening in Wandsworth prison, where the inspirational governor, Ian Bickers, has taken 50 prisoners with

Level 3 qualifications – he is paying them and has given them a uniform … That is an excellent initiative.'[12]

This illustrates the difficulty in effectively scrutinising prisons. Everyone who could contradict Bickers' testimony either works for him or is behind bars. Lying to Parliament is a serious offence, but I don't think he was being intentionally misleading. He only spends two days a week in Wandsworth, and obviously has little idea of what's going on in his own prison.

We've now been a reform prison for eight months, and there are a few signs of its wasted potential. The Graffiti Project promises to nurture artistic talent, while brightening up our surroundings. Sid, one of the Annexe posse, is an experienced street artist, and has been given permission to do some 'throw-ups' on E Wing. His vivid paintings are all based on inspirational quotes, such as 'Only in the darkness can you see the stars.' The artwork makes an immeasurable difference, but unfortunately nobody consulted the E Wing governor. He takes one look at Sid's oeuvre and orders it to be obliterated by a coat of white paint.

The Graffiti Project is more successful on Trinity. One afternoon we head out to the exercise yard and see an explosion of chaotic colour on the far wall. Close inspection reveals that it's actually the word 'Wandsworth', with each letter drawn by a different inmate. A little launch event is organised, attended by some senior officers and a photographer from the local paper. It's only when they're all assembled that they realise nobody has unlocked the prisoners who did the actual painting.

5 February

My mother has been taken severely ill in Sri Lanka. I find out while calling my brother about something else entirely. It's impossible to speak to my folks on the phone, and I spend hours paralysed by my sheer impotence. My distress stems from a total lack of control over my mother's health. Thankfully my father has a tendency to over-insure, so my mum gets the best medical care. It turns out to be a nasty strain of encephalitis, and she slowly starts to recover.

Control freaks

Much has been written about whether we have a hand in our own destiny, but at least in the outside world it *feels* as if we have some involvement in our fate. Prison not only robs inmates of control, but also denies them the illusion of agency. They are constantly reminded that they have no impact on anything, which has long been cited as a cause of mental illness.

In 1971, the experimental psychologist Jay Weiss did a series of experiments on rats. He first trained them to avoid electric shocks by pressing a lever. He then changed the system so that they could no longer control the shocks. The rats initially became hyper vigilant, pressing the lever wildly and trying to control the shock even when it wasn't being delivered. The image of rats pressing inactive levers is chillingly reminiscent of rows of lights outside cells flashing as call bells routinely go unanswered. Weiss's rats then descended into a state of ruinous anxiety, caused by their constantly activated stress responses. They eventually realised that they couldn't prevent the ongoing shocks, and stopped pressing the lever. The animals then became completely inactive and unable to learn any new strategies for avoiding the shocks.[13] Psychologists call this state 'learned helplessness'.

The prison environment enforced learned helplessness on an industrial scale, as we lost every last vestige of agency. Some people tried to re-exert control in any way they could, which was yet another cause of self-harm. It explained why many prisoners kept their cells brutally spotless, while others spent hours obsessing over their canteen orders.

6 February

I get another slip explaining why I've been refused my Cat D:

1) Apparently I have a new case starting at Southwark Crown Court later in February. Thanks to my lawyer's lack of action, OMU are unaware that it's just a five-minute confiscation hearing that I don't even have to attend.

2) 'Offender cannot go to open conditions as he has too long to serve.' Maths is evidently not OMU's strong point. Prisoners are eligible for open conditions at 24 months, and I have currently just over 22 months to go.

3) The last one is a bit of a curveball. OMU thinks I'm unsuitable for open prison as I'm a 'persistent and prolific offender', which is difficult to square with the fact that this is my first conviction.

This slip is actually quite heartening. OMU's reasons for rejecting my Cat D are demonstrably bollocks, so it should be easy to win an appeal. I've already booked a slot on this week's surgery to make my case.

8 February

I lie awake all night, terrified of screwing up my recategorisation. In the morning, I head down to Governor Daniels' office, and wait nervously for my OMU slot. Further down the landing I can see Sally, the head of the activities department, trying to coerce prisoners into a focus group. Several civil servants have just arrived, but only one inmate has turned up to meet them.

Daniels arrives 20 minutes late. He's clearly hung-over, and clutching a mug of lukewarm tea. As soon as he opens his door, I dart into his office and launch into my carefully prepared spiel.

'Next week's court date isn't a new case. It's just a tiny confiscation hearing. I don't even need to be there.'

Daniels' hangover actually works in my favour, as he starts agreeing with me just to speed things up. 'OK, that shouldn't be a problem. How much is your confiscation going to be?'

'A hundred grand.'

He sniffs. 'That's bugger all. Why did you get five years?'

'Judge Beddoe.'

'Ah, right. Well, a hundred K confiscation won't keep you here. Put something in writing confirming that figure, and you'll get your Cat D on appeal.'

I float back to H Wing feeling better than I can remember in my entire life. It's as if the prison doors are creaking open, and the world outside is brighter and more magical than ever before. In the cell I turn on the radio just as Abba's 'Dancing Queen' comes on. I decide that this will be my Shawshank moment, and crank up the volume. It's freeflow, and dozens of inmates stroll past and start to sing along. Officer O'Reilly belts out the chorus, and even does a couple of twirls.

11 February

I'm called to the Listener Suite, and meet a huge Asian lad called Ash. He's completely bald, with a massive beard, and has severe learning difficulties. He keeps breaking off the conversation and babbling meaninglessly, then suddenly punching his hand shouting 'BOOM! That's where the money is!' Ash regularly self-harms and has attempted suicide on several occasions.

'How long have you got left?' I ask.

'Dunno, bruv, dunno. I'm IPP, innit. Gonna keep me here forever.'

Ash's problems stem from the fact that he doesn't have a release date. He's one of many prisoners who are serving a sentence of Imprisonment for Public Protection. He received his sentence back in 2007, and was given a minimum tariff of just one year. He is still in prison 10 years later, and has lost a decade of his life thanks to the Kafkaesque nature of the parole system. In order for him to be released, he has to prove that he's no longer a threat to the public. This is an extraordinarily hard thing to do, especially if, like Ash, you have learning difficulties and are functionally illiterate. He has been instructed to do a specific offender behaviour course to demonstrate that he's reduced his risk. But despite the plethora of rehabilitation programmes in Wandsworth, the prison doesn't run the course that he needs to complete. He's unable to move to a jail that runs the necessary programme, so he's stuck in a horrific limbo. He simply has no idea when, if ever, he will get out, which is having a catastrophic impact on his mental health. This becomes a vicious cycle: the uncertainty causes greater behavioural problems, which are then used against him in his parole hearings. The longer he's inside, the less chance he has of getting out.

It's almost impossible to empathise with Ash's nightmare predicament. I've frequently struggled to get my head round my own sentence, but at least I know when I'm getting out. My release date sits as an unmovable beacon in the future, pulling me inexorably forwards even in my darkest moments. IPP prisoners like Ash have no such magnet, and instead drown in a sea of lethal uncertainty.

Eternal unrest

IPP sentences were introduced in 2003 by the then Home Secretary David Blunkett, and were only intended for serious violent offences. The judge would issue a short minimum tariff, but the prisoner would stay incarcerated until they could prove they were no longer a risk. The Home Office anticipated just 900 offenders with IPP sentences, but by 2010 the number had hit 10,000. In 2012, these unjust punishments were abolished, but this wasn't retrospective, so thousands of IPP offenders remained stuck in the system.[14] As of August 2017, there were 3,300 IPP prisoners incarcerated without a release date. Nick Hardwick, the former Chief Inspector of Prisons and head of the Parole Board, called IPPs a 'blot on the system. The level of suicide, assault, and self-harm is unacceptably high.'[15] The Prisons and Probations Ombudsman found that IPP offenders had

> a far higher chance of committing suicide than normal prisoners.[16]
> Even David Blunkett admitted, 'We certainly got the implementation
> wrong. The consequence of bringing that Act in has led, in some
> cases, to an injustice and I regret that.'[17]

13 February

I have become quietly obsessed with the plethora of offending behaviour courses on offer at Wandsworth. I don't actually have to complete any myself, as my crime isn't deemed sufficiently serious, but prisoners convicted for drugs or violence are barred from open prison until they've completed certain rehabilitation programmes. Chief among these is Victim Awareness, which promises to 'explore the effects of crime on victims, offenders, and the community, and discuss what it would mean to take responsibility for their personal actions'.

Out of curiosity, I slip into one of the Victim Awareness sessions. It's run by a young man called Gideon, who looks utterly terrified standing in front of 15 hardened prisoners. He tells the story of a sinful tax collector called Zac, who unsurprisingly sees the error of his ways. This is a rehash of the parable of Zaccheus, and I realise that the programme is run by a Christian charity. Much of it is a ham-fisted attempt to turn prisoners towards Jesus, which feels slightly unethical given that I'm the only person here through choice.

That said, the assembled prisoners all enthusiastically engage with the programme. Gideon asks for someone to publicly reflect on their own crimes, and Chaz, a career criminal I vaguely know, quickly volunteers.

'I used to be a right scumbag, God's truth. I didn't give two fucks about no one. But thanks to Gideon and the Victim Awareness course, I now understand the full impact of my offending. Not just on my victims, but on wider society and my own family. I can honestly say that I'm never going to commit crime again.'

He sits down to heavy applause, while Gideon looks like he's about to be canonised. I tell Chaz that I'm impressed with his brutal honesty. He gives me a wink, and whispers, 'Load of old crap, innit. Got to play the game to get my Cat D.' I later ask him if he's learnt anything from the course. 'Loads,' he replies. 'I picked up all the lingo that they like to hear – "offending pathways", "mitigating risk", all that shit. You trot them buzzwords out to OMU, and then you're off to Ford in a heartbeat.' Chaz's performance will help unlock his Cat D, even though he's already planning his next crime.

Would I lie to you?

There is a gaping paradox at the heart of most offending behaviour programmes. Prisoners are forced to engage with certain courses in order to get better conditions, and will therefore happily admit to killing JFK if it means they can go to open prison.

Official studies show that the majority of these programmes have no impact on reoffending whatsoever. Forensic psychologist Dr Robert Forde is a fierce critic. 'I first thought these courses would be good and recommended a few people to do them. It was only later I began to question the evidence and looked it up. I was horrified because there appeared to be almost no evidence at all. And what evidence there was didn't seem to be very supportive.'[18]

Some of these courses actually make criminal behaviour worse. The Sex Offender Treatment Programme ran in British prisons for 20 years, costing over £100 million. A 2012 study found that prisoners taking the course were more likely to reoffend than those who were just locked in their cells. This was because the programme normalised their horrific behaviour, and taught them how to emulate empathy rather than experience it. The MoJ sat on the report for five years while the author was bullied out of a job.[19] The study was eventually leaked to the *Mail on Sunday* in 2017, Liz Truss was castigated for suppressing the report, and the programme was eventually abandoned.[20] Another study showed that mindfulness courses, which are bizarrely quite prolific in British prisons, were also likely to increase reoffending. It was argued that the techniques encouraged prisoners to avoid taking responsibility for their actions, which could make criminality more likely.[21]

14 February

The BBC is heavily trailing tonight's *Panorama*, which is an investigation into HMP Northumberland.[22] It's been secretly filmed by a reporter who trained as a prison officer and worked undercover in the jail for two months. Gary and I tune in, and it's a riveting watch. The prison is saturated with drugs and the reporter finds two kilos of spice on his very first day. One of the officers actually passes out from a spice attack, which Gary finds hysterical.

'They don't fuck about up north! Even the screws are knocking back the spice.'

The hapless screw claims that he collapsed after inhaling second-hand smoke. I find this highly implausible. For months I've been walking around G Wing, where everyone is permanently blazing spice, and I've never had so much as a head rush. The drug culture at HMP Northumberland will horrify the public, but I suspect their OMU will be inundated with requests to be transferred into the prison. I'm more shocked that the reporter spent nine weeks undercover without being rumbled. This means that he sneaked in a secret camera every day without being searched, which could easily have been drugs instead.

15 February

My final confiscation hearing is due to take place tomorrow. The judge agreed for me to appear by video link, but there's no indication that this has been arranged. I call my lawyer repeatedly, but only get through to a paralegal. She keeps calling it 'video clink', which doesn't fill me with confidence.

I'm about to end the call when she adds as an afterthought, 'Of course the hearing's been postponed a few days.'

'Really? Why?'

'I think it's because it's been delayed.'

This sends me into a complete tailspin. I track down the reception orderly, who says that my property box has been pulled for tomorrow, meaning that the prison still intends to send me to court. I call Lottie and ask her to email my lawyer, explaining that Wandsworth is planning to dispatch me to Southwark.

Hours later, Lottie gets a testy response. My solicitor insists that the hearing has been postponed, and indicates that Wandsworth won't try to take me to court the next day.

The next morning a screw opens our door at 6 a.m.

'Get dressed, Atkins, you're going to court.'

'My hearing's been pushed back.'

'You're on the list. We're sending you to Southwark.'

'There's no fucking hearing. I'm not going.' I return to bed to cement my position.

'You'll need to sign a form,' he flaps.

'Whatever.'

Ten minutes later, he returns. 'The photocopier's broken. I'll just tell them, er, something.'

'You do that.' I lie awake cursing my lawyer.

19 February

My admin services are still in great demand. Today I'm visited by

Giggs, a likeable young tearaway who's recently been refused his Cat D, perhaps understandably given that he's the most prolific drug dealer on the wing.

Sceptical about its likely success, I type a letter to OMU. It argues that Giggs has been fully rehabilitated, and that he can be completely trusted in open prison.

Tall stories

I wrote out hundreds of applications, letters and forms for various inmates. As well as alleviating the boredom, it gave me an opportunity to help prisoners who lacked the basic literacy to advocate their own cause. Occasionally I would include statements I knew to be quite untrue. I had few qualms about this at the time, as it didn't seem any different from defence lawyers proposing unbelievable scenarios in court. I had little loyalty to the prison system, which routinely dispensed unfair and arbitrary decisions. Providing admin services also ensured I never experienced any violence, as I was known as a useful person to have onside.

Giggs is delighted with my work and offers me a variety of narcotics as payment. I politely decline, and instead ask about his dealing operation.

He tells me that he mainly trades in spice. He buys in a batch of 'eight balls', which are about two grams each, and splits these in half into a 'benz'. These are then subdivided into 10 'five shots', which are the standard doses that he sells about the jail.

'A five shot from anyone else is only good for two spliffs. *My* five shots gonna give you four spliffs – guaranteed.'

This competitive edge has enabled Giggs to. corner the Trinity market, and the profits are phenomenal. Outside prison, an ounce of spice costs £150, which has a value inside of around £2,800. Giggs prefers to be paid in packs of burn. His customers give him tobacco they've ordered off the canteen, and he is quietly stockpiling in preparation for the prison smoking ban, which is due to start in June.

'Price of burn gonna go up tenfold, innit. Man gonna make *mad* profit, you get me.'

I'm extremely impressed. 'Have you ever considered a career at Goldman Sachs?'

Giggs stashes his burn supplies in other prisoners' cells to spread the risk. He'll ask a friend to sit on five packs, and give them a sixth to smoke as payment.

'How are the drugs coming into prison?' I ask quietly.

'Got a bent screw on the mains, innit.' Giggs would never risk using a drone, and sees a corrupt officer as far more reliable. This view is supported by a Radio 4 documentary this week – *The Prison Contraband Crisis* – which claims that the bulk of smuggled goods come in with staff.[23]

The doc challenges the government narrative that drones are responsible for spice in prisons. The programme interviews a former screw who was caught bringing in drugs, and who claims to have been corrupted by a scheming prisoner. The ex-officer describes how the Machiavellian inmate alighted on the fact that he liked football, which was apparently enough to lure him to the dark side. Naked greed, coupled with the miserly wages paid to prison staff, seemingly played no part in his downfall whatsoever.

Puppets on a string

I watched a lot of news coverage about prisons, and 95% of the time inmates were presented as voiceless, zombified simpletons, stumbling between self-harming and spice attacks. But occasionally it served the authorities' interests to elevate us to veritable Moriartys, who could coerce clueless prison officers into our devious schemes. A female officer was caught having an intimate relationship with a prisoner and sending him racy texts. The judge decided that she was 'terribly compromised and vulnerable to being manipulated'.[24] Another female screw at HMP Whitemoor was busted for sneaking in spice for a convicted murderer. In court she pleaded that she was under the spell of some kind of evil genius, and got away with a suspended sentence.[25] The judge didn't buy the more obvious motive that she wanted the money to pay for an extra week in Lanzarote.

22 February

I'm settling in for the evening when Mini Me opens our door.

'Can you do a Listen?'

'Not my night. It's Faisal's shift.'

'I just went to unlock Faisal but he was spiced to fuck. I'm not letting him out like that. I thought all you Listeners were clean.'

Being wasted on duty is a real no-no. The Trinity Listeners generally enjoy a good relationship with the officers, which will be squandered if they think we're spiced up. The screws could easily stop us seeing contacts, leading to the same desperate situation as on the mains. The problem is that I don't know what to do with this information. Grasses are not popular in prison, and usually get moved to the nonce wing for their own protection.

23 February

There is a bizarre interview with Liz Truss in today's paper: 'She is a big fan of movies about prison; her favourite is *The Shawshank Redemption*. And she wants to harness a little of the spirit of the 1994 thriller. "It shows prisons can be very difficult places where people have a hard time and are separated from their family. But they can also be places of hope where people decide to do things differently.'"[26] This makes me wonder if Truss has watched the whole film. I've seen it dozens of times, and Shawshank prison does indeed 'do things differently': an inmate is beaten to death on his first night, Tim Robbins' character is repeatedly gang-raped, and another prisoner is shot dead by the head officer. Shawshank is so full of hope that Robbins digs through 40 feet of concrete to escape.

Truss then goes on *The Andrew Marr Show*, where she's asked if the nation's prisons are in crisis.[27] She replies extremely carefully. 'There is a very difficult situation in our prisons.' She tortuously avoids using the word 'crisis', and instead doggedly tries to accentuate the positives. 'We do have a plan, we're recruiting more officers.' She doesn't mention that officers are quitting almost as fast as they're being hired. During her tenure a recruitment drive to employ more prison officers saw just 22 extra staff in all the government-run prisons in London.[28]

She blunders on. 'Every prison officer, they will have a case load of six offenders that they are supervising. They're encouraging them to do the English and maths they need to get off drugs. And that number works.'

Away with the fairies

One of the great myths of the prison system was that every inmate was individually supervised by a 'personal officer'. They were purportedly responsible for our welfare and progression, and we could approach them with any problems or concerns.[29] In reality, nobody ever heard from a personal officer, and they became a running joke. Whenever we were confronted by cancelled S&Ds, delayed visits, lost post, broken phones or freezing showers, we'd shake our heads and say we'd be raising it with our personal

---

officer. I once saw a sign asking: *Struggling in prison? Speak to your personal officer. If you don't know who your personal officer is, then speak to Officer Donnelly.* Needless to say, Officer Donnelly had left the prison several years previously.

One afternoon, Jack, one of my regular Listener contacts, popped in to say goodbye as he was about to be released. He revealed that he'd just met his personal officer. It was a very short encounter; the officer just asked Jack if he had any problems. Jack said he didn't, as he was being released in 48 hours, so they shook hands and said goodbye. This smacked of a tick-box exercise, so the authorities could claim that prisoners had the support of a personal officer, even if it was just to hold the door open as they left.

Liz Truss ends her TV interview by insisting that she's in the job for the long haul. 'This will take time, it's not something you can sort out in weeks or months. But I'm absolutely determined to deal with that.' Three months later, she is replaced as Justice Secretary.[30]

24 February

It's finally time for my last confiscation hearing. I have completely failed to attend by video link, so I will have to go in person. I barely sleep. Around 4 a.m., Gary farts loudly, and I sit bolt upright shouting 'Hello?!' Gary finds this terribly funny. I don't.

At half five, I rise to get dressed. I've previously discussed my sartorial choices with Connor, who is a seasoned veteran of the dock. I'm loath to wear my court clothes again, and Connor has assured me that informal attire will not prejudice the outcome. However, he did receive his 15-year sentence in a hoodie, so perhaps I shouldn't heed his advice. I pull on a tracksuit anyway, and am led through the darkened wings.

I'm put in the holding cell with the other prisoners bound for Southwark. One guy, Taki, is completely off his trolley. He keeps kicking the door, howling that he doesn't need to go to court. Five screws appear in blue gloves, which is a sign that things are about to get messy. I stand back while Taki is forcibly carried out to the van.

I'm then pushed into a cubicle and strip-searched. The reception staff are all on high alert after a recent breakout in Liverpool. A murderer has just escaped from a hospital visit, after a gun-wielding pair came to his aid.[31] One of the officers confiscates my pen. I point out that the Liverpudlian accomplices were armed with gun, knife and pepper spray, not plastic biros, but it does no good. I'm put in the van, and we drive across central London.

The journey is less unsettling than last time, despite Taki kicking the van constantly and screaming 'I NOT GO COURT, I NOT GO COURT!' We soon arrive at Southwark, where he absorbs everyone's attention. My hearing isn't until the afternoon, and I'm led down to a kennel. I've brought some psychology work, but I can't actually do any of it as I don't have a pen. It's pretty frustrating, but would be disastrous if I was actually trying to mount a defence.

My only entertainment is Taki down the corridor. He's still hooting demonically, and keeps thumping his kennel door. The court staff respond by swearing and laughing at him. After an hour, one of the guards sheepishly admits that he has indeed been brought to Southwark by accident. Learning that he was right all along does not lighten Taki's outlook.

Hot boxes

Whatever the complaints about conditions in Wandsworth, the treatment of prisoners being transported to court was often far worse. A 2015 report found vulnerable people being left to languish for 10 hours in squalid graffiti-covered courtroom cells. Custody staff from contractor GEOAmey described one transgender suspect as 'the thing', and told detainees that the only right they had was the 'right to breathe'.[32] This right was withheld from Rafal Sochacki, who died of heatstroke at Westminster Magistrates court in 2017, after he was held for five hours in a cell on one of the hottest days of the year.[33]

At 2 p.m. I'm led up to Court 5 once more. Judge Beddoe expresses frustration that I've been physically produced, given that he expressly said I didn't need to be there. I give an exaggerated thumbs-up from the dock. Beddoe reads out the confiscation order and prosecution costs, which together come to over £200,000. The bad news is that I will now have to sell my house to pay this demand. The good news is that I can finally take these figures to OMU, which should convince them to let me out of Wandsworth.

25 February

I come back to the cell to find the radio on full blast and Gary dancing round the room.

'Just got my fucking Cat D!' he yells, and we have a proper man hug. My reaction is intensely bittersweet – elation that our efforts have prevailed, mixed with deep sadness that I'm losing a close friend.

Gary joins the gaggle of Cat D inmates on Trinity who are all trying to get to Ford. OMU deliberately keep lags ignorant of upcoming transfers, to prevent anyone arranging an escape. The recent breakout in Liverpool has made the authorities even more tight-lipped, and the information vacuum is filled with speculation and gossip. A primary source of confusion is Gerald, the reception orderly. His job involves finding the property boxes of inmates who are due to be shipped out. For a suitable fee, he will tip off prisoners that they're about to depart. Unfortunately, he also smokes industrial quantities of weed, so his travel information is as accurate as Southern Rail. I sometimes wonder if his half-baked intel is secretly orchestrated by OMU, all part of a cunning misinformation campaign. It's pretty pointless keeping Cat D prisoners in the dark anyway, given that they're being dispatched to open prison. If they have itchy feet, they can simply wait until they get to Ford and abscond on the first night.

There are only a few days left to appeal against my recategorisation, and I desperately need to tell OMU how much my confiscation is. I assumed this would be a simple task, but my solicitor has just sent me a letter with the wrong figures on it. If it's seen by OMU, they'll think I owe more than I do and reject my appeal.

26 February

Nigel, the last of the original White Collar Club, is finally going home on Friday. He sits in my cell enthusing about the steak and wine he'll consume on his first night of freedom. I really want to be happy for him, but wish he'd bugger off and stop tormenting me. Out of sight and out of mind is the only way to survive without my former luxuries.

Other inmates get very stressed as they approach their release date. Prisoners being released without accommodation are just given a list of homeless shelters and £47,[34] which won't get them very far in London. I'm fortunate to have a support network for when I get out, but a lot of offenders have nothing waiting for them.

Derry, a chirpy Irish lad nearing release, still has a POCA benefit figure outstanding. The court acknowledged that he didn't have any assets, so it won't result in extra time, but future earnings can technically be confiscated to clear the debt. While in Wandsworth, he has worked as a biohazard cleaner, which is the best paid job in the prison, and accumulated £700 in his prison account so he could put down a deposit on a flat. Days before his release, his meagre nest egg is seized to go towards his confiscation. It will barely make a dent in the outstanding figure, but he now doesn't have anywhere to live. Being homeless is unlikely to help his efforts to go straight.

Inside job

Offenders released with accommodation and employment have far less chance of committing further crimes.[35] In fairness, this fact was fully acknowledged by Governor Bickers, who championed vocational programmes like dry lining. This was run by the charity Bounceback, which claimed to 'act as a bridge between prison and full-time employment'.[36] Inmates were taught skills during their sentence, and Bounceback tried to find them a job for their release.

I once saw an internal report showing that 20 prisoners completed the dry-lining course, which was bloody good by Wandsworth's standards. I then noticed that only one inmate actually had a job lined up for when they got out. This turned out to be Dylan, the tool thief I remembered fondly from my own dry-lining days. He was released a couple of weeks later, but word soon filtered back that he hadn't turned up for work. His disappearance was solved when it emerged that he had just been re-arrested. This breached his licence conditions and triggered an automatic recall to jail. The poster child for the Bounceback scheme had only succeeded in bouncing right back into prison.

Another prisoner employment scheme was Cells Pitch, which promised to 'bridge the gap between prisoners and entrepreneurship'.[37] Inmates were encouraged to develop their own business ideas, which they then pitched to a panel of investors. The winner was given £250 on release, to turn their inspiration into reality. Unfortunately, whoever cooked up this idea had spent more time watching *Dragons' Den* than they had in prison. It ignored the appalling literacy problems: half of Wandsworth's residents would struggle to read their own charging sheet, let alone manage a profit-and-loss account. Most offenders leaving the prison didn't have anywhere to live, either, so whoever won this award would probably have to launch their business empire from a park bench.

28 February

Things have deteriorated since Faisal was discovered spiced up on Listener duty. Several officers have recently made barbed comments about the Listeners being on drugs, and hinting that we shouldn't be let out to do our work. This afternoon I run into Arthur from the Samaritans, and ask him for a quiet word.

'Faisal was on duty the other night,' I blurt out. 'One of the officers refused to unlock him.'

'Why was that?'

'He was spiced off his face.' This is the only time I grass someone up in prison. It's a colossal risk, but I have the strange urge to prove that I still have a moral compass.

Arthur pats me on the shoulder. 'Thanks for telling me. I'll have a quiet word.'

Prison is definitely changing me. Six months ago I wouldn't have dreamed of ratting someone out, but I've now got a solid core of confidence growing inside me. Days later, I pop into the centre office to get the visit slips.

'They've been picked up,' grunts an officer.

'Who by?'

'Dobby.'

Dobbs is an epic brown-noser, and this isn't the first time he's moved onto someone else's patch. I am extremely reticent to lose the visit slips, as they provide a bulletproof excuse to move around Trinity. I tell Gary what's happened, and he insists that I confront the issue head on. Before I can stop him, he marches onto the landing.

'Dobby! Chris wants a word with you.'

Dobby slithers into the cell, and Gary shuts the door firmly behind him. I stay seated, while Dobby stands in front of me like a naughty schoolboy.

'Why have you taken my visit slips?' I demand. 'I've been delivering them for months.'

'I, er, I was told to hand them out by Officer Monaghan. He said if I didn't do it I'd get a nicking.'

This is extremely doubtful. Monaghan is a remarkably chilled officer, and is only ever officious about his own fag breaks. Dobby attempts, somewhat unconvincingly, to further substantiate his story. I can see why he was found guilty and got seven years.

'Those slips are the only way I can get a proper conversation with my son.' My voice is starting to rise. 'If I can't talk to Kit, then things are going to become unpleasant.'

Gary hovers threateningly in the background, and I can't deny that I'm getting a kick out of this. Dobby reluctantly hands over the slips, and Gary opens the door to indicate that the meeting is over. I feel like Mr Bridger in *The Italian Job*.

1 March

Liz Truss announces yet another plan to tackle the prison crisis. She wants existing staff to get specialist training to help prevent inmates self-harming and attempting suicide.[38] I can see why this proposal is attractive, as it avoids hiring any more staff. And it would be a good start. But it's often the screws themselves who are fuelling the anxiety and stress. One of my regular Listener contacts is Amin, who is completely incapable of dealing with authority. He keeps fighting losing battles with the officers, which results in him being put on Basic. I can't say I blame the officers for this, but he's been locked in his cell for weeks, and is now seriously self-harming. The officers are the root cause of his distress, and therefore the last people he's going to trust. Asking the screws to alleviate the suffering of prisoners like Amin is a bit like training a torturer in first aid.

2 March

Faisal, the spiced-up Listener, bounces up to me in the exercise yard. I assume that he's discovered I've grassed him up, and practically soil myself. It transpires that he's just being friendly, and we walk a few laps of the yard. Confident that I'm not going to get shanked, I ask him how he ended up in prison.

'Got convicted of aggravated robbery, but that's bullshit. I didn't steal nuffink. All I did was put a cigarette out on that cunt's head. He was being right cheeky, innit.'

'Fucking liberty,' I tut soothingly. 'How did you get caught?'

'Did it in front of CCTV, innit.'

Faisal now deeply regrets his actions. This is less about the impact on the victim, and more about the CCTV being on several news websites. His worst actions are eternally enshrined on the internet, which will haunt him for ever more.

3 March

Gary has been told by five different people that he's going to Ford tomorrow. Two of his sources are officers, but he is still keeping this news under wraps, as OMU remains highly paranoid about prisoners knowing their travel plans. One of the cleaners, Hank, recently discovered that he was heading to Highpoint. He went round saying goodbye to all the screws, and even shook the hand of the SO, who promptly cancelled his transfer. Gary is determined to avoid the same trap, and is doggedly feigning ignorance of his impending departure.

We've planned a fun-packed evening in the cell – a final backgammon championship and the last four episodes of *The Sopranos*, Season 3. At the end of S&Ds, we're locked up by Mr Lancha, an enormous African officer. For reasons I'm still not entirely sure of, I jovially announce, 'This is Gary's last night – he's off to Ford tomorrow!'

Gary looks like he's having an epic spice attack. I remember, too late, that Mr Lancha also works for Security, and is by far the worst officer to spill the beans to. He looks at us with pained eyes. 'Guys, you aren't supposed to know your movement details. Who told you?'

Gary frantically tries to unfuck my fuck-up, stammering, 'I don't know … Am I moving? Nobody's told me anything.'

It's taken six weeks' campaigning to get him his Cat D, and I've just kiboshed it in three seconds. I desperately try to convince Lancha that I was only joking, which is somewhat undermined by the stream of cons coming up to bid Gary farewell. Lancha bangs us up, and a heavy atmosphere descends in the cell.

Prison transfer slips are handed out around 7.30 p.m., so we have to wait an hour to learn if Gary is still going to Ford. We play an unbearably tense game of backgammon. Both of us are straining to hear the jangle of keys that might herald an incoming slip. Half seven comes and goes, and nothing appears under the door. I pour out an abject apology, taking full responsibility for killing Gary's transfer. He insists that it's not my fault, even though it blatantly is. Halfway through my grovelling, a screw calls Gary's name at the door. We sprint over, and a note comes in informing Gary that he's going to Ford tomorrow. I collapse to my knees, and Gary leans against the wall sighing heavily.

The next morning I head out on freeflow, while Gary remains locked in. All of Trinity now knows that he is going to Ford, but he's still segregated to prevent him telling anyone. I call Lottie, who texts Gary's mum about the move. If she holds up the prison van with a shotgun, then I am in deep trouble.

By his own admission, Gary was a drug-addled loser when he came to prison. He used the incarceration to his advantage and got himself completely clean. But he was only really tested when he was given the extra six months. His family blamed him, his girlfriend nearly walked, and even I thought he'd start using drugs again. But he proved everyone wrong, keeping his family and girlfriend onside and marshalling every resource to turn the situation around. I wave goodbye to my friend convinced that he'll never return to prison again.

11

Paedophiles and Prizes

In which I pull every last move to get out of Wandsworth. I meet a paranoid sex offender, and fail to persuade Lunn to leave H Wing.

Things I learn:

1) The appalling lack of healthcare provision

2) Appeals are a double-edged sword

3) Don't come to prison with a Louis Vuitton trunk

I finally board a lifeboat, alongside the captain of the sinking ship.

4 March

I now have a spare bed to fill. I swoop in on Wilson, a banker who has recently arrived on the wing. He's only been inside three weeks, and he couldn't be more middle class if he had a Waitrose tattoo. He jumps at a place in the Executive Suite, and we quickly move his stuff in.

'Welcome to club class,' I say, handing him Gary's cell key. 'The in-flight movie is Season 4 of *The Sopranos.*'

I find Miss Black and inform her that Wilson has moved into H2-09. She raises an eyebrow. 'You do realise that *I'm* supposed to arrange all cell moves?'

Thankfully she doesn't kick up a fuss, but the other Listeners soon start circling.

'So, Gary's gone. Which Listener are you moving in?'

'Wilson,' I reply. 'He's already in.'

'He isn't a Listener!'

'He'll start training in a couple of weeks.' In reality, the training doesn't start for three more months.

Wilson takes a bit of time to settle in. Despite our shared class roots, we are poles apart in our prison careers. I'm a Wandsworth veteran of eight months, while he's been inside for under a month and is still reeling from the shock of conviction. He'll sometimes tail off mid sentence, and I keep catching him staring at the ceiling with moist eyes. This is how I must have appeared to Ted when I first arrived.

5 March

Lunn is suffering acute problems with his accommodation. Ninety-five per cent of inmates have to share two-bed cells, as single pads are very rare and the source of much bitterness and jealousy. H Wing has a dozen single-bed cells on the Ones, which are reserved for the servery workers. Very occasionally, other prisoners have got normal cells redesignated as single pads. Lunn has been lobbying hard for this for some time. He definitely deserves a single, as he's quite old and works tirelessly as the Listener coordinator. After much wrangling, the SO finally agrees that he can live in his current cell on his own.

This information is not widely shared. At 2 a.m., Lunn's door is opened by a night officer, who introduces him to a new cellmate. Swaying in the doorway and stinking like a Wetherspoons is the unwanted guest, who has just arrived from a nearby police station. The cops often send remand suspects to Wandsworth after dark, as we have the only night-time reception in London. New prisoners are supposed to stay on E Wing, but it's frequently full, and H Wing is used as an overspill. Night officers will routinely circulate our landings trying to offload aggressive inebriates. They keep stopping at Lunn's cell, as it looks like he's got a spare bed. Lunn then has to argue that his cell has been officially redesignated as a single. So far he has kept the intruders out.

As time goes on, these relentless nocturnal awakenings take their toll. Lunn lies awake, fearful of the next home invasion, and even the sound of jangling keys gives him a panic attack. Meanwhile a spice dealer moves into one of the official single cells downstairs. He sits in his cell all day, blasting out drum and bass while openly plying his trade.

6 March

Today there is another wing rep meeting, which I attend for the sheer comedy value. These gatherings remind me of *Waiting for Godot*: nothing happens, everything is uncertain. Each scene is just like the one that precedes it, with witless characters engaging in mindlessly trivial conversations. Today's proceedings are also visited by a pair of random clowns, aka two guys from Carillion. The residents of Trinity are ably represented by myself, Teasnitch, Fenton and Les.

Governor Yeti starts off by noting that the wings are quite grubby. He proudly unveils his vision to appoint 'Cleaning Champions to own the hygiene journey'. This is exactly what he said last time, but as yet no one has volunteered for this unpaid role.

'Let's mark that one as pending,' Yeti mutters to himself.

'Brilliant!' chirps Les, who is looking increasingly fried these days. He's still waiting to be sentenced, but his hearing keeps getting postponed. The uncertainty is crippling, and he still believes that sucking up to the prison authorities will get him a more lenient punishment. I have tried explaining that Governor Yeti has as much influence over the judge's decisions as I do, but Les's deranged sycophancy continues unabated.

Next item – Yeti's vision for a comment box, into which prisoners can deposit ideas on improving conditions. I'm dubious that this will attract constructive messages, or indeed anything in written form. It emerges that there's a box ready for action, but it has no sign advertising its purpose.

Yeti nods thoughtfully. 'So it hasn't actually gone live yet?' I very nearly crease at this point. The governor evidently thinks he's launching a new iPhone rather than a small wooden box. Fenton volunteers to arrange an appropriate sign.

Yeti beams. 'All *right*, let's launch it at the end of the week. That's what I'm about, right there.' He's like David Brent in a turban.

Les punches the air. 'Brilliant!'

Next item – the perilous state of H Wing showers.

I raise a hand. 'The water is now scalding hot. It's actually quite dangerous.'

The Carillion guys have a little chuckle at us snowflake prisoners. 'Last we heard it was too cold, now it's too hot. We can't win!'

'Brilliant!' grunts Les.

I take a deep breath. 'Over Christmas, the showers were freezing cold, which incidentally was the cause of a riot at HMP Birmingham. Then someone turned our thermostat up to boiling, so the water now actually burns the skin. The temperature we are looking for …' I pause for dramatic effect, 'is warm.'

The Carillion guys reluctantly agree to have a look. After the meeting, I accompany them down to the shower room, which is just as well as they have no idea where it is.

'When did you last visit the showers?' I ask.

'Er, when we installed them.'

The shower room is full of steam, and a prisoner stands next to a shower head in his pants. His body is gleaming red, as if he's fallen asleep pissed in Magaluf. The bloke from Carillion turns on one of the showers and sticks his hand under the jet.

'JESUS!' He recoils as if he's touched an electric fence. 'This place is a death trap! I'll get it turned down to a safe temperature within twenty-four hours.'

We never see the Carillion guys again, and the water remains boiling hot until I leave.

7 March

Wandsworth is currently hosting an academic programme with Middlesex University: 'The Learning Together approach brings together students from universities and from within prisons to learn together ... in an innovative method of knowledge exchange and discussion.'[1]

Soft focus

Wandsworth constantly struggled to recruit officers, nurses and maintenance staff, but there was never any shortage of well-meaning academics. During my sentence I met dozens of visiting professors, criminologists and PhD students, usually in slightly surreal focus groups. At first I enthusiastically signed up to these gatherings, as they got me out of the cell and would usually have nice biscuits. I soon became bored, but must have been on a list called 'Will give good focus group', as I kept getting randomly hauled into events. The visiting academics were invariably horrified at the revolting conditions in Wandsworth, and insisted that something must be done to improve prisons. They'd then promptly bugger off and absolutely nothing would change.

This programme is struggling for numbers, and today Linda from Education sticks her head round my door.

'Can you get some more lags signed up to this criminology

course? There's only three guys on it at the moment, and they're only there to learn how to not get caught.'

I ask Lunn if he wants to sign up.

'How long is it?' he asks.

'Eight weeks.'

He smiles and shakes his head. 'There's no point me starting. I'll be out in a few weeks when my appeal comes through.' Lunn was given five years for tax fraud, but is appealing both his sentence and his conviction. Appeals can be extremely stressful; the judges deliberate in private for months, and then announce their decision without notice. Only 11% of conviction applications and 25% of sentence appeals are successful.[2] Lunn has been waiting ages for his result, and is convinced he's going to win. I really hope he does, as I've grown very fond of the old man, but being optimistic in prison is a risky business. I've succumbed to similar wishful thinking myself, confidently telling everyone that I'll be out of Wandsworth by the end of January.

8 March

Governor Yeti's cleanest wing competition goes live. A big sign appears in the Trinity centre: CLEANEST WING COMPETITION ON TRINITY! We will be doing random spot checks over the coming weeks, and a PRIZE will go to whichever wing has the cleanest landings.

After an initial flurry of excitement, the competition has no discernible impact. This is due to the prize being awarded to the officer supervising the cleaning, rather than the prisoners actually doing the work. It later emerges that the cleaning on all three Trinity wings is supervised by the same screw, who will therefore pocket the award irrespective of which wing wins.

9 March

Lunn has lost his appeal. The poor man is completely gutted, as he'd been banking on a positive outcome.

I try and find a silver lining. 'At least you can get your Cat D and go down to Ford.' Prisoners going through appeals are often kept in Wandsworth so they can easily attend court. Now that it's all over, Lunn can finally move to open conditions.

'I'm not going to Ford,' he replies. 'I'm needed here.'

'Are you out of your fucking mind?'

'Governor Bickers has asked me to stay and support the chaplaincy. And Arthur really needs my help with the Listener training.'

I doubt Bickers has a clue who Lunn even is, and it's highly unlikely that Arthur would pressurise anyone to remain in Wandsworth. I fear that losing his appeal has made Lunn cling to the stability of H Wing. It reminds me of Brooks, the elderly character in *The Shawshank Redemption*, who's so terrified of leaving prison that he nearly kills another inmate to prevent his release.

At the eleventh hour, I finally get a letter from my solicitor with the correct confiscation figures. I immediately photocopy it and distribute it widely around the prison.

10 March

I'm doing the inductions on E Wing when a whistle goes downstairs. Connor and I take up our usual position on the Threes to watch the ensuing ruckus below. Several screws run into a cell and start wrestling with a troublesome prisoner. Supervising the melee is a large senior officer who I realise is CM Chaplin from OMU. I quickly skip down the stairs to buttonhole him.

'Mr Chaplin? I wondered if I could ask you about my recat appeal?'

My patter is not helped by the blood-curdling screams emanating from the nearby cell.

'PUT THAT DOWN OR YOU'LL GET A WEEK IN THE BLOCK!'

Chaplin calmly sips his tea. 'You're Atkins, aren't you?'

'I CAN'T BREATHE!'

'We emailed the court. They said that your confiscation was two hundred grand.'

'IF YOU STOP SPITTING THEN I'LL GET OFF YOUR BACK.'

'That's not *quite* correct,' I say, trying not to sound like a smartarse. 'Over half of that is actually prosecution costs, which are in fact a civil penalty.'

'GO FUCK YOUR MOTHER, YOU FAT CUNT!'

'I spoke to Ford and they've said they'll have you at that figure,' replies Chaplin.

'STAFF! WE NEED MORE STAFF!'

'We still have to process your recat appeal. It shouldn't take long.'

It's really time to quit while I'm ahead. 'I don't suppose I can get on tomorrow's bus?' I venture.

Chaplin laughs and finishes his tea, indicating that the conversation is over. He then goes to assist in pummelling eight cans of crap out of the guy in the cell.

11 March

Around 10 p.m., Lunn and I are called into the Listener Suite. The door soon crashes open, and a frenetic, twitching mess flies in.

'I'm a fucking dead man. Gonna string up, stop them getting me first.' Ross, a stocky Essex boy in his mid twenties, paces constantly round the room. 'I was on A Wing, yeah, and I fucked with the wrong people.' Apparently he eavesdropped on some members of a notorious London gang and overheard where they kept their drugs on a nearby estate. He tipped off one of his associates on the outside, who went and stole the gang's stash. It soon emerged that Ross was the inside man in Wandsworth, and his neighbours demanded retribution. He has since received several kickings, and was beaten with a loo seat so badly that he couldn't walk. He is covered in scars and bruises but has refused medical treatment to prevent the officers getting involved.

'I've told the lads they can have the stash back. But they just want to fuck me up to send out a message to everyone else.'

Ross moved to Trinity to get away from the gang, but went into a cell opposite the brother of the guy who was robbed. I know who he's referring to, and he could not have picked worse enemies. He has locked himself in his cell all week, while his would-be assassins hiss death threats through the door. He can't sleep, and hasn't showered or called home for ages. I've never seen a contact so scared; he is clearly in desperate fear for his life.

'I know I've fucked up. I deserve the beatings, and they owe me a few more. But these boys want to put me in the ground.' He's still got a year to serve, and can't face living like this any more.

Ross's predicament is entirely self-inflicted, but I still feel sorry for him. The standard Listening approach – encouraging the contact to talk about their feelings – seems utterly redundant.

'Have you asked about moving to a different jail?' I say.

'The screws don't care. They think I'm a total lowlife who deserves what he's getting.'

I have no idea what to do, but thankfully Lunn has a plan. 'You might not believe this, but you're in a bit of luck. It's the Safer Custody meeting tomorrow. With your permission, I'll raise your situation with the governors.'

A tiny ray of hope appears in Ross's eyes. 'What can they do?'

'I'll put it on the record that you have to move prison. If they refuse, and you die, they'll have to explain themselves at your inquest.' Lunn speaks with such calm authority that Ross seems ever so slightly relieved. I doubt this will work, but it's given him something to look forward to. Suicidal people can feel that every path forwards is closed off. Giving them something – anything – in the immediate future can make all the difference.

A day later, I check in on him. He is sharing with a tramp who came in at Christmas and for some reason is still here. He looks like

Treebeard from *The Lord of the Rings*, and has absurdly long toenails. I tap on the glass, causing Ross to leap off the bed like a jackrabbit. When he realises it's only me, he slinks up to the door.

'What's the latest?' he whispers.

'Lunn spoke at the Safer Custody meeting. I don't know what's been decided.'

Ross is paranoid that Treebeard will overhear us, and is desperate to talk in private. I ask several screws to escort him to the Listener Suite, but they're all too busy.

The following day, I nip back up to his cell and see Treebeard sitting on his own.

'What happened to your padmate?'

'Shipped out. Winchester.'

I run back to H Wing and tell Lunn that his gambit has been successful. The old man smiles to himself, but never mentions it again. Ross was as unsympathetic as they come, and most people would have let him get his comeuppance. Lunn's altruism brings into sharp contrast the two different perspectives of his character. When he was convicted, the prosecutors portrayed him as the accounting equivalent of Dr Crippen. This couldn't be further from the compassionate and decent man who probably just saved Ross's life.

12 March

Our door is opened by a podgy middle-aged man in a checked shirt and jeans. He looks like a farmer who's wandered in from a nearby hayfield.

'Are you Atkins?'

'Yes.'

'I'm temping at OMU. I've got to do your recategorisation appeal.'

I instinctively shake his hand, before realising that I've just washed and my hands are dripping wet. The OMU farmer recoils, and I have to assure him that it was just water. He gets out a folder and flicks through some notes.

'There's an issue with your confiscation,' he says sternly. 'The concern is that you'll abscond from open prison to avoid paying it.'

'OK.'

'I need to do an assessment and check that you're suitable for Category D status.'

This is it. This moment will decide if I'm stuck in Wandsworth for another six months. I summon all my concentration for the impending grilling.

'So ... Are you going to pay your confiscation?'

'Yes, guv.'

The farmer nods. 'Good. I'm going to give you your Cat D.' Before I can thank him, he beetles off the wing.

The news takes a few hours to sink in, and a huge weight starts to lift off my shoulders. It quickly becomes public knowledge. Friends float in to congratulate me, before asking to inherit items of my furniture.

I can finally join the gaggle of Cat D inmates on H Wing, all furtively swapping rumours about impending buses. One is a seasoned con who's been to Ford before and talks longingly of a nearby brothel.

'I always nip down for a bit of day release, if you know what I mean.'

This establishment even offers 'Ford discounts', to build their customer base. It makes strong commercial sense, as sex-starved prisoners are going to take significantly less time than standard clientele.

14 March

There is a serious problem with the outgoing post. The H Wing mailbox hasn't been emptied for a week, and it's so full that I can't even push my envelopes through the slit. It's causing a lot of anxiety as we approach Mother's Day. I overhear a huge inmate telling a terrified screw, 'If my mum doesn't get my card, I will do a Strangeways.'

I track down the Hitler Youth SO and explain that things will get ugly if they don't empty the mailbox.

'Someone has lost the key,' he flaps. 'There's no way to open it.'

It's impossible to reply without being patronising. 'Guv, we're surrounded by hundreds of experienced criminals. If we put the call out, we could get this lock picked in five minutes.'

My incoming correspondence has slowed significantly since the new year. This isn't necessarily a bad thing, as I'd often get stressed about replying in good time. It's also becoming increasingly difficult to relate to some of my friends' lives on the outside. I sometimes struggle to write things like 'I'm so sorry about your faulty guttering … delighted your three-week holiday to India was a success … thrilled that your film is getting positive reviews' while I'm begging for loo roll and watching teenagers self-harm. It feels as if I'm dispatching messages from a spaceship that is drifting ever further into the abyss.

16 March

Most Listener contacts I see just once, but there's always a handful of regular customers. At the moment our most frequent caller is Jules, a small, furtive prisoner in his thirties. He requests a Listener pretty much every day, often in the small hours. Despite this persistence, he never seems troubled by anything remotely serious. I've seen him half a dozen times, and he just complains that he's 'cheesed off' that nobody has responded to his general apps. Given the appalling suffering in Wandsworth, I don't offer him much sympathy. Jules's time-wasting has caused so much frustration among the other Listeners that they've refused to see him at all.

Tonight I'm roused at 3 a.m. and led to his door.

'I can't sleep,' he moans. 'I'm worrying about what's been going on with my apps.'

I give him 10 minutes, then go back to bed. The next day I corner Lunn.

'Can I blacklist Jules as well? I can't face seeing him again.'

Lunn quietly explains that Jules is 'presenting' – telling us something innocuous because he's too ashamed to divulge his real problem. Apparently he is inside for sexual assault, and is petrified of this being discovered by other inmates. Most sex offenders live on the Vulnerable Prisoner Unit, but some choose to sweat it out in general population. This secret explains why Jules is getting tongue-tied, and also makes me feel quite conflicted. The Listener scheme is supposed to be for everyone, but it's difficult being empathetic with someone responsible for such a vile crime.

Days later, I'm called to his cell again, and he starts bleating about his sodding application forms. I take a deep breath. 'You really need to be honest with me about your problems.'

'I told you!' he storms. 'I'm annoyed that they've ignored my dry-lining application.'

'Listeners are only here to talk to prisoners who are self-harming or suicidal. Good night.'

Two days later, I'm called into the Listener Suite. My heart sinks when I see Jules's twitchy eyes waiting for me.

'Hi, Jules, what's the problem?'

'I'm feeling suicidal.'

'I'm really sorry. Why do you feel like that?'

'Well, I've submitted these general apps and nobody's responding to me.'

'I'm going to press the bell now. This session is over.'

The officer arrives and takes Jules away. I add my name to the list of Listeners who won't take call-outs from him.

Talking nonce sense

The authorities strongly recommended that sex offenders lived on the Vulnerable Prisoner Unit (VPU), which was a sealed unit at the far end of C Wing. It was also home to several ex-cops, a few grasses and even a former judge. Vulnerable prisoners still got to work in some prison jobs, and even had their own entrance to the kitchens. This door was overlooked by one of the cells I briefly shared with Ted. Every day I'd be awoken by him yelling out of the window: 'Morning, nonces! Don't slip with that kitchen knife!' Sex offenders were detested by the rest of the inmates, who desperately wanted to feel that there were others lower down the social chain. It was the ultimate form of virtue signalling; castigating paedophiles allowed 'normal' prisoners to paint their own crimes as comparatively innocent misdemeanours.

The only contact I had with sex offenders was when Danielle brought me their induction tests to mark. Surprisingly, the nonces' standard of English and maths was far higher than the Wandsworth average. Their tests were administered by an orderly on the VPU called Fred, who had previously worked as Danielle's orderly when he was on remand for sexually assaulting a child. This didn't faze Danielle, who had worked in prisons for years, and Fred fulfilled his duties efficiently enough. When he got to trial, he was found not guilty, and immediately left the prison.

Several months on, Danielle was visiting the local library with her young son, and saw Fred hanging round the kids' section. Her first instinct was to call the police, but Fred had been acquitted and wasn't doing anything illegal. They talked awkwardly, Danielle nervously wondering if he was scoping out new victims or just borrowing a book. A few weeks later, she walked onto C Wing and saw Fred coming down the stairs. He'd just been charged with new sexual offences. He was looking for a prison job, so she rehired him as her orderly.

18 March

I have completely failed to convince Lunn to leave Wandsworth. He's got his Cat D, without even asking for it, but wants to remain on Trinity to support the Lord's work. Religious provision has been on its knees since the departure of the prison chaplain. I find his loyalty to the prison completely barmy, especially as he keeps being roused at 3 a.m. to repel inebriated would-be cellmates.

'You'd be fucking mad to swerve a bus to Ford,' I keep telling him.

'I assure you that I'm completely sane. I'm staying entirely of my own free will.'

To me these are mutually contradictory statements.

The next morning, another prisoner appears at our door in a tizz. 'Lunn has got a movement slip! They're sending him to Ford!'

I nip down to see Lunn beaming through his observation panel, waving his transfer slip. 'I'm not going. I'm on hold!' This refers to a process by which inmates are blocked from moving to a different jail. It is clearly not infallible, given that Lunn is demonstrably being shipped out. It occurs to me that his intransigence could actually work in my favour.

'Can we do *A Tale of Two Cities*?' I ask.

Lunn fortunately understands the Dickens reference, and agrees that I should try to take his place. I rush around and find the movements officer.

'Guv, Lunn doesn't want to go to Ford.'

'Is he insane?'

'Pretty much. Can I go instead? I've had my Cat D for ages.' This is a complete lie, but I know this officer won't check or care.

'Dunno, it's not exactly a common situation. I'll find out and let you know.'

This is screw parlance for 'forget it'. Nonetheless, word of my departure flies round the wing. I go up to the education department and have a wildly unproductive morning. Every time I hear a jangle of keys, I snap round, thinking it's an officer coming to whisk me away. Generally it turns out to be Linda going for a fag.

The minutes tick by, and it becomes obvious that I won't be leaving Wandsworth today. I slouch back to the wing, where Lunn is still banged up. The officers tried to get him onto the van three times, and Lunn just kept repeating, 'I'm on hold!' He told them to give me his place, but the SO decided it was too late to do a risk assessment. I struggle to see how a bus ride to Ford could be any riskier than staying in Wandsworth.

19 March

I'm walking past the phones just as Pops, the elderly Greek man on the Ones, slides down to the floor, wheezing loudly. Fenton and I run over and carry him down to his cell. The old man has three types of cancer, and is on a complex mix of medication, which has just been screwed up by the nurses. His problems are exacerbated by having to stand around waiting to use the phones. He was previously allowed to call for an unlimited time, rather than being cut off after five minutes, but this privilege has been inexplicably stopped. Pops should clearly be in open prison, but OMU have refused his Cat D, claiming that he's an escape risk. This is despite the old man being unable to stand unaided.

20 March

Our cell door is suddenly unlocked and a huge screw marches in. He looks round our pad and whistles. 'Fuck me, this is a big cell!'

'We're going to knock through and build an extension for a home cinema.' I use this gag a lot.

'Are you Atkins?'

'Yes, guv.'

'You've been here since July. According to my list, you never got a second-day screening.'

As the name suggests, the second-day screening is a medical check that all inmates are supposed to receive on their second day in prison. The screw beckons in a nurse who has been lurking outside. She obviously doesn't let the Data Protection Act get in the way of her work, and is happy to conduct a private examination in front of an officer and another prisoner.

'Have you got any medical problems?' she says.

'Well, since you ask, my glasses broke when I arrived.'

She hands me a piece of paper. 'You need to fill in an app.'

'I've sent in about twenty and nothing has happened.'

The officer looks at his watch. 'So you've had your second-day screening now. Can I tick you off my list?'

'Technically it's my two-hundred-and-sixty-fourth-day screening, but you go right ahead.'

The officer and the nurse troop out. Wilson is mildly flabbergasted, but I'm actually quite pleased. Wandsworth's management is notorious for fixing the stats to make it look as if things are running better than they are. Often prisoners are given vital services just before they leave so the authorities can claim that provision has been made. Bizarrely enough, being given a ridiculously late medical screening indicates that I will soon be transferred to Ford.

21 March

A rumour swirls that Governor Bickers has called an emergency staff meeting in the chapel this afternoon. Every officer has to attend, and freeflow is duly cancelled. At the start of my sentence this would have made me furious. Now I see the extra bang-up as a nice bonus, as I'll get a few hours' quiet studying in the cell. We are unlocked mid afternoon, and I bump into Montague, the irritating Listener who now lives opposite. He's moping about as if he's just been bereaved.

'What's up?' I ask.

'Ian is leaving us,' he says mournfully.

Prison is a strictly surnames place. 'Ian who?'

Montague shakes his head patronisingly. 'Ian. Ian Bickers? He's going next week.'

Once I get over Montague believing that he's on first-name terms with the governor, I'm rocked to learn of Bickers' departure. He became executive governor just before I arrived, and has been the biggest cheerleader of the government's reform policy. The staff meeting was so that he could announce his exit, and the officers drift back in a pretty mutinous mood. They've been continually assured that calmer seas lie ahead, as long as Bickers steers the good ship *Reform*. It now transpires that the captain has nabbed the last lifeboat, just as the icebergs hove into view.

Days later, the *Guardian* breaks the story, attributing Bickers' departure to the demise of the Purple Army: 'HMP Wandsworth governor leaves after failure of idea to give duties to prisoners … Most of the "peer advisers" have been kept locked in their cells … Of the 50 prisoners recruited to be peer advisers … just 15 have been partially trained since September.'[3]

I knew that the Purple Army was being routed, but didn't realise our defeat had pushed the general out the door. (Apologies for the military metaphors.)

22 March

Wilson develops a nasty swelling on his elbow. He is convinced that it's bursitis, which he's had before. By the evening, his elbow has grown to the size of a tennis ball and turns an angry shade of purple. He obviously requires medical attention, so I hit the emergency bell.

Twenty minutes later, a night officer appears outside. He's just over five foot tall, and can barely see through the obs panel. After some persuasion he agrees to call the night nurse over the radio. She's quite reticent to attend, as 'it doesn't sound very bad'. I ask the officer to tell her that she ought to clap eyes on the patient before making that call. The nurse eventually arrives, but can't examine Wilson as nobody has a cell key. She peers at his elbow through the obs panel, and reluctantly agrees to call 'Hotel 3', the roving prison medical team. They turn up half an hour later, and we now have three officers and three nurses in attendance. They cautiously open our cell door and start examining him.

'Have you lost any blood?'

'Do you think it's fatal?'

Their questioning is clearly geared towards concluding that he doesn't require immediate treatment. The male nurse blatantly hasn't seen this condition before, and just keeps poking Wilson's engorged elbow, like Kit inserting his finger into every cake in a bakery. The young female night officer looks barely qualified to drive, let alone administer medical triage. Nevertheless, she enthusiastically joins in the diagnosis game. Producing a magic marker, she draws a line around the swelling to see if it gets any bigger, ignoring the fact that it's already dangerously large.

Unsurprisingly, they all conclude that Wilson needs to be locked in his cell with a couple of painkillers. I'm guessing this is their stock response for every conceivable ailment. Black Death? Two paracetamol and behind your door. Severed artery? Two paracetamol and behind your door.

Wilson explains that he's had bursitis previously, and needs emergency antibiotics to prevent septic shock. The night officer nods compassionately and starts to lock the door.

I finally pipe up. 'If this was anywhere else, you'd take him straight to A and E. Shutting him in a box with headache tablets is grossly negligent.'

The young screw gets quite snippy. 'We have this in hand, *buddy*. We've even drawn a line round the swelling.'

'I'm no doctor, but a line of black ink won't stop the poison entering his bloodstream.'

She orders me to 'butt out' and slams the door shut. The nurse assures Wilson that someone will check on him every hour through the night.

Wilson remains pretty stoical. He crawls into bed muttering, 'If I die in my sleep, don't wake me up.'

23 March

Nobody comes back to check on Wilson in the night. He's still alive in the morning, but the swelling has doubled in size. We're unlocked for freeflow, and he staggers off to see the duty nurse. She acknowledges that it's very serious and promises to get the doctor. I assume that my cellmate is in good hands and head off to work.

When I return, Wilson looks terrible, and he reports glumly that he still hasn't seen a doctor. I stomp out of the cell and track down SO Owen, who is usually dependable when things really matter. I explain that we're about to have a medical emergency, and she gets on the radio.

'Tell that fucking doctor to get here *now*.'

The doctor goes to K Wing by accident, and I run over and lead him back to our cell. Thankfully he knows more about medicine than he does about the layout of the prison.

'This is septic bursitis,' he says after 20 seconds. 'He needs to go to A and E right now, or he'll go into septic shock.'

Wilson is handcuffed to an officer and taken in a taxi to St George's. He returns to the cell at 9 p.m. and updates me on his trip. He had a nice dinner and was put on an IV drip of strong antibiotics. 'I have to return to the hospital every day for a week to repeat the treatment.'

'Good luck with that,' I reply.

24 March

In the morning, we're visited by the tall, friendly officer universally known as the BFG. He makes sure no one else is around and whispers to Wilson, 'You're going to hospital at lunchtime. Don't tell anyone that you know, or they'll cancel the trip.' The authorities are still on high alert following the Liverpudlian breakout, which happened on a doctor's visit. Wilson promises to keep shtum.

I come back from work at 4 p.m. to see that he is still here. No one came to collect him for his appointment. He didn't want to complain as it would involve admitting he knew he was going. I march off and ask Miss Black why Wilson hasn't gone to hospital. She instinctively blames the prisoner, and suggests that his visit was cancelled as he obviously knew he was heading to St George's. This is a Catch-22, as doctors have to tell patients about their impending treatment.

I find SO Owen again. She calls the mains centre, who tell her that Wilson's appointment was cancelled by Healthcare.

'They're lying pricks,' she spits. 'Healthcare wouldn't kill the trip, as they'll get the blame if he croaks.'

The swelling is now about 10 inches long and covers most of Wilson's arm. Owen tells the centre that he has to go to hospital immediately. The centre radio back insisting that this is impossible. SO Owen mutters, 'Fuck the centre,' and escorts Wilson over to the mains herself.

The evening wears on and Wilson does not return. It strikes me that this is the first time I've had a cell to myself. I can't say I particularly like it.

25 March

No sign of Wilson. Somewhat ominously, his name starts disappearing from prison lists. His sandwich doesn't come in at lunchtime, and his copy of *The Times* stops being delivered. I call out to a passing officer, 'Guv, does Wilson's missus know that he's in hospital?'

The screw gets quite upset. 'You're not supposed to know where he is!'

I motion round the empty cell. 'Well, he didn't come back last night. So he's either in hospital, escaped or dead.'

The officer refuses to engage with my *reductio ad absurdum*. 'We only notify next of kin if it's life-threatening.'

26 March

Still no sign of Wilson. His missus must be tearing her hair out wondering what's happened to him. I find her number among his things and try and give it to an officer.

'Guv, can someone contact Wilson's wife? Just so she knows that he's in hospital.'

The screw leaps back. 'That would mean telling *you* that he's at the hospital!'

I call Lottie and ask her to phone Wilson's wife and tell her what's going on.

27 March

No Wilson. I'm now firmly on bus watch, and keep gossiping with the other Cat D guys about impending transports.

'Have you heard anything?'

'The SO on visits hinted there was a van tomorrow.'

'Gerald said there were two buses to Ford on Friday.'

'Did he say who was going?'

'Nah. I'll let you know if I hear any more.'

We all pretend to help each other, but any one of us would happily leapfrog the queue given half a chance. It reminds me of the fall of Saigon, where everyone was fighting to get on the last choppers before the Vietnamese arrived.

I call Lottie and Kit to say goodnight. I'm strangely unsettled and I want to say something important, but don't know what it is. I drop in on Lunn, who's in his usual chipper mood. I joke that he'll probably get another transfer slip tonight.

'I'm not going anywhere,' he insists. 'The governor needs me here. I'm on hold.'

After bang-up, I sit alone trying to read. Throughout these last nine months I've craved solitude, but now that I'm finally alone, I feel desperately lonely.

'ATKINS!' an officer shouts from the door. A piece of A4 paper is passed through, simply stating PRISONER TRANSFER NOTIFICATION: ATKINS – HMP FORD.

'Are you sure this is for me?' This is a pretty idiotic question, given that the slip has my name on.

The officer sighs. 'You're going to Ford tomorrow. Do you understand?'

She walks off, and I'm hit by a rising tide of panic and joy. I feel I should celebrate, so I attempt a cartwheel and nearly sprain my ankle. I desperately want to share this momentous news. I even consider calling a Listener for the first time, just to gloat with someone that I'm finally leaving. I check the rota to see who's on duty, and it turns out to be me.

The door suddenly swings open and Wilson stumbles in. I make him a cup of tea, and he recounts the last four days. SO Owen took him to the mains, where the ranking officer refused to let him go to hospital, claiming that his elbow didn't look very serious. The prison doctor said that it was bloody serious, and they spent an hour arguing. Meanwhile Wilson was locked in a holding cell with an overflowing loo and shit up the walls. Hardly an appropriate location for someone with a severe infection.

Eventually an officer took him to the hospital. The screw wanted to return him to Wandsworth immediately after the treatment, but the doctor refused to let him go until he'd finished the course of antibiotics. He was then chained to an officer on a hospital ward. The other patients kept giving him 'I wonder what he's done?' looks, while the screw sat by the bed watching films on an iPad.

As the week went on, Wilson found himself being guarded by increasingly senior officers. By the end he was being minded by three-stripe custody managers, who'd normally be running several wings. Word had clearly spread that supervising him was a really cushy number, so the top brass piled in to get the overtime. Following Lottie's tip-off, his missus drove straight to St George's, and the nurses just sent her up to the ward. After some discussion, the screws let her visit as long as Wilson stayed chained up. She came in every day bringing goodies from M&S. He was constantly on an IV drip of powerful antibiotics, and is now back to good health.

The doctor won't see you now

Prison healthcare is straight out of the Middle Ages. It wouldn't have been out of place if they'd started dispensing leeches. I was once asked to deliver some medical slips, and every time I dropped one into a cell, the occupant went completely nuts. I looked through the remaining pieces of paper and realised they were notifying prisoners of doctor's appointments that had taken place the previous day. 'Discretion is the better part of valour,' I muttered to myself, and chucked the remaining slips in a bin.

The MoJ insists that 'Prisoners get the same healthcare and treatment as anyone outside of prison.'[4] As with so many MoJ statements, that's flatly contradicted by a mountain of evidence. The Wandsworth Independent Monitoring Board said in its 2017 report: 'The existing prison healthcare facilities were substandard ... The majority of the clinic rooms breached infection control requirements ... Cancellation of clinics for Healthcare operational reasons continued to be high ... On average two hospital appointments a week were missed due to the unavailability of an officer escort.'[5]

The national picture remains just as bad. In 2017, there was a damning leak of doctors' emails, claiming that prison healthcare was so bad that it would be shut down on the outside. 'There is a higher than average percentage of chronic disease and no nursing or GP capacity to manage them.'[6] Annabella Landsberg collapsed in HMP Peterborough in 2017 showing obvious symptoms of diabetes. The staff decided she was faking and she was locked in her cell for 21 hours until she died.[7] In 2019, a mental health trust in Sussex was fined £200,000 after a vulnerable teenager died on the hospital wing of HMP Lewes.[8]

I pack my things, while offloading useful tips to Wilson. 'Take my slips job, it'll get you off the wing to call home. If anyone gives you hassle, talk to Giggs upstairs. He's a bit of a nutter, but I've done his recat appeal and he owes me a favour.'

There's a three-bag limit on prison transports, and my stuff is currently taking up six. The main problem is my books, which have been arriving at a faster rate than I've been reading them. I take down the photos of Kit, now enhanced by a dab of toothpaste and Wandsworth paint, and look round fondly at this dank, dingy but comparatively roomy cell. It's difficult to believe that it's been my home for six months; it feels like I only just moved in. I'm suddenly strangely scared about what lies ahead.

28 March

A gate is unlocked outside, and I snap awake with a flood of adrenaline. Wilson stirs next to me.

'What time is it?' he asks groggily.

'Seven forty-five,' I respond without looking.

Wilson staggers to his feet and crosses the room to the tiny clock. 'It's seven forty-five exactly.'

This means that I can now tell the precise time in Wandsworth from the little sounds of the routine. It really is time to get the hell out of here.

Wilson and I say goodbye. We've got on fine, but haven't had the bromance I shared with Martyn, Scott and Gary. The door opens and he goes out, leaving me banged up inside. A few people come to my door to say goodbye, but it's nothing like the throng that gathered for Scott.

Lunn's smiling face appears outside. 'I've got a Ford movement slip as well. I'm not going – I'm on hold.'

'Are you *sure* you're on hold? OMU seem hell-bent on getting rid of you.'

He laughs. 'I'm going to the chapel.'

Linda comes by. We normally enjoy friendly, sweary bants, but today she's quite distant and stiff. It doesn't help that we're saying goodbye through a thick steel door. I thank her profusely for sorting out my psychology course, and for generally being a good laugh. She tells me to write to her, and then she's gone.

I haven't made any headway on scaling down my possessions, and I'm hit by severe luggage anxiety. I bin a load of OU paperwork and bequeath all my food to Wilson, which gets me down to five bags.

Miss Dooley unlocks the door. 'Are you ready to go?'

'I'm actually staying till June. I need the loyalty points.'

I commandeer a laundry trolley for my bags and drag it off H Wing. Les is in the centre, and he gives me a restrained man hug. This involves us gently bumping chests with our hands in our pockets. It's a move he's copied from young gang members, but he can't quite pull it off.

I get to the end of K Wing and wait to be escorted to the mains. The trolley has to stay here, and I desperately need help moving my crap. Danielle appears; she'd heard that I was going and has run over to say goodbye. I tell her that she's been a total saint, and a constant source of humanity in this inhumane world. We instinctively want to hug, but there are officers up the landing, so we exchange an oddly formal handshake.

Lurking nearby is a new inmate called Rudd. He's quite friendly and has been asking around for a decent job. I introduce him to Danielle, and strongly recommend that he replaces me as education orderly. Danielle takes my word for it and tells him that he can start tomorrow. Once she has gone, I inform Rudd that the price for this prime job is helping me lug my bags to reception.

We're taken to the mains, and I soak up the towering Victorian walls for the last time. Wandsworth is a festering shithole, unlike anywhere else I've been in my life, but I'm still weirdly sad to be leaving. We go through E Wing and I call around for Connor. Someone says that he's 'training', which means he's still asleep. I'm gutted that we can't say goodbye.

In reception, I'm locked in a busy holding cell, and the officer eyes my towering pile of stuff.

'Just three bags on the van,' he grunts. I try once more to rationalise my possessions, while a Scouse prisoner brags about his experiences in a Brazilian jail, droning on about the appalling conditions in Pernambuco. A grizzled Scottish con retaliates with a diatribe about his time in an Indian prison. It's like being in an episode of *Banged Up Abroad*.

I manage to compress my worldly goods down to four bags. Sitting next to me is a butch Kosovan who's also going to Ford; he offers to take one of my bags as his. We've never spoken before, and I'm extremely touched by his generosity. I think back to my first hours in Wandsworth, and the unsolicited kindness I received from Hitchins and Ted. It's a good day for mankind when people help strangers in a place like this.

Danielle pops up at the window, with Connor's grinning face behind her. She's obviously kicked him out of bed to send me off. The screw refuses to open the door, but he's mercilessly bullied by Danielle until he lets me out. I quickly hug Connor goodbye. His sanguine attitude to his horribly long sentence has been a constant source of inspiration.

I'm sent back round the dirty Yellow Brick Road. They strip-search me, which seems pretty pointless given that I'm going to an open prison notoriously awash with drugs. The officer then produces my prop box, and I lift the lid with giddy anticipation. At the top is my court clobber. The curry stains now easily qualify as a public health risk.

'Guv, can I chuck these clothes away? They're going to give someone cholera.'

'Got to take everything with you. Those are the rules.'

I'd actually be disappointed if they started introducing common sense at this stage. I'm thrilled to be reunited with my Argos watch, which was swiped on arrival for having a stopwatch function. I start to put it on, but realise that it's broken. I pull out the Christmas decorations that were deemed too dangerous for H Wing. At the bottom is a book of cryptic crosswords, which I was sent by a friend. Even the reception officer has no idea why this was confiscated. I've since concluded that it's because of Prison Rule (PSI) 49/2011 – 11.3/f: 'Correspondence may not contain the following: obscure or coded messages which are not readily intelligible or decipherable.'[9]

I'm bundled into a final holding cell, which turns out to be the first room I sat in when I arrived in Wandsworth. It still has the wildly misleading posters, promising spotless cells and smiling officers. All the other transfer vans have now left, and it's just our Ford bus waiting to go. There are supposed to be five of us on it, but Lunn is nowhere to be seen. Outside we can hear a screw shouting down the phone, 'Where is the old git? I don't care if he's on hold. If he's not here sharpish, we're cancelling the bus.'

We all become extremely fretful that Lunn will trap us in Wandsworth. The Kosovan even offers to take him aside for five minutes to change his mind. We then see an enormous officer manhandling Lunn, and he's thrust into our holding cell.

'I told them I was on hold and that I wasn't going to Ford,' he says, voice shaking. 'The officers got me from the chapel and marched me to the SO's office. He screamed that if I wasn't in reception in five minutes, he'd bend me up and throw me in the block.' It's tragic to see him abused by the very system that he's so desperate to help. He's obviously terrified of moving somewhere new, and deep down I know how he feels.

We're soon led out to the van, and I'm driven away from Wandsworth for the last time. Several prisoners have previously warned me, 'Don't look back, or you'll come back.' I can't resist a cheeky peek, and watch the crumbling Gothic edifice shrinking in the distance. London quickly fades away, and I see green fields for the first time in nine months.

We soon arrive at HMP Ford, which is near Arundel Castle on the Sussex coast. As the van backs up, Martyn and Gary dash into the car park. They're both smiling and sporting fine suntans, and they bang on the side of the van shouting my name.

Once I'm off the van, I find that there aren't any locked doors and we're free to roam about. Ford was formerly an RAF base, and most of the prisoners live in the old billets, which are dotted around a big field. The expanse of space does my head in; I can't focus on anything more than 20 metres away. I try to call Lottie, but can't remember the number, even though I've been dialling it every day for months. I go to my new room and curl up in bed, desperate for the world to stop spinning.

My brutal reaction to leaving Wandsworth indicates just how institutionalised I've become. People who've never been to prison use the word in a derogatory and patronising sense, implying that our minds have become dulled by the crushing routine. But it's actually about changing and adapting to survive. Much of my normal functioning did diminish over those crazy months, but only because it was completely redundant. I instead developed mechanisms to cope with the extraordinary challenges of Wandsworth life. I became a well-oiled cog in a completely broken engine. Yanking me out was always going to be rough.

Over the next few days, I quickly adapt to the radically different environment. There is booze and drugs everywhere. Every night a bag of goodies is thrown over the fence, and lots of inmates are permanently arseholed. That said, the atmosphere is far more peaceful than Wandsworth. The weather is amazing, and I quickly lose my flaky white pallor. Lunn keeps insisting that he'd rather be back on H Wing. This changes as soon as we have our first visits. The Ford visits hall is like an airport lounge, with only two officers sitting quietly in the corner. We're allowed to move around, and there's even an outside picnic area. Visits last for two whole hours, and I spend most of the time playing hide-and-seek with Kit. I can't think what Lottie has been teaching him, as he's frankly rubbish at hiding. I usually felt terrible at the end of a Wandsworth visit, but I skip out of the hall on a massive high. Lunn has just spent two hours with his wife, and pats me on the shoulder. 'You know, it might have been a good idea leaving Wandsworth after all.'

* * *

This is where my prison diary came to an end. My life became pretty boring once I was at Ford, and there wasn't much more to write about. I soon moved to HMP Springhill, another open prison in Oxfordshire. Halfway through my time inside, I was allowed out on day release, and Lottie drove me and Kit to Whipsnade Zoo. It was extremely odd being out in public again, I half expected people to be flying around on hoverboards. The only thing that had really changed was that everyone was even more obsessed with their smartphones. I'd been paranoid that people would point at me in horror, but nobody paid me the blindest bit of attention.

Kit played with me as though I hadn't been away a day. I'd had recurring nightmares that he would forget who I was, but the father–son bond was as strong as ever. This was solely down to Lottie, who'd worked tirelessly to keep us close since I went inside.

For the last half of my sentence I spent most of my waking hours in the outside world, mostly studying psychology at Oxford Brookes University. In the final nine months I was allowed to stay out overnight for a few days at a time. This meant I could put Kit to bed and take him to school again, and it was downhill all the way to the end.

As I approached the finish line, I received some unexpected help from something I'd done during my time in Wandsworth. While languishing on H Wing, I'd create spurious and elaborate markers to track the passage of time. I'd tell myself, 'It's soon ten per cent of my whole time inside', or 'In three days I'll have done a third of my time in a closed prison.' These milestones gave me something to look forward to in the near future, but were usually met with crushing disappointment as they brought no change to my circumstances. But they became extremely valuable in the second half of my sentence, as they helped me to envisage the time left to the finish. I knew exactly what 10% of my sentence felt like, as I could remember precisely when that point was back in Wandsworth. It was as if I'd climbed a mountain and accidentally left a line of cairns, which became a vital guide to getting back down.

The countdown to the end was incredible, like I'd discovered the best drug in the world, albeit one where you have the horrific comedown first. On 28 December 2018, I walked out of the prison gates for the last time, and Kit was waiting dressed in a fox onesie. He bounded up to hug me so forcefully that we both nearly fell over.

Martyn got out a few months before me, and remains irrepressibly cheerful. I have no doubt he will land on his feet whatever happens.

When Gary departed Ford, his girlfriend picked him up in a camper van and they drove off for a holiday in Wales. I got a card that simply said: *If the van's rockin', don't come knockin'!* Exactly nine months later, Emma gave birth to their first son, and they are all thriving. Connor still has a few years to go, and is doing a diploma in business management. Apparently he has been scoring over 90% in his exams. Scott is also still inside, and I am now visiting him, which is extraordinarily weird. The first time, he somehow got the café hatch to present me with a whole cake that I was allowed to take home.

And as for me? Well, my jail experience wasn't wholly negative. I sometimes think that everyone should spend a little bit of time in prison, though it's probably best done before having children. I try and think of those incredible nine months in Wandsworth as a unique social experiment. It's comforting to know that there's humour, hope and kindness in even the darkest corners of the world. I learnt a lot about human nature, but probably even more about myself. Before my incarceration I was a bit of a judgemental prick. This was a driving force of much of my film-making, where I was essentially finger-wagging on TV, accompanied by jaunty music and colourful graphics. As Scott predicted, the Listening work has definitely changed me for the better. I now try to listen and understand more, and condemn a little less. The world is also less judgemental of me than I feared; lots of people have been very kind and forgiving about my predicament. I don't think I'll be secretly filming people and splashing it on the front of national newspapers any more, but I was getting pretty sick of that anyway.

Many people were extremely shocked that I got five years, but if I'd been handed a shorter sentence this book would never have been written. If Judge Beddoe had given me four years, I'd have only spent a fortnight in Wandsworth. Five years was the lowest possible sentence to enjoy the full Wandsworth experience. Maybe Beddoe knew that, and hoped that I'd do something sensible with my time there.

Whatever I do with the rest of my life, it's going to be easier than fixing glasses with a biro top, or dodging psychopaths on G Wing, or wearing the same clothes for two months. Nothing in my future can be as taxing as Wandsworth, and it's quite liberating to know it's all behind me. From now on, I intend to face every setback, difficulty and challenge with a simple mantra: *It's not Wandsworth, baby. It's not Wandsworth.*

Epilogue

It's important to stress that my prison experience was very different from the norm. I had unswerving support from family and friends, and I was looked after by a decent bunch of people inside Wandsworth, so I survived pretty much unscathed. It also helped that I was educated, white, middle class, relatively affluent, and I didn't have a mental illness. This is not the case for the huge majority of other prisoners, and incarceration does irreparable damage to them and their families. You may well think that it's justly deserved, as they've broken the law, but this argument does nothing to tackle reoffending. Dostoevsky once said that 'the degree of civilisation in a society can be judged by entering its prisons'. On that basis, we are turning into a very uncivilised country indeed.

Since I've just written a whole book castigating the prison system, I should also add some suggestions on how it could be improved. Before I get on my soap box, however, it's worth catching up on recent developments. Weeks after I left Wandsworth, the prison's reform journey came to an abrupt end. The *Guardian* reported that 'The future of the government's reform prisons has been thrown into doubt after Wandsworth prison, seen as the flagship of the scheme, lost its status and reverted back to a normal prison.'[1]

Since then there have been no new reform prisons, and the entire programme has died a death. It was the latest in a long line of tenuous political initiatives that sounded great in press conferences but did nothing to address the prison crisis. Liz Truss, who had constantly championed the reform programme, quit the following month.[2] David Liddington was appointed Justice Secretary and made similar noises about enacting radical change,[3] but things continued to deteriorate. In 2017, there were 12% more prison assaults, a 12% increase in self-harm,[4] and riots at the Mount, Long Lartin and Birmingham (again). Liddington departed after a few months, having made no discernible impact, and was replaced by David Gauke.[5] To be fair to Gauke, and his eccentric prisons minister Rory Stewart, they both proposed more progressive measures than any of their recent predecessors.[6] They suggested scrapping sentences of under 12 months[7] and slightly humanised the IEP system to get rid of Entry level.[8]

This didn't stop the crisis intensifying throughout 2018. HMP Liverpool hit the headlines for having the 'worst conditions inspectors have seen'. Peter Clarke, the head prison inspector, apportioned much of the blame to the national leadership of the prison system.[9] Rory Stewart subsequently declared that he'd resign as prisons minister if the 10 most failing jails did not improve in the next year.[10] He didn't wait to face the music, and instead provided the comic relief during the 2019 Tory leadership election. In 2019, there was an 11% rise in assaults, self-inflicted deaths rose from 81 to 86, and there was a staggering increase in self-harm of 24% to an all-time high of 57,968 incidents. The MoJ revealed that one in seven prisons had a performance of 'serious concern' – the highest proportion since ratings began.[11]

Boris Johnson became prime minister in the summer of 2019 and law and order policy took a sharp turn to the right. Robert Buckland QC was appointed Justice Secretary,[12] and Priti Patel (who had previously advocated the death penalty) became Home

Secretary.[13] The government immediately announced its intention to create 10,000 new prison places[14] and proposals to increase sentence lengths.[15]

There were five different Justice Secretaries over my 30-month sentence. Even Premiership football managers have more job stability. This situation has been heavily criticised by a former Chief Inspector of Prisons: 'One of the main causes of the failure of the prison system is the lack of dedicated, knowledgeable and experienced leadership … The chief executives of the Justice Ministry … are politicians, who have no working knowledge of the Prison Service, no management experience of leading large complex organisations, and who create instability of purpose and policy with their frequent replacements.'[16]

Chris Grayling, whose absurd reforms were responsible for much of the current crisis, was promoted to Transport Secretary, where he famously gave a ferry contract to a company that didn't have any ships.[17]

After quitting Wandsworth, Ian Bickers was promoted to Director of Immigration Removal Centres. He swiftly moved job once again, to something called Deputy Director – Data Driven Department & Culture Change Team.[18] Any suggestions as to what this title actually means will be gratefully received. Months later, he (honestly) went to run something called the New Futures Network.[19] Despite my sarcastic barbs, I genuinely think that Bickers desperately wanted to turn Wandsworth around. His cherished Purple Army was a very good idea, but like so many modernising reforms, it was stymied by the Prison Officers Association.

In October 2017, Mark Fairhurst took over the POA. He immediately advocated that some prisoners should be locked up for 23 hours a day and be forced to wear orange Guantanamo jumpsuits. 'The only language they are going to understand is violence because they are used to getting their own way by being violent … All their visits would be behind glass, and they would be handcuffed …

It's really harsh but we need to do it because we need a change to incentivise people to start behaving.'[20]

In February 2018, the inquest was held for Osvaldas Pagirys, the Lithuanian teenager who killed himself while I was in Wandsworth. The Probation and Prisons Ombudsman found that 'Wandsworth staff had not satisfactorily acknowledged his vulnerability or taken adequate action to tackle his deteriorating mental health, and had failed to manage his suicide risk ... The delay in responding to Mr Pagirys's cell bell on the day he was discovered hanging was unacceptable ... Had staff responded to [his] cell bell within that timeframe his life might have been saved.'[21]

CCTV emerged showing Osvaldas' emergency light flashing, while a female officer sits drinking tea in front of the TV. The officer then attends to the adjacent cell, but doesn't see the blinking red light just inches away. She finally goes to Osvaldas' cell and sounds the alarm, by which time it's too late. These shocking CCTV images were later broadcast by ITV's *Exposure* as part of a searing documentary on the prison crisis. The Ministry of Justice refused to comment on Osvaldas' death, not even to express regret or extend condolences to his family. This encapsulates the official indifference to how prisons are routinely killing the most damaged people in our society.

I hope that this book has provided enough evidence that Wandsworth, and the prison system as a whole, is failing on an epic scale. Failing to stop mentally ill people self-harming and committing suicide, failing to provide a safe and decent environment for inmates and officers, and failing the public by releasing offenders who commit even more crimes. This crisis has festered under a cloak of national ignorance, as most ordinary citizens believe that bad prisons don't affect them. But this couldn't be further from the truth, as the collapse of the prison system has coincided with an explosion in violent crime. The violent crime rate in England and Wales has doubled in the last three years. In Wandsworth I met dozens of young men who had been convicted of gun and knife crime. They were usually repeat offenders, and had served several earlier sentences for minor offences. If prisons were more effective, these lads might have been steered away from their later serious offending.

There are many complex and interconnected reasons for the rise in criminal behaviour, and prisons are just a piece of the puzzle. But there are plenty of examples of how reforming prisons can drastically cut crime. Swedish prisons are humane and fair, and focus on educating and rehabilitating offenders rather than fixating on punishment. It's led to a huge drop in reoffending, and the closure of many prisons.[22] This is doubly cost-effective, as less money is spent catching criminals, and fewer people need locking up.

So in the highly unlikely event that I'm appointed Justice Secretary, these are the changes I would introduce:

Mental health. We need many more secure mental health units, where the most disturbed individuals can be properly looked after. This would lower the rates of suicide and self-harm, and significantly help the rest of the prison system. Officers currently spend far too much time dealing with a small number of highly disruptive inmates, who are usually severely mentally ill. Removing these troubled offenders from general population would free up more time for officers to deal with everyone else.

Officer numbers. Many problems can be traced back to plummeting staff levels. Teachers sit in empty classrooms, as there aren't enough officers to unlock inmates for lessons. Healthcare is on its knees because prisoners are unable to attend medical appointments. Fewer officers leads to more bang-up, which directly increases violence. Raising staffing levels would make jails safer, and improve many other key areas.

Offending behaviour courses. There are well over 100 rehabilitation programmes accredited to run in British prisons, but there's scant evidence that any of them are effective. Officials still cling to the belief that these courses work, as acknowledging otherwise means admitting that they've wasted a fortune over many years. The MoJ should abandon any cognitive behaviour course that doesn't have concrete supporting evidence, and divert money towards employment and educational programmes.

Employment. Offenders who leave prison into paid jobs are significantly less likely to reoffend.[23] Some big employers, such as Pret, DHL and Timpson, are now deliberately hiring ex-prisoners. James Timpson believes that his former-offender employees are 'more loyal and, after being in prison, obsessed with turning up on time'.[24] The Brexit labour shortage should encourage others to capitalise on this untapped manpower. More open prisons should be built, which would increase the number of offenders getting paid jobs. This would also save money, as open prisons are much cheaper to run.

Education. Inmates who gain skills and qualifications are much more employable on release. Rather than being locked in cells all day, prisoners should be working on their English, maths and IT. More than half of serving prisoners were excluded from school,[25] so jail provides an opportunity for them to get the basic education they missed the first time round. Fifty per cent of inmates are functionally illiterate, and pushing more literacy programmes will pay dividends.

Prison numbers. Between 1993 and 2012, the prison population of England and Wales almost doubled to over 86,000,[26] and has remained around that level ever since – the highest prison population in the EU.[27] This is a consequence of a long-running political arms race, as politicians keep increasing sentences to demonstrate they are tough on crime. But there is precious little proof that extending sentences actually acts as a deterrent.[28] It's also quite clear that giving drug smugglers ludicrously long sentences and criminalising addicts does nothing to curtail drug use.

IPP sentences. These indefinite sentences are now completely discredited, and were abolished in 2012. As of 2018, however, there were still 2,300 IPP prisoners in the system who were over their original tariff.[29] They are still being forced to prove that they don't pose a risk to society, which is often impossible. This is causing widespread mental health problems, and increasing levels of self-harm and suicide. The only just and humane option is to release every IPP prisoner who is currently over tariff.

IEP system. This has been widely criticised as ineffective, counter-productive, a waste of officers' time, and wide open to abuse.[30] Forbidding adults to wear their own clothes is stigmatising and dehumanising, and prisoners start loathing the authorities on day one. The whole IEP system should just be abandoned, allowing prisoners to wear their own clothes and access basic necessities. This would free up thousands of hours of officers' time, allowing them to focus on areas that actually tackle reoffending.

Telephones. Countless incidents of violence and self-harm are caused by prisoners being unable to use the phone. Some jails have recently installed phones in cells, which has led to a sharp drop in violence.[31] In-cell phones should be rolled out nationally, which would also reduce the demand for illicit mobiles. The call rates from prison phones to mobiles are extortionate, and should match the rates paid by the general public.

Bureaucracy. Running prisons with paper-based admin is grossly inefficient, and systems need to be brought into the twenty-first century. Some modern prisons have abolished all paper admin, and have fitted consoles in cells so that inmates can electronically access their visits, canteen, menus, etc. This digitisation creates huge efficiency savings, and should be rolled out across the entire prison estate.

Healthcare. Basic healthcare is a human right, and it's not soft justice to demand that all inmates should have proper medical treatment. Increasing officer numbers would make an immediate difference to medical standards, as more inmates could get unlocked for appointments. Prisons need more nurses, doctors and medical facilities, and officers shouldn't be able to block hospital visits just to make their own lives easier.

Visits. If the authorities genuinely believe that maintaining family ties is the key to rehabilitation, inmates should be allowed a humane allocation of visits. There are over 200,000 children with parents in prison, so denying meaningful contact just breeds a whole new generation of criminals.

These are the key changes needed at a political level if we are to stand a chance of tackling the prison crisis. I'm certainly not alone in this view, and you'll find similar recommendations from politicians of all stripes, leading criminologists, the Prison Reform Trust and the Howard League for Penal Reform. It will take greater financial investment to turn the crisis around, and no political party ever won an election by promising to spend more on prisons. But cutting prison spending just costs more in the long term, as reoffending rates remain stubbornly high. The entire prison budget in 2017/2018 was £4.34 billion,[32] but the cost of reoffending was more than three times this, and is estimated at £15 billion a year.[33]

If you want to do something personally, then I'd strongly recommend donating to the Samaritans, who run the Listener scheme, and the Shannon Trust, which manages the excellent Toe by Toe literacy programme. If you are an employer, try giving a break to an ex-prisoner. I think you'll be pleasantly surprised. Chances are that you'll know someone who ends up inside, so do write them a letter or an email, and maybe send them a few quid to buy some biscuits.

Most of all, I'd suggest you bring some balance to the prison debate. Yes, most prisoners have done something wrong. Yes, they deserve to be punished, sometimes by incarcerating them for quite some time. But what's frequently ignored is that deprivation of liberty is a punishment all by itself. If I'd been locked in a cheap hotel for 30 months, it would have been almost as horrible, as I'd still have been separated from my son, which was by far the worst part of my imprisonment. Putting the boot in and inflicting subhuman treatment is wildly counterproductive, as it's unlikely to foster a sense of civic responsibility.

The British public has developed a sadistic mindset towards prisons, and fiercely resists any policies that actually rehabilitate offenders. But it's the public that suffers the effects of reoffending, as inmates walk out of the gate more damaged than before they went in, and commit even more crimes. Things can only change when attitudes shift towards more progressive and effective methods. Once the public gives the government the space it needs to make radical and modernising change, prisons might finally start encouraging offenders to turn their backs on crime.

References

Introduction

1 https://www.theguardian.com/society/2017/apr/27/prison-statistics-reveal-big-rise-in-assaults-on-staff-and-self-harm

2 https://www.independent.co.uk/news/uk/home-news/uk-prison-population-conditions-government-urged-reduce-a7991351.html

3 https://assets.publishing.service.gov.uk/government/uploads/system/uploads/attachment_data/file/724526/HMI-Prisons_Annual_Report_2017-18.pdf

4 https://www.mirror.co.uk/news/uk-news/holiday-camp-prison-scout-group-9911810

5 https://www.theguardian.com/society/2018/feb/20/ombudsman-terms-teenagers-death-in-prison-appalling-osvaldas-pagirys

6 http://www.prisonreformtrust.org.uk/Portals/0/Documents/Bromley%20Briefings/Summer%202018%20factfile.pdf

7 https://publications.parliament.uk/pa/cm201617/cmselect/cmworpen/58/5804.htm

8 https://www.channel4.com/news/new-allegations-of-sexual-assault-against-mohamed-al-fayed-by-three-women-including-15-year-old-employee

9 https://www.theguardian.com/film/2017/dec/08/dustin-hoffman-sexual-harassment-broadway

Chapter 1: Trauma and Toothpaste

1 https://assets.publishing.service.gov.uk/government/uploads/system/uploads/attachment_data/file/317904/Fact_Sheet_-_Overview_of_POCA__2_.pdf

2 https://www.bbc.co.uk/news/uk-36384729

3 https://drug.addictionblog.org/does-spice-show-up-on-drug-tests/

4 https://www.telegraph.co.uk/news/2017/09/22/letters-sent-prison-photocopied-amid-fears-soaked-drugs/

5 https://www.dailystar.co.uk/news/latest-news/597499/Superdrugs-UK-prisons-lag-reveals-synthetic-taking-hundreds-casualties-Brit-jails

6 https://www.bbc.co.uk/news/uk-england-dorset-41319812

7 https://www.theguardian.com/technology/2015/jul/23/panopticon-digital-surveillance-jeremy-bentham

8 https://prisonjobs.blog.gov.uk/your-a-d-guide-on-prison-categories/

Chapter 2: Lockdowns and Love Actually

1 https://www.itv.com/news/anglia/update/2016-07-14/norfolk-mp-liz-truss-promoted-to-justice-secretary/

2 https://www.theguardian.com/society/2016/jul/19/prisons-legal-highs-peter-clarke-new-psychoactive-substances

3 https://www.theguardian.com/society/2016/may/20/wandsworth-governor-ian-bickers-jail-disorder-prison-reform

4 https://www.standard.co.uk/news/crime/prison-perks-offenders-will-have-to-earn-privileges-in-rules-shake-up-8596716.html

5 http://www.prisonreformtrust.org.uk/ForPrisonersFamilies/PrisonerInformationPages/IncentivesandEarnedPrivileges

6 https://www.justice.gov.uk/downloads/offenders/psipso/psi-2011/psi_2011_11_incentives_and_earned_privileges.doc

Chapter 3: Showers and Slips

1 https://uk.reuters.com/article/uk-trial-insidertrading-sentences/ex-deutsche-banker-and-accountant-jailed-for-insider-dealing-idUKKCN0Y31TG

2 https://www.elizabethtruss.com/news/elizabeth-truss-outlines-her-views-sentencing-and-size-prison-population-centre-social-justice

3 https://www.theguardian.com/society/datablog/2016/nov/18/fewer-prison-officers-and-more-assaults-how-uk-prison-staffing-has-changed

4 https://www.theguardian.com/society/2014/jul/20/moj-recruits-redundant-staff-ease-jails-crisis

5 https://www.theguardian.com/society/2014/mar/24/ban-books-prisoners-england-wales-authors

6 https://www.theguardian.com/society/2014/dec/05/prison-book-ban-unlawful-court-chris-grayling

7 https://news.sky.com/story/transport-secretary-chris-grayling-should-resign-over-chaotic-railway-timetables-11571187

8 https://www.theguardian.com/society/2019/jan/29/more-than-half-young-people-jail-are-of-bme-background

9 http://www.dailymail.co.uk/news/article-3751059/New-isolation-cells-hate-preachers-t-spread-poison-jail-Units-stop-dangerous-inmates-inciting-join-Islamic-State.html

Chapter 4: Goodfellas and Goldilocks

1 http://www.wandsworthguardian.co.uk/news/14636741.display/

2 https://www.theguardian.com/politics/2013/mar/13/wandsworth-prison-jail-chris-huhne

3 http://www.swlondoner.co.uk/hmp-wandsworth-criticised-desperate-state-prisoners-suicides-behind-bars-rise-dramatically/

4 https://www.thetimes.co.uk/article/jail-rejects-inmates-after-blunders-by-repair-firm-on-200m-contract-qcmxwg6mc

5 https://www.independent.co.uk/news/uk/politics/chris-grayling-carillion-rory-stewart-prison-maintenance-contract-justice-minister-a8417496.html

6 https://www.theguardian.com/society/2018/jan/23/carillion-prisons-terrible-state-andrea-albutt-prison-governors-chief

7 https://www.telegraph.co.uk/news/uknews/law-and-order/12185138/Crackdown-on-compensation-payouts-for-prisoners.html

8 http://www.politics.co.uk/comment-analysis/2016/09/07/prison-reform-looks-dead-in-the-water-under-liz-truss

9 https://www.theguardian.com/books/2016/oct/01/nobel-prize-laureates-money-award

10 https://www.dailymail.co.uk/news/article-3807325/We-deserved-truth-25-years-ago-Ben-Needham-s-mother-slams-mystery-witness-not-coming-forward-earlier-police-start-latest-dig-hunt-missing-toddler.html

Chapter 5: Biohazard and Back Rubs

1 https://www.sentencingcouncil.org.uk/about-sentencing/types-of-sentence/life-sentences/

2 https://www.gov.uk/government/publications/home-detention-curfew

3 https://www.simplypsychology.org/milgram.html

4 https://www.theguardian.com/uk-news/2016/oct/18/one-arrested-after-man-killed-in-pentonville-prison

5 https://www.bbc.co.uk/news/uk-england-london-37698780

6 https://www.bbc.co.uk/news/av/uk-36327325/bbc-exclusive-a-look-inside-wandsworth-prison

7 https://www.samaritans.org/how-we-can-help/prisons/listener-scheme/

8 https://www.youtube.com/watch?v=1Qr8JYi5XEA

9 https://www.theguardian.com/uk-news/2016/aug/09/woman-dies-police-pursuit-crash-after-drone-over-wandsworth-prison

10 https://www.standard.co.uk/news/london/revealed-number-of-banned-items-thrown-into-london-prisons-up-by-more-than-400-per-cent-a3249746.html

11 https://www.nao.org.uk/report/confiscation-orders-2/

12 https://www.theguardian.com/society/2017/oct/22/prison-officers-to-get-body-worn-cameras-in-3m-jail-safety-boost

13 https://assets.publishing.service.gov.uk/government/uploads/system/uploads/attachment_data/file/726874/The_demand_for_and_use_of_illicit_phones_in_prison_web_.pdf

14 http://www.prisonreformtrust.org.uk/PressPolicy/News/vw/1/ItemID/13

Chapter 6: Suicide and Sellotape

1 http://www.bbc.co.uk/news/uk-37854358

2 https://www.thesun.co.uk/news/2093823/furious-prison-officers-threaten-to-take-control-of-every-jail-in-the-country-in-protest-at-explosion-in-violence-behind-bars/

3 http://www.bbc.co.uk/news/uk-37854358

4 http://www.thisislocallondon.co.uk/news/14551413.display/

5 https://chicagounbound.uchicago.edu/cgi/viewcontent.cgi?article=2471&context=journal_articles

6 http://pricetheory.uchicago.edu/levitt/Papers/DonohueLevittTheImpactOfLegalized2001.pdf

7 https://www.theguardian.com/society/2016/nov/02/prisons-in-england-and-wales-given-boost-of-2500-new-staff-to-tackle-violence

8 https://www.theguardian.com/commentisfree/2016/nov/03/liz-truss-prison-officers-prisons-staff-prisoner

9 https://justicejobs.tal.net/vx/mobile-0/appcentre-1/brand-13/candidate/so/pm/1/pl/3/opp/14284-14284-Operational-Support-Grade-OSG/en-GB

10 https://www.stgilestrust.org.uk/article/our-peer-advisor-programme-returns-home-to-HMPWandsworth

11 https://www.theguardian.com/society/2016/nov/02/prisons-in-england-and-wales-given-boost-of-2500-new-staff-to-tackle-violence

12 https://www.theguardian.com/society/2017/mar/29/hmp-wandsworth-ian-bickers-governor-leaves-prisoners

13 http://www.bbc.co.uk/news/uk-england-london-37899401

14 https://www.bbc.co.uk/news/uk-england-london-40293767

15 15 https://www.bbc.co.uk/news/uk-england-london-40293767; http://www.dailymail.co.uk/news/article-3920286/Chilling-footage-filmed-prisons-reveals-violent-world-bars.html

16 https://s3-eu-west-2.amazonaws.com/ppo-prod-storage-1g9rkhjhkjmgw/uploads/2018/02/M248-16_Death-of-Mr-Osvaldas-Pagirys_HMP-Wandsworth_14.11.16_SID_18-21.pdf

17 https://www.independent.co.uk/news/uk/home-news/thousands-of-prison-officers-just-decided-to-go-on-strike-a7418016.html

18 https://www.bbc.co.uk/news/uk-37984479

19 https://www.washingtonpost.com/posteverything/wp/2016/02/02/denmark-doesnt-treat-its-prisoners-like-prisoners-and-its-good-for-everyone/?utm_term=.1b9349c58cd6

20 http://www.prisonreformtrust.org.uk/Portals/0/Documents/Bromley%20
Briefings/Summer%202018%20factfile.pdf

21 https://www.bbc.co.uk/programmes/b0834tmt

22 https://www.barnardos.org.uk/what_we_do/our_projects/children_of_
prisoners.htm

23 https://www.barnardos.org.uk/what_we_do/our_projects/children_of_
prisoners.htm

24 https://www.justice.gov.uk/downloads/offenders/psipso/psi-2013/PSI-30-
2013-incentives-and-earned-privileges.doc

25 http://www.prisonreformtrust.org.uk/ForPrisonersFamilies/
PrisonerInformationPages/IncentivesandEarnedPrivileges

26 https://www.gov.uk/government/publications/multi-agency-public-
protection-arrangements-mappa--2

27 https://www.justice.gov.uk/downloads/offenders/psipso/pso/PSO_2205_
offender_assessment_and_sentence_management.doc

Chapter 7: Spinsters and Spiceheads

1 https://assets.publishing.service.gov.uk/government/uploads/system/uploads/
attachment_data/file/449290/glossary-of-programmes.pdf; https://www.gov.
uk/government/collections/justice-data-lab-pilot-statistics

2 http://www.equinoxcare.org.uk/wp-content/uploads/2018/07/JD-Prison-
Offender-Resettlement-Workers-NEW.doc

3 https://www.sparkinside.org/our-work/heros-journey

4 http://www.safeground.org.uk/prisons/man-up/

5 http://www.safeground.org.uk/impact-evidence/full-list-programme-
evaluations/

6 https://s3-eu-west-2.amazonaws.com/imb-prod-storage-1ocod6bqky0vo/
uploads/2017/09/Wandsworth-2016-2017.pdf

7 https://www.thesun.co.uk/news/2844087/time-added-on-to-prisoners-
sentences-for-attacking-each-other-more-than-doubles-in-five-years/

8 https://www.justice.gov.uk/downloads/offenders/psipso/psi-2011/psi-64-2011-
safer-custody.doc

9 http://edition.cnn.com/2009/CRIME/05/29/spector.sentencing/index.html

Chapter 8: Murder and Mutiny

1 https://www.thetimes.co.uk/article/rioting-inmates-at-winson-green-
birmingham-used-keys-from-warden-to-unlock-cells-589f30k0w

2 https://www.birminghammail.co.uk/news/midlands-news/winson-green-
priosn-riots-inmates-12332465

3 https://www.expressandstar.com/news/crime/2017/09/29/hmp-birmingham-
riots-six-convicted-of-mutiny-after-worst-prison-riot-since-strangeways/

4 https://www.theguardian.com/business/2016/may/12/painstaking-investigation-deutsche-bank-insider-trading

5 https://www.thesun.co.uk/news/2463202/riot-breaks-out-at-prison-as-60-inmates-take-control/

6 https://www.bbc.co.uk/news/uk-england-kent-42217789

7 https://www.itv.com/news/story/2013-11-01/18-rated-movies-prison-ban/

8 https://yjlc.uk/age-2/

9 https://www.independent.co.uk/news/uk/politics/criminals-under-25-should-not-go-to-adult-prison-mps-commons-justice-select-committee-a7379811.html

Chapter 9: Courtrooms and Cheeseburgers

1 https://www.imb.org.uk/independent-monitoring-boards/

2 https://www.politics.co.uk/comment-analysis/2016/09/07/prison-reform-looks-dead-in-the-water-under-liz-truss

3 https://www.dailymail.co.uk/news/article-1392885/Prisoner-allowed-father-child-jail-human-right-family-life.html

4 https://www.thesun.co.uk/news/2057116/prison-officer-found-guilty-of-misconduct-after-collecting-lags-sperm-in-syringe-in-plan-to-conceive-chocolate-baby/

5 https://www.edp24.co.uk/news/crime/career-paedophile-roy-reynolds-sentenced-to-16-months-in-jail-1-4844055

6 https://www.bbc.co.uk/news/uk-northern-ireland-38586271

7 https://www.express.co.uk/news/uk/750588/paedophile-sex-children-convicted-jail-spare-free-judge-sick-Daniel-Taylor

8 https://www.imb.org.uk/report/wandsworth-2017-18-annual-report/

9 http://www.transformjustice.org.uk/wp-content/uploads/2018/03/TJ_March2018report.pdf

10 http://www.ppo.gov.uk/app/uploads/2014/07/Risk_thematic_final_web.pdf

11 https://www.itv.com/news/2015-07-21/hunt-for-inmate-mistakenly-freed-from-wandsworth-prison/

12 https://www.dailymail.co.uk/news/article-5178663/The-number-prisoners-wrongly-released-jail-10.html

13 https://www.dailymail.co.uk/news/article-3947584/Prisoners-cushy-life-Ministers-want-jail-softer.html

14 https://www.thesun.co.uk/news/2987950/hmp-berwyn-wrexham-uk-cells-cost/

15 https://www.mirror.co.uk/news/uk-news/exposed-prisoners-partying-drugs-vodka-11305994

16 https://www.dailymail.co.uk/news/article-2205824/Ill-stop-jails-like-holiday-camps-says-new-minister-justice.html

17 https://www.lbc.co.uk/radio/presenters/nick-ferrari/nick-ferrari-sort-out-holiday-camp-prisons/
18 https://www.theguardian.com/inequality/2017/jun/15/reading-for-freedom-life-changing-scheme-dreamt-up-by-prison-pen-pals-shannon-trust-action-for-equity-award
19 https://www.justiceinspectorates.gov.uk/cjji/media/press-releases/2015/03/learningdisbailitiespt2news/
20 https://www.theguardian.com/society/2016/jan/05/jail-reading-scheme-letter-tom-shannon-trust
21 https://www.shannontrust.org.uk/support-us/

Chapter 10: Despair and Dancing Queen

1   https://publications.parliament.uk/pa/cm201719/cmselect/cmpubacc/400/400.pdf
2   https://twitter.com/MoJGovUK/status/733345232117436416
3   https://www.theguardian.com/society/2017/jan/26/prison-suicides-in-england-and-wales-reaches-record-high
4   http://www.swlondoner.co.uk/revealed-wandsworth-prisons-tragic-suicide-rates-highest-country/
5   https://www.dailymail.co.uk/news/article-4183510/HBOS-banker-jailed-11-years-1bn-fraud.html
6   https://www.thesun.co.uk/news/2786265/hbos-rotters-used-posh-yacht-to-scam-fortune-during-1bn-asset-stripping-trial/
7   https://www.theguardian.com/business/2017/feb/02/hbos-manager-and-other-city-financiers-jailed-over-245m-loans-scam
8   https://www.theguardian.com/business/2017/jan/30/cash-cruises-sex-parties-hbos-manager-lynden-scourfield
9   https://www.parliament.uk/business/publications/written-questions-answers-statements/written-question/Lords/2017-12-21/HL4432/
10 http://data.parliament.uk/writtenevidence/committeeevidence.svc/evidencedocument/justice-committee/prison-reform/oral/44534.html
11 http://www.mirror.co.uk/news/uk-news/jail-go-up-like-dynamite-10601487
12 https://hansard.parliament.uk/pdf/Commons/2017-01-25
13 https://psycnet.apa.org/record/1972-04417-001
14 https://www.newstatesman.com/politics/uk/2017/08/im-blame-blunketts-indefinite-prison-sentences-and-thousands-still-locked
15 https://www.theguardian.com/society/2017/aug/14/liz-truss-get-grip-backlog-prisoners-held-beyond-interdeminate-sentence-ipp
16 http://www.ppo.gov.uk/app/uploads/2014/07/Risk_thematic_final_web.pdf
17 https://www.bbc.co.uk/news/uk-26561380
18 https://inews.co.uk/news/worboys-forensic-psychologist-horrified-lack-evidence-behind-prison-sex-offender-courses/

19 https://www.bbc.co.uk/news/uk-48683296
20 https://www.dailymail.co.uk/news/article-4635876/Scandal-100million-sex-crime-cure-hubs.html
21 https://www.thetimes.co.uk/article/why-mindfulness-makes-criminals-worse-3sd6xf5fh
22 https://www.bbc.co.uk/news/uk-38931580
23 https://www.bbc.co.uk/programmes/b08hnpml
24 https://www.dailymail.co.uk/news/article-5674345/Female-prison-officer-25-started-personal-relationship-prisoner.html
25 https://www.dailymail.co.uk/news/article-3865078/Prison-guard-inmate-said-pretty-smuggled-phones-jail-send-sex-texts-murderer-infatuated-him.html
26 https://www.thesun.co.uk/news/2900379/prison-crackdown-will-include-tough-but-fair-agenda-to-prevent-lags-reoffending/
27 https://www.bbc.co.uk/programmes/p04tczmv
28 https://www.bbc.co.uk/news/uk-england-london-43115364
29 https://www.doingtime.co.uk/how-prisons-work/the-first-weeks-in-custody/personal-officer/
30 https://www.ft.com/content/eb01cd18-4f63-11e7-bfb8-997009366969
31 http://www.dailymail.co.uk/news/article-4246586/Police-hunt-murderer-two-armed-men-help-escape.html
32 https://www.independent.co.uk/news/uk/crime/prisoners-being-left-in-squalid-courtroom-cells-by-private-escort-companies-and-told-they-have-only-a6723336.html
33 https://www.bbc.co.uk/news/uk-england-london-48747398
34 https://www.crisis.org.uk/ending-homelessness/law-and-rights/prison-leavers/
35 https://webarchive.nationalarchives.gov.uk/+/http:/www.cabinetoffice.gov.uk/media/cabinetoffice/social_exclusion_task_force/assets/publications_1997_to_2006/reducing_summary.pdf
36 http://bouncebackproject.com
37 http://www.cellspitch.com
38 https://www.thesun.co.uk/news/2900379/prison-crackdown-will-include-tough-but-fair-agenda-to-prevent-lags-reoffending/

Chapter 11: Paedophiles and Prizes

1 https://www.mdx.ac.uk/our-research/research-groups/prisons-research-group/learning-together
2 https://www.judiciary.uk/announcements/coa-news-release-crim-appeals-heard-more-quickly-11122012/
3 https://www.theguardian.com/society/2017/mar/29/hmp-wandsworth-ian-bickers-governor-leaves-prisoners
4 https://www.gov.uk/life-in-prison/healthcare-in-prison

5   https://www.imb.org.uk/report/wandsworth-imb-2016-17-annual-report/
6   https://www.theguardian.com/society/2017/aug/22/prison-healthcare-so-bad-it-would-be-shut-down-on-outside-say-doctors
7   https://www.theguardian.com/commentisfree/2019/apr/05/healthcare-jails-killing-female-prisoners-black-women-annabella-landsberg
8   https://www.nursingtimes.net/news/mental-health/cqc-prosecutes-mental-health-trust-over-prisoner-suicide/7029362.article
9   http://www.justice.gov.uk/downloads/offenders/psipso/psi-2011/psi-49-2011-prisoner-comms-services.doc

Epilogue

1   https://www.theguardian.com/society/2017/jun/04/hmp-wandsworth-loses-reform-prison-status-ian-bickers
2   https://www.ft.com/content/eb01cd18-4f63-11e7-bfb8-997009366969
3   https://www.gov.uk/government/speeches/prison-reform-open-letter-from-the-justice-secretary
4   https://www.independent.co.uk/news/uk/home-news/prison-violence-self-injury-uk-highest-level-record-inmates-figures-hmp-liverpool-nottingham-a8177286.html
5   https://www.gov.uk/government/ministers/secretary-of-state-for-justice
6   https://www.gov.uk/government/news/justice-secretary-david-gauke-sets-out-long-term-for-justice
7   https://www.telegraph.co.uk/politics/2018/06/26/scrap-jail-terms-less-12-months-serious-offences-says-prisons/
8   https://www.gov.uk/government/news/fairer-prisoner-incentives-to-encourage-rehabilitation
9   https://www.theguardian.com/society/2018/jan/19/liverpool-prison-worst-conditions-inspectors-report
10 https://www.bbc.co.uk/news/uk-45214414
11 https://www.bbc.co.uk/news/uk-49110327
12 https://www.newstatesman.com/politics/uk/2019/07/cabinet-audit-what-does-appointment-robert-buckland-justice-secretary-mean
13 https://www.newstatesman.com/politics/uk/2019/07/cabinet-audit-what-does-appointment-priti-patel-home-secretary-mean-policy
14 https://www.bbc.co.uk/news/uk-49309112
15 https://www.channel4.com/news/boris-johnson-pledges-to-increase-prison-sentences-for-violent-and-sexual-crimes
16 https://tpa.typepad.com/home/files/the_failure_of_the_prison_service_in_the_uk.pdf
17 https://www.theguardian.com/politics/2019/mar/01/grayling-reaches-33m-settlement-over-brexit-ferry-fiasco-court-case-eurotunnel
18 https://uk.linkedin.com/in/ian-bickers-a4515625

19 https://twitter.com/ian_bickers/status/1033990834881011712?lang=en

20 https://www.mirror.co.uk/news/uk-news/violent-prisoners-should-locked-up-11068061

21 https://www.theguardian.com/society/2018/feb/20/ombudsman-terms-teenagers-death-in-prison-appalling-osvaldas-pagirys

22 https://www.theguardian.com/society/2013/dec/01/why-sweden-closing-prisons

23 https://www.gov.uk/government/news/jobs-strategy-aims-to-cut-reoffending

24 https://www.telegraph.co.uk/finance/newsbysector/retailandconsumer/10266250/Timpson-has-key-to-giving-ex-convicts-second-chance.html

25 https://www.theguardian.com/education/2017/oct/10/school-exclusion-figures-date-england-only-tip-iceberg

26 https://assets.publishing.service.gov.uk/government/uploads/system/uploads/attachment_data/file/218185/story-prison-population.pdf

27 https://www.thetimes.co.uk/article/britain-has-the-highest-prison-population-in-the-eu-m32052srz

28 http://www.bbc.com/future/story/20180514-do-long-prison-sentences-deter-crime

29 https://www.theyworkforyou.com/wrans/?id=2019-01-21.210573.h

30 http://www.prisonreformtrust.org.uk/portals/0/documents/punishment without purpose final2941007.pdf

31 https://www.bbc.co.uk/news/uk-england-merseyside-43462060

32 https://www.statista.com/statistics/298654/united-kingdom-uk-public-sector-expenditure-prisons/

33 https://assets.publishing.service.gov.uk/government/uploads/system/uploads/attachment_data/file/565014/cm-9350-prison-safety-and-reform-_web_.pdf

Acknowledgements

This book would simply not exist without three special people who worked with me intensely on it over months and years. Lottie Moggach (aside from looking after my son and providing constant emotional support) somehow found the time to give priceless guidance on its very earliest versions. Lottie's wonderful mother Deborah Moggach looked after me as though I was her own son, and helped me through some very dark times. Debby also pored over countless drafts, helping me develop the shape, tone and style of the book. The third member of this holy trinity is my amazing agent Gordon Wise at Curtis Brown. He took on the book after seeing a pretty erratic early manuscript, and helped me enormously in whipping it into shape. Without these three amazing people, *A Bit of a Stretch* would never have got off the ground, and I'm forever in their debt.

I'd like to thank everyone at Atlantic Books, who took a massive punt on the bedraggled ex-con who stumbled into their offices. Mike Harpley immediately got what I was trying to do, and has been a huge champion of the book. His incisive edits have elevated the project massively. I also need to thank the folks at Audible for their dedicated work in helping me record my own audiobook reading.

Copyeditor Jane Selley needs a big cheer for sorting out my highly dysfunctional grammar. Mega thanks to Nicola Thatcher at Keystone Law for keeping the book on the right side of the law. There are lots of people behind the scenes at Curtis Brown who made all this happen, including Niall, Alice and Luke.

I only had the headspace to write this book because I was supported throughout my prison journey by a wonderful group of friends. They were with me every step of the way, even during my trial – I'm pretty sure a rota was organised to ensure I could always see a friendly face in the courtroom. As soon as I arrived in Wandsworth, I was inundated with letters, photos and emails, which helped me get through the loneliest times. Corresponding with my friends also served as a fantastic sounding board for the stories and jokes in these pages. So in no particular order, enormous love and thanks to Tom P, Annie, Chris M, Ana, Katie, Pete, Mariya, Tim, Rach, Bex, Charles, Lou, Victoria, Jay, Chris S, Tess, Chloe, Heydon, Rich P, Carla, Harry, Greg, Kurt, Charlotte, EJ, Daisy, Simon B, Daniel P, Jobbo, Catherine, John S, Nicky, Dan, David B, Paul B, Larushka, Tom, Marc S, Ian N, Declan, Jonny S, Uncle Tony, Fiona, Lawrence, Georgia and Adam. You really are the most wonderful friends anyone could hope for.

In particular I need to thank my best friend Nazia (to whom this book is dedicated) for looking after my affairs for two and a half years. She kept my life together far more effectively than I was ever able to while I was at liberty. Vanessa also deserves a special mention for all the beautiful and amazing drawings; they really helped more than words can say.

My brother Duncan and my parents Vicky and Patrick went through a pretty grim time as well, but were unwavering in their support and love. My cousin Alex also worked tirelessly on my behalf. Kit's childminder Danielle and her mum Wendy stepped up and helped out enormously while I was away. Also big thanks to Sathnam and Horatio for looking after my son a great deal.

Huge thanks to Simon Goldberg, Razwana Akram, Razi Mireskandari, Louis Charalambous, Anthony Burton and most of the team at SMAB for their advice and support. Big thumbs-up to Simon Pentol (now a QC, get you!) and Kathryn Arnot Drummond for their legendary efforts during my trial. I'd also like to thank Steve Dagworthy and the team at Prison Consultants.

Special shout-out to Martyn Dodgson and Christopher Lunn, who both allowed me to use their real names in this book. Neither asked for anything to be changed, and I value their friendship enormously. I'd also like to thank my friends 'Ted', 'Scott', 'Connor' and 'Gary' for letting me delve into their private lives and experiences, as well as being an emotional crutch. There were certain officers and staff at HMP Wandsworth who showed extraordinary kindness towards me: particular appreciation to 'Linda' and 'Danielle'; you really are both superstars. I will get a load of shit on WhatsApp if I don't thank my mates from Springhill, so hat tip to Ryan, David C, Ed, Ali, Yankee, Abs, Marc C, Marc H, Marc O, Andrew, Max, Dre, Ram, and especially Amanda 'Harvester' Burnham – you all helped me get through those long, boring months at open prison.

Everyone should thank the Samaritans team who trained me to be a Listener and supported me and all the other Listeners at Wandsworth. There have been Samaritans working unpaid across the prison estate for 25 years, and they do a tireless and gruelling job that saves lives every day.

Finally, I really need to thank my son Kit, who was the light at the end of that long, dark tunnel. He really is such an awesome and happy child. I love you, buster.